THE
HOLIDAY
KOSHER BAKER

THE

HOLIDAY
KOSHER BAKER

TRADITIONAL & CONTEMPORARY
HOLIDAY DESSERTS

PAULA SHOYER

STERLING
New York

STERLING
New York

An Imprint of Sterling Publishing
387 Park Avenue South
New York, NY 10016

ISBN 978-1-4549-0714-5

Library of Congress Cataloging-in-Publication Data

Shoyer, Paula.
  The holiday kosher baker : traditional & contemporary holiday desserts / Paula Shoyer ; photographs
by Michael Bennett Kress.
    pages cm
  ISBN 978-1-4549-0714-5 (hardback)
 1. Jewish cooking. 2. Desserts. 3. Baking. 4. Holiday cooking. I. Title.
  TX724.S533 2013
  641.5'676--dc23
                                2013017403

Distributed in Canada by Sterling Publishing
c/o Canadian Manda Group, 165 Dufferin Street
Toronto, Ontario, Canada M6K 3H6
Distributed in the United Kingdom by GMC Distribution Services
Castle Place, 166 High Street, Lewes, East Sussex, England BN7 1XU
Distributed in Australia by Capricorn Link (Australia) Pty. Ltd.
P.O. Box 704, Windsor, NSW 2756, Australia

For information about custom editions, special sales, and premium and corporate purchases,
please contact Sterling Special Sales at 800-805-5489 or specialsales@sterlingpublishing.com.

Manufactured in Canada

2 4 6 8 10 9 7 5 3 1

www.sterlingpublishing.com

Photographs by Michael Bennett Kress

This book is dedicated to my five favorite people in the entire world:
My loving and supportive husband, Andy,
and my amazing children, Emily, Sam, Jake, and Joey.
My wish is that you stay as sweet as you already are.

CONTENTS

The Revolution Continues

Three years ago, one of my greatest dreams was realized with the publication of *The Kosher Baker: 160 Dairy-Free Desserts from Traditional to Trendy* (Brandeis 2010). It took me five years to get that book into the world. I was certain that the kosher community needed it, because every *kiddush* and event I went to was still serving the same boring parve desserts I had eaten since I was a child. Kosher food was becoming more gourmet and kosher desserts needed to catch up. *The Kosher Baker* started my kosher baking revolution.

Since then, I have been on a book tour that never seems to end. I have traveled throughout the United States and Canada conducting baking demonstrations for Jewish groups—and learning that home bakers are among the happiest people you will ever meet. Several miracles, big and small, happened along the way.

First, I will relate the bigger miracles. One day, back in December 2010, I received an email from a woman named Brochi from Chabad of Sea Gate, Brooklyn, inquiring about my availability to do a cooking demonstration for her community. Sea Gate is where my mother grew up. I called Brochi and asked if her Chabad house was located at 3844 Lyme Avenue and she replied, "Yeeesss?!" I proceeded to tell her that 3844 Lyme Avenue was once my grandparents' house. I knew that it had become a Chabad house because, when my grandmother died at the age of 98—after a lifetime of baking—the rabbi who officiated at her funeral was the rabbi of Chabad of Sea Gate. Then Rivkah Brikman, the rabbi's wife, got on the phone and she could not believe that the person she was speaking to, and whom she wanted for the cooking class, was the granddaughter of the family she had heard so much about.

Where would I be doing the demonstration? In my grandmother's kitchen!—The same grandma to whom *The Kosher Baker* book is dedicated, and the grandma who gave me my first taste of delicious homemade desserts.

I taught the class to 45 women, some of whom had connections to my grandparents. My daughter Emily, my aunt Ethelind Wiener, and my parents Reubin and Toby Marcus were there too. I expected to be overwhelmed with emotion. Instead, I felt extremely calm, happy, and at peace, as if it were the most natural thing in the world to be back in my grandmother's house after 24 years. At that moment I knew that I was exactly where I was supposed to be, doing precisely what I was meant to be doing.

The second miracle was more of my own creation. For several years I had auditioned for television cooking shows, and though I was never cast, the experiences gave me great material for comedy at speaking engagements. At one audition, for example, I was asked to show them "a dance move." When I read about a new dessert competition show, I auditioned simply to get more material. This time, however, the joke was on me, and I was cast for the first season of Food

Network's *Sweet Genius*. I did not win, but I had a really great time. It was the hardest professional day I have ever experienced, but it was quite exciting to be on the beautiful set and prove to myself that, even in my late forties, I could challenge myself in a whole new way. I was happy with my performance, particularly because judge Ron Ben Israel enjoyed the taste of my creations, and my cookbook and the word "kosher" were mentioned on national television. I had never thought of myself as a brave person before, but being on that show made me feel like a warrior, albeit one channeling Julia Child.

The smaller miracles are no less important. In the past few years I have heard from people who told me that my book inspired them to start baking. A new bride wrote that my recipes connected her with her grandmothers who had long since died. My nursery school teacher ended up in the audience of a class I taught in New York City. A woman in New Jersey started a small business selling desserts based on my recipes to help support her family. I inspired a teenage boy to sell babkas out of his house. A man in his eighties was my assistant when I baked for an event in Michigan. The kosher bakers of the Midwest, who have no kosher bakeries for miles and miles, made me feel like I had written the book just for them.

These beautiful experiences nourished my soul and convinced me that I had to keep going, pushing the community toward even better, more contemporary, easier, and healthier desserts. The kosher baking revolution continues.

While *The Kosher Baker* is meant to be your weekly Shabbat dessert handbook, *The Holiday Kosher Baker* will become, I hope, your new holiday baking manifesto. It is designed to fit the way you think about holiday desserts. For every Jewish holiday you need beautiful desserts for entertaining at festive meals, but for major, longer holidays you also need snacks. *The Holiday Kosher Baker* has recipes that are gluten-free, vegan, nut-free, and low in sugar. In other words, in this book, there's something for everyone in the Jewish community. It includes contemporary twists on traditional desserts to remind people of their grandmothers, yet it brings the desserts they love completely up to date.

Each holiday chapter includes easy, one-bowl desserts, as well as fancier, multiple-step desserts. This arrangement will help busy cooks find the elegant desserts they need for evening and Shabbat/holiday dinners and the quick recipes they want as snacks for themselves, their kids, houseguests, and anyone else who might show up.

The Holiday Kosher Baker includes my best dairy recipes, mostly for the holiday of Shavuot. During my book tour, many Jewish bakers who do not need dairy-free desserts approached me, requesting dairy recipes. Since then, I have helped them to successfully reengineer my dairy-free recipes back into dairy recipes.

As we all know, Passover is the standout holiday that truly demands high-quality desserts. The Jewish people have been lulled by years of baking the same old recipes into thinking that Passover desserts have to be leaden and tasteless. This book proves them wrong.

The recipes here reflect a modern sensibility for healthier desserts and an exciting fusion of flavors, with a generous peppering of international desserts. This is a new era for Jewish bakers to showcase—at home—the same desserts they see in the mainstream. Now you have a guidebook that shows you how to create new, creative, and yet holiday-appropriate desserts that no longer reflect the "same old, same old" approach that we have used for a generation. It is time to take a step forward, get into the kitchen, and realize that a new world of baking is at your fingertips. Join my revolution.

Your Kosher Baking Encyclopedia

The skills you'll learn here will not only help you perfect the recipes in this book—they can also be applied to all the dessert recipes you make, and give you the confidence to ensure success every time you bake.

HOW TO USE THIS BOOK

Every major holiday has two distinct baking needs: elegant desserts for Seders, Shabbat, and holiday dinners, and snack desserts for daytime. Most chapters of this book are divided into two sections, so you can easily find the perfect dessert to match your entertaining and snacking needs. You will find low-sugar, gluten-free, vegan, and even nut-free desserts in this book—something for everyone. Each recipe tells you how easy or challenging it is, but do not be frightened by recipes that have long instructions—they are simply meant to carefully walk you through the steps:

EASY These are usually one-step or very simple two-step desserts that do not require any special skills. Most easy recipes require no more than 15 minutes of active prep time, but some recipes may require chilling dough or batter overnight.

MODERATE These recipes are often two-step desserts, a cookie or cake with a filling or glaze, desserts that require special shaping of the dough, or more than 20 minutes of preparation time.

MULTIPLE-STEP These desserts are not necessarily difficult—the recipes simply have two to three parts. For example, a recipe might include a dough plus a cooked filling, along with a rising or chilling time, and require more sophisticated baking skills. These desserts typically demand more than 30 minutes of preparation time or have several parts that take about ten minutes each.

To help you follow special diets or customs, recipes are labeled with the following designations:

Dairy
Gluten-free
Low sugar
Nut-free
Parve
Vegan

For Passover

Non-gebrokts (no combination of matzoh cake meal and liquids)

BASIC BAKING EQUIPMENT

A kosher kitchen is a jam-packed place, so you want to store only what you truly need. You also need to have certain equipment that makes baking easier and faster. Here is my list of essentials, the equipment I use over and over again:

* Food processor
* Electric mixer, preferably a stand mixer with whisk, hook, and paddle attachments

* Measuring cups and spoons (at least two sets)
* Waxed paper
* Parchment paper or silicone baking mats
* Wooden spoon
* Wire whisk
* Juicer
* Vegetable peeler
* Heatproof bowl
* Mixing bowls
* Zester
* Silicone spatulas
* Candy thermometer
* Kitchen scissors
* Pastry brushes
* Dough scraper
* Digital scale
* Wire cooling racks

NOTE: Additional baking equipment is listed in the individual sections that follow.

IF YOU'RE USING A CONVECTION OVEN

The recipes in this book were tested in non-convection ovens because not every oven has the convection feature. If you use a convection oven, reduce the temperature by 25 degrees Fahrenheit (4 degrees Celsius) and reduce the baking time by 5 to 8 minutes for cake recipes; and 2 to 3 minutes for cookie recipes. Everyone's oven is different. The first time you try a new recipe, reduce the baking time by 2 to 5 minutes and check the dessert for doneness. You can always *add* baking time, but you cannot take it away.

COOKIES

Everyone loves cookies—they're a great snack to have on hand or in the freezer to serve when people show up or when you want to treat yourself with a small bite of something delicious. Cookie-baking success depends on three things: the right equipment so your cookies bake evenly, knowing the tips to roll or shape your cookies, and how to check for doneness.

* Cookie sheets—Cookie sheets are one type of pan that cannot be replaced by disposable substitutes. Disposable sheet pans are flimsy, and cookies do not bake evenly on them. Use sturdy cookie sheets. It is worth having at least two good cookie sheets and then baking in batches. I have found that heavy-gauge, light-colored aluminum pans are best for most cookies; they will not buckle with use (buckling will cause cookie dough/batter to spread in unattractive ways). Darker-colored cookie sheets absorb more heat, so if you use them your cookies will bake faster. I keep two kinds of sheets in my collection: jelly roll pans and flat pans with a small lip on one side to allow me to slide parchment and cookies off easily.

Additional Essential Cookie-baking Equipment

* Cookie cutters, different sizes
* Rolling pin
* Silicone baking mats (such as Silpat)
* Long and wide metal spatulas

Cookie Doneness, or You Are the Cookie Boss

I always tell bakers to shave about two minutes off the baking time the first time they follow a new cookie recipe and then check the cookies for doneness, because everyone's oven is a little different. If your cookies are done to your taste,

These Pistachio Cookies (page 126) are chewy. Try the "press test" below to make sure they are done the way you like them.

take them out of the oven; if not, check them again in another minute. In each of my recipes, I give a range for baking time, as well as a visual description of what the cookies should look like when they are done. Remember that, just like roasted meats and chickens, cookies (even perfectly soft ones) will continue to bake after they are removed from the oven.

FOR CRISP COOKIES, you want to bake them until the edges are golden, but the center can still be a light color. If you bake cookies until the centers are the same color as the edges, they will be dry.

FOR CHEWY COOKIES, try the press test. If you can press your finger down on top of the cookie all the way to the bottom, it is not yet done. If you can press halfway through the cookie, remove it and the rest of the batch from the oven and let

them cool; they will harden up just a bit yet remain chewy. If you press the top of a cookie and can barely press down, it is already crisp and over-baked (for a chewy cookie).

I recommend doing a test batch of six cookies or fewer to see how they bake in your oven. If they come out badly, you have not lost much dough and you will have learned precisely how long to bake your cookies so they come out perfectly. Remember, "perfect" means how *you* like them.

Decorating and Plating Cookies

When I was in cooking school in Paris, one of the youngest instructors taught me that most desserts can be fixed or even reassembled to look better. For example, to save a burnt cookie edge, the first line of defense is to take out your vegetable peeler and scrape off the burned parts, keeping the round shape of the cookie. A knife will leave evidence that you tried to fix it. If your cookie did not brown evenly or is simply not as pretty as you hoped it would be, you can always dust the top with cinnamon or confectioners' sugar (either

COOKIE BAKING TIPS

1. Always line your cookie sheets with parchment paper or a silicone baking mat.
2. As you shape cookies, try to make them the same size so that they bake at the same rate.
3. Even if you set your oven to the "convection" setting, you should still rotate the cookie sheets and switch the pans to different racks halfway through baking.
4. Trust yourself—you know how you like your cookies; bake them the way YOU want to eat them.

straight or mixed with cocoa). To dust one-third or one-half a cookie, cover the part that does not need dusting with a strip of parchment or waxed paper.

I also like to decorate cookies with dark or white chocolate, both for fun and to cover any blemishes. You can dip part of a cookie into melted chocolate, drizzle lines of chocolate onto your cookies, or use a pastry bag to make chocolate dots, squiggly lines, or any other decoration. Let chocolate-decorated cookies dry before placing them in storage containers.

When plating cookies, use a platter of a contrasting color. Chocolate cookies look great on blue, turquoise, pink, or other bright-colored plates. Vanilla cookies should be placed on darker plates. Discount kitchen and home stores are great places to buy interesting plates and platters.

I like to display cookies overlapping in rows. If you have more than one type of cookie to serve, place them in alternating rows. I will sometimes take a batch of simple cookies, dust half of them with confectioners' sugar, and decorate the remainder with dark chocolate so it appears that there are two entirely different types of cookies on the platter, when I have only baked one.

Freezing Cookie Dough and Storing Cookies

I often freeze rolls of cookie dough and then slice and bake as needed. You could also bake all the cookies for an entire holiday at one time—just label and place them in the freezer, and pull them out as needed. Cookies do thaw pretty quickly, often in less than an hour, and I usually remove them from the freezer before we sit down for dinner. The best way to keep cookies looking good during freezing is to place the cool, freshly baked cookies on a cookie sheet and freeze them for half an hour. When the cookies are firm, you can stack them in a freezer bag and they will retain their shape and not crumble into each other. Layering

cooled cookies between sheets of waxed paper and freezing them in large plastic containers also works well. Containers prevent breakage, particularly for delicate cookies, although fewer broken cookies result in fewer treats for you. Freezer bags work just fine for sturdy cookies. Most cookies will store well in a freezer for up to three months.

CAKES

All bakers need a handful of cake recipes that they have mastered to celebrate the holidays and occasions of their lives. The equipment and tips below will help you create cakes that are baked properly and that release easily from the pan. I have also armed you with techniques for making your cakes look as beautiful as possible with little effort.

If you make a lot of cakes, the best piece of equipment you can buy is either a stand mixer or an electric hand mixer.

Additional Essential Cake-baking Equipment

* Baking pans—If you do not have exactly the same size pan as the one that is called for in a recipe, do not worry—just use a pan that is about one inch smaller or larger.
* Bundt pan—I use silicone ones with a 12-cup (2.8-liter) capacity
* 8 to 9-inch (20 to 23-cm) round baking pans—use nonstick pans
* 8-inch (20-cm) square pan
* 9 x 13-inch (23 x 33-cm) pan
* 11 x 14-inch (28 x 36-cm) pan
* 12-inch (30-cm) loaf pan
* Muffin tin and muffin liners
* Springform pan
* Jelly roll pans—12 x 18 inches (30 x 46cm)

Tools for Decorating and Glazing Cakes

* Small flat metal spatula
* Large flat metal offset spatula

* Disposable pastry bags
* Pastry tips—3 different sizes of circles, the largest ½-inch (1.25-cm) wide; 2 star tips in different sizes; and a tip with a flat side to allow you to make ½-inch (1.25-cm) stripes on your cakes.
* Long serrated knife for slicing cake layers
* Cardboard circles
* Decorating turntable
* Skewers to test for doneness

Greasing Pans

Other than during Passover (when dietary restrictions prevent it), the easiest way to grease a cake pan is with spray oil that contains flour. You can also grease a pan with regular spray oil, oil, melted butter, or margarine. Add two tablespoons of flour to the pan, shake it all around to cover and then tap out the excess flour. When I use round,

square, or rectangular baking pans, I often trace the bottom of the pan on parchment paper, cut out the shape, grease the pan with oil, press in the cut parchment, and grease the top of the parchment. This method makes it super easy to pop a cake out of the pan.

Testing Doneness

Toothpicks are too short to insert into a large cake to test for doneness. Buy long wooden kebab skewers and store them near your oven; they allow you to test the deepest part of your cake. Once the inserted skewer comes out clean, the cake is done. For layer cakes, err on the side of baking a moment or two longer; it is easier to slice and assemble an overbaked cake than an underbaked one.

Other Cake-baking Tips, Techniques, and Tools

EGGS Cakes come out best when eggs are at room temperature.

BEATING EGG WHITES The whites should be at room temperature (leave them out for at least an hour). First whip them on medium speed until foamy. Then turn the speed to low and add a pinch of salt or a few drops of lemon juice, which will stabilize the beaten egg whites. Bring the speed up to medium for a few seconds and then up to high. If your recipe calls for soft peaks, the whites should bend slightly when you gently lift the whisk. If your recipe requires stiff peaks, beat the egg whites until the peaks stand straight up.

COOLING Unless a recipe states otherwise (such as for sponge cakes), let the cake cool in the pan for 10 minutes and then turn it out onto a wire rack to cool completely. Every 20 minutes or so, move the cake around so it does not stick to the rack.

FILLING CUPCAKE PANS Do not fill more than ¾ of the muffin cup with batter or the batter will overflow. Usually somewhere between ⅔ and ¾ full will result in a relatively flat-topped and not overly large muffin or cupcake.

EVEN BAKING If you are baking several cakes at one time, rotate the pans halfway through baking time—and move them to different racks to help them bake evenly.

SLICING CAKE LAYERS First place your cake on top of a piece of waxed paper. Trim the top and sides of the cake to make them flat. Use a knife to mark on the side of the cake where you will slice it. Hold a long serrated knife in one hand and place the other hand palm-down on top of the cake. Slice about 2 to 3 inches (5 to 8cm) into the cake while turning the cake with the other hand. Keep turning until you have sliced 2 to 3 inches (5 to 8cm) in all around. After you have cut all around, place the knife into one cut part and pull straight across to join the cuts. Leave the slice on top of the cake and repeat for as many additional slices of cake as are necessary. Your slices do not need

to be perfect because they will be hidden inside a layer cake.

EVEN OUT THE LAYERS As you frost the layers, every time you add a cake layer to a cake, bend down in order to see the cake at eye level and check the top to make sure it is level. If it's uneven, gently press down on the part of the cake that is higher than the rest, or add more icing or glaze to level it out. (You can also use the same method to fill in the side of a cake that needs to be evened out).

FILLING AND USING A PASTRY BAG To use any pastry bag, place the coupler inside the bag, position the tip you've chosen on the outside, and secure it with a ring. Fold down the top of the bag about 3 to 4 inches (8 to 10cm), and fill three-quarters of it. Then lift up the sides of the bag, making sure to keep the filling inside. Bring the sides together and use your hand to squeeze the filling down toward the tip of the bag. Twist the top of the bag and hold it in your hand, using your thumb to prevent the bag from untwisting. Use that hand to squeeze out the filling and your other hand to guide where you want the filling to go. To refill the bag, turn down the sides, fill it three-quarters of the way, and then press down and twist the top of the bag.

CRUMB COAT One of the challenges of cake decorating is keeping the icing free of crumbs. The best way to accomplish this is to spread a thin coat of icing on the cake and then put it in the freezer for at least twenty minutes. When you spread the next coat of icing on top of the first, there will be no crumbs to pick up. Be careful to avoid getting crumbs in your icing bowl. Use a decorating turntable to ice cakes.

EASY CAKE DECORATIONS You can never go wrong with a bar of chocolate and a vegetable peeler. You can shave the chocolate directly onto the top of the cake or scrape the shavings into a bowl and then press them into the sides of the cake. You can also press dry coconut or chopped nuts into the sides of a cake. Another easy option is to melt chocolate (dark or white), place it into a pastry bag fitted with a small round tip, and squeeze out swirls, lines, dots or anything else on top of your cake. If you have pretty fruit, you can decorate the top or sides of the cake with strawberry slices, berries, or any other sliced or cut fruit (see the introduction to Classic Cheesecake on page 192)—but be sure to add the fruit just before serving the cake to keep it fresh. If you are ambitious, you can buy white fondant, dye it any color you like, roll it out on waxed paper sprinkled with confectioners' sugar, cut it into shapes, and then press the shapes into the cake icing.

STORING Cakes made without fruit can be easily frozen, though apple cakes freeze just fine. Once you've unmolded and cooled a cake, wrap it in plastic and freeze it. You can also freeze cakes that have been assembled and frosted. First freeze the frosted cake on a cookie sheet and, after it is frozen solid, wrap it in plastic and put it back in the freezer for up to three months.

TARTS, MOUSSES, AND PASTRIES

When you are having guests for the holidays, it is nice to present a dessert that looks like you spent hours in the kitchen on it, when you actually didn't. This book has several fruit tarts and pies for different holidays. With the right equipment and techniques, you can achieve a truly professional look. I have also included easy mousses and pastries, many of which can be made and frozen in advance of a holiday.

WHIPPING CREAM Place chilled cream into the bowl of a stand mixer and beat with a wire whisk at high speed until the mixture forms thick ribbons.

THAWING PUFF PASTRY SHEETS If you have time, let the pastry sit at room temperature for about 45 minutes and then unroll it. If you are rushed, remove the package of pastry from the box and place in the microwave oven. Use the "defrost" function of the microwave and thaw for one minute. Turn the package over and defrost for another minute. Remove the sheets from the package and place them on a clean towel to finish thawing until you are ready to use them.

Tools for Tarts and Pies

* Use a long wooden rolling pin without handles—it will roll more of the dough's surface and you can put pressure exactly where you want it in order to roll out the dough as evenly as possible.
* 9-inch (23-cm) pie plate
* Tart pan with a removable bottom

Rolling Cookie, Pie, and Pastry Dough

Place a large piece of parchment paper on your counter and sprinkle it generously with flour. Place the dough on top of the parchment paper, sprinkle it with more flour, and then cover the dough with parchment paper. Roll the rolling pin over the parchment paper. Turn the bottom parchment paper several times to roll the dough in different directions in order to even it out. Lift the top piece of parchment from time to time and sprinkle the dough with a little more flour. To place the dough into a pie pan, remove the top piece of parchment, place your hand under the bottom piece of parchment, lift the dough, and turn it into the pie pan. Remove the parchment paper and use your fingers to press the dough into place.

PLATING DESSERTS

Here are some tips for plating your desserts:
* Choose contrasting colors for sauces.
* Cut your cake into interesting shapes (such as triangles).
* Add chocolate decorations.
* Plated desserts should have a mix of colors and textures (creamy and crunchy, for example).
* Make sure that not everything on a plate is either very sweet or very tart.

TIMING AND PLANNING HOLIDAYS

Two weeks before every holiday, start planning. Make your shopping list and decide what you want to make. Consider the number of people for whom you'll be cooking, and take into account any food allergies. When you're planning what to make for dessert, try to balance the heaviness of the menu with lighter desserts and offer something light for friends who want a small treat, rather than a full portion of dessert. It is nice to offer both fruit and chocolate desserts.

As you consider recipes for holiday meals, see which parts of various desserts can be made in advance. Doughs and cake layers, for example, can be frozen and made weeks beforehand. Spread out the work. If you are making an elaborate meal, do not choose a dessert recipe that requires last-minute assembly or decoration.

Although every recipe in this book indicates the number of servings, bear in mind that if you are making several desserts, not everyone will have a serving of each.

I've found that these guidelines work well:
* For 10 people—one large dessert, such as a cake or pudding + one batch of cookies
* For 20 people—two large desserts + two batches of cookies.

BAKING FOR JEWISH LIFE-CYCLE EVENTS

Although the following section does not pertain to holidays, I have included it because many people I meet on my book tour ask me how to bake for these life-cycle events.

A NOTE ABOUT BAKING FOR SHIVA

The Jewish custom is that when a close family member passes away, the mourning family sits shiva (meaning seven, for the number of days one sits), and friends and family come to visit and pay their respects. There is often way too much food at a shiva, and you should always see who is doing the coordinating and ask what is needed before you start baking. It is always a good idea to bring the dessert sliced on a disposable platter so that no one has to do any work, and ask the host whether they want to serve it or save it for later. If the person who has passed is elderly, consider bringing a low-sugar dessert, because there will likely be several people in the crowd who are diabetic. Also, think about bringing comfort desserts that will not make a mess.

Some suggestions:
* Babka Bites (page 8)
* Everything Rugelach (page 52)
* Chewy Chocolate Olive Oil Cookies (page 76)
* Cheese Babka (page 198)
* Madeleines (pages 11 and 13)
* Nana's Holiday Apple Cake (page 26)

* Cranberry and Orange Spelt Scones
  (page 17)
* Sugar-Free Pumpkin Bread (page 48)

A NOTE ABOUT BAKING FOR A BRIS OR BABY NAMING

When you bring desserts to a bris or baby naming, consider whether your goal is to feed the crowd or the mom. If you know the mom well, then you know what she would like to nosh on. When my daughter Emily was born in Switzerland, my friend Esther Lack came to the hospital with a huge bag of mandelbread. The nurses in Geneva made me drink tea every hour (to help with lactation) and I had a great snack to go with it. I often bring the moms a babka, challah, or cookies for themselves and then something grander, like a layer cake, for the guests. It's tricky, however, to slice anything while you're holding a baby. Always bring a dessert that a mom can grab with one hand.

For the Mom

* Babka Bites (page 8)
* Tea Sandwich Cookies (page 44)
* Gingerbread Cookies (page 73)
* Decorated Cookies with Royal Icing (page 70)
* Chocolate Chip Cookie Bars (page 129)
* Pignons (page 14)
* Everything Rugelach (page 52)

For the Crowd

* Whole-Wheat Chocolate Babka (page 20)
* Vanilla and Chocolate 12-Layer Cake
  (page 28)
* Ombré Layer Cake—suggestions: blue or green for a boy and pink or orange for a girl (page 32)
* Red Velvet Layer Cake with Vanilla and Chocolate Frostings (page 59)
* Almond and Olive Oil Cake (page 74)
* Cream Cheese Flan (page 195)

HIGH ALTITUDE BAKING

At high altitudes, desserts take longer to bake, and liquids evaporate faster from batters and dough. To achieve successful desserts, Susan Purdy, author of *Pie in the Sky*, suggests a range of recipe adjustments, depending on altitude. For best results, she suggests increasing the amount of liquids in recipes by 2 to 4 tablespoons (30 to 60ml); increasing the amount of dry ingredients (and in the case of Passover baking, the cake meal and potato starch) by 2 to 4 tablespoons (15 to 30g); decreasing sugar by 2 to 4 tablespoons (25 to 50g); and decreasing baking powder by ⅛ to ½ teaspoon. Adjusting recipes for high altitude baking is not an exact science and may require some trial and error on your part. Be sure to keep notes on the results.

Rosh Hashanah
and Yom Kippur

The two-day holiday of Rosh Hashanah is the Jewish New Year. It is the anniversary of the creation of humanity, a time when we acknowledge G-d as Creator of the entire universe. We recognize not only G-d's historic role in the world but G-d's continuous presence in our lives. During services we pray to G-d to grant us a happy and healthy new year. The shofar (an instrument made of a ram's horn) is blown to serve as a wake-up call to repentance.

For a month before Rosh Hashanah, the shofar is blown every morning in synagogue to alert us to the upcoming holiday. In my neighborhood, Rosh Hashanah's imminent arrival is signaled every year by the delivery of honey from the Starr family. My friend Lily Starr spends months choosing the honey, the bottle, designing the label, choosing the ribbon, the perfect box, and writing a lovely New Year blessing. The honey tastes different every year; some years it is sweeter and some years it is less intense, just like life. On the first night of Rosh Hashanah, we drizzle the Starr family honey on our challah and dip apples in it and wish each other a sweet new year. Indeed, Rosh Hashanah desserts are traditionally made with apples and honey to symbolize the desire for a sweet year.

This chapter has contemporary desserts but also ones that will remind you of your grandmother's, such as apple cake, strudel, and babka. On Rosh Hashanah, rather than serving a huge buffet of deserts, I often serve a plated dessert, which is sufficient after a meal that simply includes too

many courses. One year I served squares of chocolate layer cake with a slice of strudel alongside. This chapter also contains recipes that serve a crowd—to enable you to bake fewer desserts but still have enough to feed your family and guests. And there are cookies and snack-type desserts to nosh on during the long afternoons.

Unless it is also Shabbat, on the first day of Rosh Hashanah we perform *tashlich*; we ceremonially cast our sins into a natural body of flowing water. The custom is to throw pieces of bread into the water. I live down the street from a creek, and every year our dear friends the Gold-Pastor family join us as we walk down to the creek, say the prayers, symbolically throw our sins away, and then come back to my house for cinnamon buns. The pecan sticky buns on page 22 are an updated version of those buns.

On Yom Kippur we fast and spend most of the day in the synagogue asking G-d for forgiveness for our sins. We read the story of Jonah, which teaches us that we all have the capacity to change. When the fast is over, we begin the year with a clean slate and a chance to improve our relationship with G-d and with the people in our lives.

Ashkenazi tradition is to break the fast with dairy food, so for desserts, my family eats breakfast-type pastries, including croissants, scones, and sticky buns (recipes for these are in this chapter). When you are contemplating ways you can improve during the coming year, consider some baking resolutions. Start baking challah for Shabbat. Warm homemade challah provides both physical and spiritual nourishment. Resolve to bake for others who need uplifting, to show them they are worth the effort you took to plan, shop, bake, and deliver something sweet. Bake from scratch more often to give your family and friends desserts that are far healthier and more flavorful than packaged and bakery treats. If you have overeaten desserts in the past year, commit to saving treats for Shabbat and holidays and forgo them the rest of the time.

As Rosh Hashanah comes right after the summer, start baking challahs in August. Once they're baked, let the challahs cool, wrap them in foil, and freeze them. Just a few hours before the festive meal, take the wrapped challahs out of the freezer and put them in the oven to warm (with the wrapping on). The Rosh Hashanah tradition is to serve round challahs, to remind us of the crowning of G-d as king and of the Jewish life cycle.

I also start baking cookies, and anything else that can be frozen, weeks before the high holidays (instructions for freezing are included with every recipe). There is plenty of last minute cooking to do for the holiday, so it helps to have challah and desserts done a few weeks beforehand.

For the break-fast meal, you need to do any baking in advance, and take the desserts out of the freezer to thaw just before you return to synagogue for Ne'ila, the last portion of the Yom Kippur service before the end of the fast.

Rosh Hashanah Snacks and Yom Kippur Break-fast Breads and Pastries

Pizza Ebraica 6

Babka Bites 8

Honey Cake Biscotti 10

Chocolate Madeleines 11

Orange and Honey Madeleines 13

Pignons 14

Cranberry and Orange Spelt Scones 17

Chocolate and Almond Croissants 18

Cheese Danish 19

Whole-Wheat Chocolate Babka 20

Pecan Sticky Buns with Butterscotch Whisky Glaze 22

Whole Grain Carrot Cake 24

Desserts for High Holiday Entertaining

Quinoa Pudding with Caramelized Apples and Honey 24

Nana's Holiday Apple Cake 26

Apricot and Berry Strudel 27

Vanilla and Chocolate 12-Layer Cake 28

Chocolate Ganache Layer Cake Squares with Fruit Sauce 31

Ombré Layer Cake 32

Apple Pizza Tart 35

Raspberry and Rose Macaron Cake 36

Apple and Honey Challah Rolls 39

Rosh Hashanah Snacks and Yom Kippur Break-fast Breads and Pastries

On Rosh Hashanah, I find I always need snack desserts for breakfast, tea time, and following *tashlich*. The desserts in this section are also easy to double and serve for a crowd for the holiday meals. The pastries in this section are perfect light desserts to serve after the fast of Yom Kippur.

EASY

PARVE

PIZZA EBRAICA

Serves everyone, until it's gone

On my blog I called Pizza Ebraica, which comes from the Jewish Ghetto in Rome, the ugliest dessert you will ever love. Every Friday, Jewish Romans line up to buy this mandelbread, which is burnt black to a crisp and filled with candied fruit (which I've replaced with apricots and cranberries). My friend Linda Watson of www.cookforgood.com, wrote a story about this recipe for the *Huffington Post* and describes Pizza Ebraica as the most frugal dessert you can make because you use any nuts or dried fruit that you happen to already have on hand (just follow the amounts indicated below). You do not need to bake the mandelbread until it is charred, but "well-browned" results in a crunchier loaf. Warning: It is very addictive.

¾ cup (180ml) extra virgin olive oil
1 large egg white
4¼ cups (530g) all-purpose flour
½ teaspoon salt
1 cup (200g) sugar
¾ cup (120g) dark raisins soaked in 1 cup (240ml)
sweet wine for ten minutes (you can also use purple grape juice)
1 cup (150g) whole almonds, with skins
½ cup (100g) dried apricots, chopped
½ cup (70g) pine nuts
¼ cup (35g) dried cranberries, chopped
½ cup (80g) golden raisins

PREHEAT OVEN to 400°F (200°C). Cover a jelly roll pan with parchment paper or a silicone baking mat. Set it aside.

PLACE THE OLIVE OIL, egg white, flour, salt, and sugar into a large mixing bowl and mix with a wooden spoon or electric mixer. The mixture will look like very dry crumbs. Add the raisins and wine and mix with a wooden spoon or your hands. Add the almonds, apricots, pine nuts, cranberries, and golden raisins and mix until combined. Place the dough on the prepared jelly roll pan and shape it into a large oval or rectangle, almost the size of the cookie sheet. Pat the top down.

BAKE for 30 to 35 minutes, or until well browned. Let cool. To eat, break into pieces. Store at room temperature for up to five days, if it lasts that long. ▪

PARCHMENT PAPER VS. SILICONE BAKING MATS

I have always preferred parchment paper to line my baking pans, because items bake faster and are crisper when they are closer to the hot pan. While writing this book I went through cases of parchment paper, so I started using silicone mats more often and am generally very happy with the results. I do, however, find that cookies and nuts baked on silicone mats need to bake a bit longer to brown well. For this dessert, parchment results in a crunchier bottom.

MODERATE

NUT-FREE • PARVE

BABKA BITES

Makes 46 to 48

Chocolate babka is my most popular dessert, and I have enjoyed teaching audiences of all ages all over the U.S. how to make it. Because it is also one of my most addictive recipes, I came up with a two-bite version so I can enjoy my beloved babka without overeating. In the end they came out so good that the risk of overeating has not been completely eliminated. Be careful not to overbake these bites or you will lose the soft interior.

Dough

¼ cup (60ml) warm water

½ ounce (2 envelopes; 14g) dry yeast

¼ cup (50g) plus 1 teaspoon sugar, divided

2½ cups (315g) all-purpose flour

dash salt

4 tablespoons (57g) margarine, at room temperature for at least 15 minutes

¼ cup (60ml) canola oil

1 large egg plus 1 egg white

Filling

½ cup (1 stick; 113g) margarine, at room temperature for at least 30 minutes

¼ cup (20g) unsweetened cocoa

¾ cup (150g) sugar

⅓ cup (60g) mini chocolate chips

To make the dough

PLACE WARM WATER, yeast, and 1 teaspoon sugar into a large mixing bowl or the bowl of a stand mixer and let it sit for 10 minutes, until the mixture bubbles and thickens. Add the ¼ cup (50g) sugar, flour, salt, margarine, oil, egg, and egg white. Combine with a wooden spoon or a dough hook in a stand mixer until all the ingredients are mixed in. Cover bowl with plastic wrap and let rise 1½ hours.

To make the filling

PLACE THE MARGARINE into a medium or large bowl and beat until creamy. Add the cocoa and sugar and beat until combined. Cover with plastic and let sit at room temperature while the dough is rising. PREHEAT OVEN to 325°F (160°C). Place mini muffin papers into a 12-cup mini muffin pan. You will need to bake Babka Bites in batches.

To assemble and bake

AFTER THE DOUGH HAS RISEN, divide it in half. On a large piece of parchment paper sprinkled with a little flour, roll each piece of dough into a 9 x 12-inch (23 x 30-cm) rectangle so that the 12-inch (30-cm) side is facing you. Sprinkle a little flour on the rolling pin if the dough starts to stick to it. Use a silicone spatula to spread half the chocolate filling all the way to the edges. Sprinkle half the chocolate chips all over the chocolate filling and roll up tightly the long way. Cut into ½-inch (1.25-cm) slices and place one into each of the muffin cups, cut side up. You will have about 24 slices. Repeat with the rest of the dough.

BAKE for 20 minutes, or until lightly golden. Serve warm or at room temperature. Store covered at room temperature for up to four days or freeze for up to three months. ◾

"YOM KIPPUR BAKING"

One year, sometime between Rosh Hashanah and Yom Kippur, I was a guest on the Martha Stewart Living radio show on XM Sirius. The title of the show was "Yom Kippur Baking," which was pretty funny, given that Yom Kippur is a fast day. We debated the merits of chocolate babka versus cinnamon buns for the break-fast, with babka emerging as the clear winner.

ROSH HASHANAH AND YOM KIPPUR 9

HONEY CAKE BISCOTTI

Makes 30

It was around Rosh Hashanah when I was getting to the end of developing recipes for this book, and my friend and great baker, Rhonda Alexander-Abt, was horrified that I did not have a honey cake recipe. I told her how much I hated honey cake. She was relentless and said I could not call this a Jewish holiday baking book without honey cake. So I challenged her to come up with a new idea that I would actually like. Rhonda came up with the idea, and I created the recipe, which tastes just like honey cake, but has a cookie crunch. This recipe makes cookies on the chewier side, but if you want them harder, just bake them a few minutes longer after they are sliced.

3 cups plus 2 tablespoons (390g) all-purpose flour

½ cup (110g) dark brown sugar, packed

½ teaspoon cinnamon

½ teaspoon ground ginger

½ teaspoon ground cloves

¼ teaspoon ground nutmeg

1 teaspoon baking powder

dash salt

½ cup (120ml) canola oil

½ cup (170g) honey

¼ cup (60ml) brewed coffee or espresso

2 large eggs

PREHEAT OVEN to 350°F (180°C). Cover a jelly roll pan or cookie sheet with parchment paper. Set it aside.

IN A LARGE BOWL, place the flour, brown sugar, cinnamon, ginger, cloves, nutmeg, baking powder, and salt and mix together. Add the oil, honey, coffee, and eggs and mix gently to combine.

DIVIDE THE DOUGH in half and shape each half into a log, 10 to 12 inches (25 to 30cm) long by 4 inches (10cm) wide, leaving 2 to 3 inches (5 to 8cm) between each loaf.

BAKE for 35 minutes, or until the loaves are set and a little browned on the bottom. Slide the parchment paper off the pan. Let the loaves sit for five minutes. Slice each loaf into ¾ to 1-inch (2cm) slices. Place a new piece of parchment paper on the pan and place the cookies on it, cut side down. Bake for five more minutes. Let the cookies cool on the pan. Store in an airtight container for up to five days or freeze for up to three months.

MODERATE

NUT-FREE • PARVE

CHOCOLATE MADELEINES

Makes 24

Madeleines are shell-shaped mini sponge cakes that are typically lemon-flavored. These cakes were made famous by a reference in Marcel Proust's *In Search of Lost Time*, where he wrote about the pleasurable memory of the taste of a madeleine dipped into a cup of tea. Each of us has foods that evoke certain memories. These are the perfect treats to create new holiday memories.

½ cup (1 stick; 113g) margarine, plus 1 tablespoon for greasing molds

⅓ cup (25g) unsweetened cocoa, plus 1 tablespoon for dusting molds

1 cup (125g) all-purpose flour, plus 1 teaspoon for dusting molds

3 large eggs, at room temperature for at least one hour

¾ cup (150g) sugar

1 teaspoon pure vanilla extract

3 ounces (85g) bittersweet chocolate

½ teaspoon baking powder

1 tablespoon confectioners' sugar for dusting, optional

Preparing the madeleine molds

PREHEAT OVEN to 375°F (190°C).

YOU WILL NEED shell-shaped madeleine molds to make these 2- to 3-inch (5- to 8-cm) cakes. Melt 1 tablespoon margarine and use a pastry brush to grease the inside of the madeleine molds, making sure to grease well. Combine the 1 tablespoon cocoa with the 1 teaspoon flour in a small bowl and sprinkle into the molds. Tap out the excess cocoa and flour into a bowl and reserve for the other batches.

Preparing the batter and baking the cakes

PLACE THE EGGS into a large bowl and beat with an electric mixer on low speed for 30 seconds. Add the sugar in four parts, beating continuously on low speed. Add the vanilla and turn the mixer to high speed and beat for 5 full minutes. The mixture should be thick and creamy.

NEXT, PLACE THE ONE STICK margarine and bittersweet chocolate into a medium microwave-safe bowl. Heat until melted, about 1 minute. Whisk well. Add the remaining cocoa and baking powder

BRINGING EGGS TO ROOM TEMPERATURE

If you're in a rush: Crack the eggs into a metal bowl. Take a second larger bowl and place an inch of hot water inside. Place the bowl with the eggs on top, and the hot water underneath will warm them. When the eggs no longer feel cold, they are ready to use.

Orange and Honey Madeleines (left), Chocolate Madeleines (right)

and whisk well. Add the remaining flour and use a silicone spatula or wooden spoon to mix into a dry-looking paste.

ADD HALF of the beaten eggs to the chocolate mixture and whisk. Put half of this mixture back into the eggs and mix on low speed until almost combined. Add the remaining chocolate mixture to the eggs and mix on low speed for 30 seconds. Turn the mixer up to high speed for 15 seconds, or until mixture is thick and smooth. Cover with plastic wrap and place in the fridge for 15 minutes. May be made a day in advance.

SPOON A TABLESPOON of the batter into each mold. Use your finger to spread the batter the long way down the mold (so that the baked cookie will

have all of the madeleine's distinctive shell shape). Cover the leftover batter and put it back in the fridge until you are ready to bake the next batch.

BAKE the little cakes for 12 to 13 minutes, or until a toothpick inserted comes out clean. Immediately remove the madeleines from the pan by tapping the pan on the counter near your wire rack. Let them cool on the rack, shell side facing up. Wash out the molds and then grease and dust them with cocoa and flour. Fill the molds with batter and bake as you did the first batch.

SERVE WARM or at room temperature sprinkled with the sifted confectioners' sugar, if desired. Store in an airtight container for up to four days or freeze for up to three months. ▪

ORANGE AND HONEY MADELEINES

Makes 30

I have included an orange-honey glaze to give the madeleine cakes a stronger honey taste. If you are short on time, you can just dust the cakes with confectioners' sugar, and they'll be just as good. Remember to serve them shell side up. You can buy madeleine molds in kitchen stores and online. I have one pan that makes 12 cakes, which I use to bake madeleines in batches. The little cakes come out of the molds easily if you grease them with spray oil that contains flour.

Cakes

4 large eggs, at room temperature for at least one hour

⅔ cup (65g) sugar

4 teaspoons orange zest (from 1–2 oranges)

2 teaspoons fresh orange juice, from zested orange

½ cup (1 stick; 113g) margarine

3 tablespoons honey

1 cup (125g) all-purpose flour

spray oil containing flour or spray oil plus 2 tablespoons flour for greasing and flouring pan

Glaze

1 cup (120g) confectioners' sugar

2 tablespoons fresh orange juice, from zested oranges

3–4 teaspoons honey, to taste

To make the cakes

PREHEAT OVEN to 375°F (190°C). Grease the madeleine molds with spray oil containing flour.

PLACE THE EGGS into a large bowl and beat with an electric mixer on low speed for one minute.

Add the sugar in four parts, beating continuously on low speed, adding more sugar after each addition is mixed in. Add the orange zest and juice and turn the mixer up to high speed and beat for five minutes. The mixture will become thick and creamy.

MELT THE MARGARINE either in the microwave oven or on the stovetop. Place in a medium bowl, and whisk in the honey. Add the flour and mix with a silicone spatula or wooden spoon until thoroughly combined. Add half of the beaten eggs to the flour, honey, and margarine mixture and mix.

SCOOP HALF of this mixture back into the eggs and mix on low speed for 15 seconds to combine. Add the other half of the flour mixture to the eggs and beat for another 15 seconds, or until just combined. Cover and place in the fridge for 30 minutes.

SPOON A HEAPING TABLESPOON of the batter into each mold. Cover the leftover batter and return to the fridge.

BAKE the madeleines for 13 to 15 minutes, or until a toothpick inserted comes out clean and a quarter inch of the outside edge is well browned. Immediately turn pan over a wire rack and tap out the cakes onto the rack. If they do not release, use a knife to gently coax them out of their molds. Wash and dry the pan and spray with more oil and flour. Repeat with the remaining batter, washing and then regreasing and re-flouring the pan before each batch.

TO GLAZE THE CAKES, place the confectioners' sugar, orange juice, and honey into a bowl and whisk well. Place a cooling rack over aluminum foil to catch the drippings. Dip the top half of the shell side into the glaze and let dry on the cooling rack, glaze side up.

STORE THE CAKES in an airtight container at room temperature for up to five days or freeze for up to three months.

MULTIPLE STEP

PARVE

PIGNONS

Makes 12

When I lived in Geneva, Switzerland, Pignons (pronounced *pinyone* in French) were in every pastry shop. They have a sweet, sugar cookie crust and are filled with almond cream and topped with pine nuts. I often make the dough and filling a few days before assembly and baking.

I bought special pignon pans in France, but, because I am generally opposed to buying and using kitchen equipment that has only one purpose, I now make them in muffin tins, which work just as well as pignon pans. To get the dough into the pan, roll it out and then cut it into circles. Press the circles into the muffin cups. Don't worry if the dough breaks or you need more to fill any holes, just use those pre-school skills of cut and paste—and no one will detect any mistakes!

Dough

2 cups (250g) all-purpose flour

1⅓ cups (160g) confectioners' sugar

½ cup (1 stick; 113g) margarine, frozen for 20 minutes and cut into tablespoons

½ teaspoon pure vanilla extract

2 large egg yolks

4 tablespoons cold water

Almond Cream

¾ cup (80g) slivered almonds

½ cup (1 stick; 113g) margarine

½ cup (100g) sugar

2 tablespoons all-purpose flour

1 large egg plus 1 egg white

2 teaspoons pure vanilla extract

1 teaspoon rum, or rum flavoring, if desired

⅓ cup (45g) pine nuts

To make the dough

PLACE THE FLOUR, confectioners' sugar, and margarine pieces into the bowl of a food processor fitted with a metal blade. Pulse for 10 seconds. Add the vanilla, egg yolks, and cold water, and mix just until the dough starts to come together into clumps. Gather the dough into a ball, flatten it, and wrap it in plastic. Put the dough in the freezer overnight.

REMOVE THE DOUGH from the freezer and let it stand until you can press it gently. Meanwhile, prepare the almond cream.

To make the almond cream

PUT THE ALMONDS in a coffee grinder or food processor and process until finely ground. Place the margarine in a medium bowl and beat with an electric mixer until creamy. Add the ground almonds, sugar, and flour and beat until combined. Scrape down the bowl. Add the egg, egg white, vanilla, and rum, and mix together. Turn the mixer speed to medium-high and beat for 1½ minutes, or until the mixture is light and airy. May be made three days in advance and stored covered in the fridge. PREHEAT OVEN to 350°F (180°C).

Assembling the pignons

USE SPRAY OIL to grease 12 muffin cups in a muffin pan. Place a piece of parchment paper on your counter and sprinkle it with flour. Place the dough on top. Sprinkle the dough with a little more flour and cover it with another piece of parchment paper. Using a rolling pin on top of the parchment, roll out the dough until it is 13 x 13 inches (33 x 33cm). You will want to peel back the top parchment a few times and sprinkle some more flour on the dough as you roll.

REMOVE THE TOP PIECE of parchment. Take a 3½-inch (9-cm) round cookie cutter or drinking glass and cut 12 circles from the dough. Use a flat metal spatula to lift the circles. Place each circle of dough into a cup in the muffin tin, pressing gently so the dough fits into the bottom, goes into the space where the bottom and sides meet, and comes up the sides. Repeat with the other 11 circles of dough. If any holes result, just patch them up with little pieces of dough.

SPOON THE ALMOND CREAM evenly into the 12 dough shells. Sprinkle a heaping teaspoon of pine nuts on top of the almond cream in each filled dough shell.

BAKE for 30 to 35 minutes, or until the crust is golden and the cream has puffed. Let the pignons cool in the pan for 10 minutes, and then remove them to a wire rack to finish cooling. Store covered at room temperature for up to four days or freeze for up to three months. ■

KEEP SOME MARGARINE STICKS IN THE FREEZER

Margarine stored in the fridge is too soft to cut into dry ingredients to make flakey crusts and cookies. Frozen margarine behaves more like cold butter.

*Cranberry and Orange Spelt Scones
(foreground), Chocolate and Almond
Croissants (center), Cheese Danish
(upper right),*

EASY

DAIRY • NUT-FREE • PARVE

CRANBERRY AND ORANGE SPELT SCONES

Makes 12 to 16

If I could, I would eat a scone every day—and almost any flavor would do. Now that I have created these whole-grain scones, I can eat them more often. Spelt is an ancient grain mentioned in the Bible. It has fifty percent more protein than common wheat and a low glycemic index. People sensitive to wheat can often tolerate spelt because it has less gluten than regular wheat. In addition, spelt is a sustainable crop, so it benefits the environment as well.

2 cups plus 2 tablespoons (265g) spelt flour, divided

½ cup (100g) plus 1 teaspoon sugar, divided

1 tablespoon baking powder

¼ teaspoon ground ginger

½ teaspoon salt

1½ teaspoons orange zest (from one large orange)

6 tablespoons (85g) unsalted butter or frozen margarine

2 large eggs, separated

⅓ cup (80ml) milk or soy milk

1 cup (110g) frozen cranberrieS

PREHEAT OVEN to 425°F (220°C). Line a baking sheet with parchment paper or a silicone baking mat. Set it aside.

PLACE TWO CUPS of flour, ½ cup sugar, baking powder, ginger, and salt into the bowl of a food processor fitted with a metal blade and mix for a few seconds. Add the orange zest and mix a few seconds to distribute. Cut the butter or margarine into small pieces and add to the dry ingredients. Process for 10 seconds.

IN A SMALL BOWL, beat one of the eggs and add to the food processor. Add the milk or soy milk and process just until the dough comes together. Sprinkle one tablespoon spelt flour on your counter. Remove the dough from the bowl and place on top of the flour. Knead gently until the dough is soft, adding the remaining tablespoon flour if the dough remains sticky. Add the frozen cranberries by pressing them into the dough so they do not roll off your counter, which they will want to do. Knead the dough, making sure the cranberries are evenly distributed throughout.

DIVIDE THE DOUGH in two and then roll each piece into a log, 1½ to 2 inches (4 to 5cm) thick and 8 inches (20cm) long. Take a sharp knife and cut the logs diagonally into wedges (triangles) making each cut in the opposite direction. Place the wedges 1½ inches (4cm) apart on the prepared baking sheet. Beat the remaining egg and use a pastry brush to glaze the top of the scones. Sprinkle the tops with the remaining teaspoon of sugar.

BAKE for 15 to 18 minutes, or until the tops are just beginning to brown. Serve warm or at room temperature. Store covered at room temperature for up to three days or freeze for up to three months. May be reheated to serve. ▪

EVEN EASIER SCONES

If you are short on time, shape the dough into a ball and then flatten it into an 8-inch (20-cm) pancake. Gently press the dough into a greased 8-inch (20-cm) round pan, brush it with egg wash, and bake for 20 to 25 minutes. Cut into wedges and serve.

MODERATE

PARVE

CHOCOLATE AND ALMOND CROISSANTS

Makes 12

I thought that a croissant could not be more perfect than one filled with a chocolate bar, until I ate my first chocolate and almond croissant. Almond cream filling is one of my favorite elements of French baking and I use it in tarts, cakes, and other pastries. You can prepare almond cream three days before you want to assemble and bake these quick and easy croissants.

1 sheet frozen puff pastry (from a 17.3-ounce or 490g box)

3 tablespoons (42g) unsalted butter or margarine

⅓ cup (40g) ground almonds (coffee grinder works best)

¼ cup (50g) sugar, plus 2 teaspoons for sprinkling on top

2 tablespoons all-purpose flour, plus extra for dusting

1 large egg, beaten, divided

1 teaspoon pure vanilla extract

6 ounces (170g) bittersweet chocolate

¼ cup (30g) sliced almonds, for decorating tops (with or without skins)

2 teaspoons water

THAW the puff pastry at room temperature for 45 minutes. The dough is ready to use when you can unroll it easily without breaking it.

PREHEAT OVEN to 450°F (230°C). Cover a cookie sheet with parchment paper and set it aside.

To make the almond cream

PLACE THE BUTTER or margarine into the bowl of a stand mixer or into a medium bowl. Beat at medium speed until soft, scraping down the bowl as necessary. Add the ground almonds, ¼ cup (50g) sugar, and flour, and mix until the mixture becomes a paste. Add half of the egg and the vanilla. Mix on low speed to incorporate and then turn the speed up to high and whip until the mixture is light and airy, about 1½ minutes. May be made up to three days in advance and stored covered in the fridge.

To make the croissants

CUT THE CHOCOLATE into small bars, about 3 inches (8cm) long and ½ inch (1.25cm) wide. Do not worry if they do not cut perfectly; you can piece together "bars" when you place the chocolate pieces into your croissants.

PLACE A PIECE OF PARCHMENT paper on the counter and sprinkle it with some flour. Unroll the pastry sheet and place it on the parchment. Use a rolling pin to smooth out the creases and roll out the dough until it is about 13 x 14 inches (33 x 36cm). Every few rolls, you will need to lift the pastry and sprinkle a little more flour underneath it so that the pastry does not stick to the parchment.

USE A FLAT, NON-SERRATED KNIFE to cut across the longer side of the dough to cut it in half. Starting from the line you just cut, cut six long triangles, with the triangle base about three to four inches wide and the sides about six inches long. Place a little less than one tablespoon of almond cream on the base of the rectangle and spread slightly across the pastry, leaving ½-inch (1.25-cm) borders on each side of the cream. Press one chocolate bar into the cream just above the triangle base, parallel to the base. Roll up the dough tightly around the chocolate bar all the way to the tip. Place on the prepared cookie sheet and bend

A KITCHEN RULER

Buy a ruler just for kitchen use and store it with your baking utensils.

the points slightly toward each other to shape the croissant into a crescent.

REPEAT for the other croissants. You should use up all the almond cream among the croissants. Place the remaining egg into a small bowl and add two teaspoons water and mix. Brush the tops of the croissants with the glaze. Sprinkle with the sliced almonds, pressing them into the glaze. If you have any leftover chocolate shavings from cutting the bars, you can sprinkle them on top of the croissants.

BAKE for 15 to 18 minutes, or until the croissants are golden. Serve warm. Store at room temperature for up to three days or freeze for up to three months. ▪

MODERATE

NUT-FREE • DAIRY

CHEESE DANISH

Serves 10 to 12

Growing up in New York, cheese Danishes were everywhere, and it always amazed me that wherever you bought them they tasted exactly the same. When I entered the food business I learned that, sadly, most Jewish bakeries buy their Danish dough commercially. Some time after the industrialization of food in the 1940s and 1950s, Jewish bakeries stopped making pastries from scratch, which is precisely why I recommend that if you like desserts you should bake them from scratch.

The one commercial ingredient I am grateful for is frozen puff pastry sheets. I have made puff pastry from scratch many times, but I know that even skilled home bakers prefer to use the frozen ones. At least you have a homemade cheese filling in this recipe! It's a nice breakfast pastry to serve either before services on Rosh Hashanah or for post Yom Kippur break-fast.

1 sheet frozen puff pastry (from a 17.3-ounce or 490g box)

12 ounces (1½ cups; 340g) cream cheese (not whipped), at room temperature for at least 30 minutes

1 large egg, separated

¼ cup sugar (50g), plus 2 teaspoons for sprinkling

2 teaspoons pure vanilla extract

1 teaspoon lemon zest (from one lemon)

dash salt

PREHEAT OVEN to 400°F (200°C). Thaw puff pastry at room temperature for 45 minutes.

PLACE THE CREAM CHEESE, egg yolk, ¼ cup sugar, vanilla, lemon zest, and salt in a medium bowl and beat together with an electric mixer until smooth. Cover and place in the fridge until the dough is ready.

TAKE A PIECE OF PARCHMENT paper the size of a jelly roll pan or a 12 x 16-inch (30 x 40-cm) cookie sheet and sprinkle the parchment paper with some flour. Unroll the pastry and use a rolling pin to roll out until it's about 12½ x 15 inches (32 x 38cm) wide. With every few rolls, lift up the pastry and sprinkle a little more flour underneath it. Turn the pastry until it's vertical. Use the back of a knife to score, but not cut through, the dough into three even, vertical columns.

REMOVE THE CHEESE FILLING from the fridge and spread it in the center column, leaving a 1-inch (2.5-cm) border on the top and bottom. Fold down the top ½-inch (2-cm) of the dough over the

cream to seal it in. Take your knife and cut the two side columns horizontally (away from the cream filling) into 1-inch (2.5-cm) long strips, leaving it attached to the dough and stopping about ¾ inch (2cm) before the cream filling. Starting at the top, take the top strip on the right side and pull over the cream at a downward angle and press into the cream. Take the top strip from the left side and cross over the first strip and press to seal. Repeat on the right side and keep alternating until you get to the bottom. When you get to the bottom two strips, cross them over each other but this time go up the pastry. Fold the bottom up about one inch to seal the filling inside.

BEAT the reserved egg white and brush the top of the pastry. Sprinkle with sugar. Bake for 30 to 35 minutes, or until golden. Serve warm. Store in the fridge for up to three days or freeze for up to three months. Reheat to serve. ▪

MULTIPLE STEP

NUT-FREE • PARVE

WHOLE-WHEAT CHOCOLATE BABKA

Makes 2 loaves, serves 25

Although my chocolate babka is extremely popular, I did hear some complaints about the amount of margarine in the recipe while I was on tour for my first book, *The Kosher Baker*. Even though I told people that they were not consuming too much margarine if they ate one slice, I nevertheless set out on a mission to create a healthier babka. Along with Esther Dayon, a serious baker who is also one of my recipe testers, I tried several options in order to reduce the fat and sugar amounts without compromising flavor. The result is a moist, chocolaty babka that will satisfy the babka cravings of even the most committed healthy eaters out there.

Dough

½ cup warm water

½ ounce (2 envelopes; 14g) dry yeast

½ cup (100g) plus 1 teaspoon sugar, divided

3 cups (375g) all-purpose flour

2 cups (250g) white whole-wheat flour

½ cup (120ml) canola oil

½ cup (1 stick; 113g) margarine, at room
  temperature at least 30 minutes

3 large eggs plus 1 egg white (reserve yolk for
  glazing)

Filling and glaze

1½ cups (300g) sugar

½ cup (40g) unsweetened cocoa

1 cup (2 sticks; 226g) margarine, at room
  temperature for at least 30 minutes

1 cup (180g) mini-chocolate chips

2 teaspoons water plus reserved egg yolk

To make the dough

PLACE warm water, yeast, and 1 teaspoon of the sugar into a large mixing bowl and let sit 10 minutes, or until thick. Add the sugar, both flours, the oil, the margarine, and the eggs. Combine with a wooden spoon or a dough hook in a stand mixer until all the ingredients are mixed together. Cover bowl with plastic wrap and let rise 2½ hours.

To make the filling

WHILE THE DOUGH IS RISING, make the filling. Combine the sugar with the cocoa. Add the margarine and mix well. You can let the filling sit out covered while the dough continues to rise.

Assembling the babka

PREHEAT OVEN to 375°F (190°C). Grease two 12-inch (30-cm) loaf pans using spray oil.

DIVIDE THE DOUGH into 4 equal pieces. On a large piece of parchment paper sprinkled with flour, roll out each piece of dough into a 10 x 7-inch (25 x 18-cm) rectangle. Spread each piece with one quarter of the filling, sprinkle it with ¼ cup (45g) of the chocolate chips, and roll up the dough length-wise. When you have two rolls, twist them around each other, keeping the seams on the bottom. Tuck the ends underneath and place into the pre-pared loaf pan. Repeat with the other pieces of dough. Brush the tops with the reserved egg yolk mixed with water.

BAKE for 40 to 45 minutes, or until well browned. Cool for 20 minutes. Run a knife around the sides of the babkas and then remove from pans and let cool on a wire rack. Store wrapped in foil at room temperature for up to two days or freeze for up to three months. ■

MODERATE

DAIRY

PECAN STICKY BUNS WITH **BUTTERSCOTCH WHISKY GLAZE**

Makes 15

These delicious, soft and buttery buns are per-fect for the break-fast after Yom Kippur and any morning, anytime, for breakfast. You can also make these parve by substituting parve marga-rine, soy milk, and parve whipping cream for the dairy equivalents.

Dough

1 cup (240ml) milk
½ ounce (2 envelopes; 14g) dry yeast
⅓ cup (65g) plus 1 teaspoon sugar, divided
4¼ cups (530g) all-purpose flour
2 large eggs
½ cup (1 stick; 113g) unsalted butter, at room temperature for at least 30 minutes
dash salt

Filling

½ cup (1 stick; 113g) unsalted butter, at room temperature for at least 30 minutes
¾ cup (165g) light brown sugar, packed
1 tablespoon cinnamon
1½ cups (180g) pecan halves, chopped, divided

Glaze

½ cup (110g) light brown sugar, packed
6 tablespoons (85g) unsalted butter, cut into small pieces
2 tablespoons Scotch whisky, I use Glengoyne single malt
⅓ cup (80ml) heavy cream
¼ teaspoon salt
2 teaspoons light corn syrup
2 tablespoons water
spray oil for greasing muffin cups

To make the dough

HEAT THE MILK until it's very warm, not hot. Pour it into a large bowl, add the yeast and 1 teaspoon sugar and stir. Let the mixture sit for 10 minutes, or until thick. Add the remaining sugar, flour, eggs, butter and salt, and mix well, using either a dough hook in a stand mixer for 2 to 3 minutes or by hand until the dough comes together into a ball. Knead the dough for another minute. Cover the bowl with plastic wrap and let the dough rise for one hour.

To prepare the filling

ABOUT FIVE MINUTES before the dough is ready, place the butter, brown sugar, and cinnamon into a medium bowl and beat with an electric mixer on medium speed until smooth. Cover and set aside.

Assembling the sticky buns

PLACE A PIECE OF PARCHMENT paper larger than 13 x 22 inches (33 x 56cm) in front of you. Sprinkle it with a little flour and place the dough on top of the paper. Sprinkle a little more flour on top of the dough. Use a rolling pin to roll out the dough until

it is 13 x 22 inches (33 x 56cm). Use a silicone spatula to spread the filling all the way to the edges. Sprinkle most of the chopped pecans on the filling, reserving ¼ to ⅓ cup (30 to 40g) to sprinkle on top of the buns after they are baked. Roll up the dough tightly lengthwise. Use a large non-serrated knife to cut the roll into 1½-inch (4-cm) slices.

PREHEAT OVEN to 350°F (180°C). Spray 15 muffin cups with spray oil. Place the buns cut side up into the muffin cups. Cover with plastic wrap and let rise 15 minutes. Bake the buns for 24 to 28 minutes, or until browned.

To prepare the glaze

WHILE THE BUNS ARE BAKING, prepare the glaze. Place the brown sugar, butter, whisky, cream, salt, corn syrup, and water into a small saucepan over medium heat. Bring to a boil and cook on medium-low heat for three minutes, stirring occasionally. The mixture will bubble and look foamy. Turn the heat to low and cook for one minute more. Set it aside.

WHEN THE BUNS ARE OUT of the oven, let them cool in the pans for five minutes. You can unmold them by twisting them back and forth to loosen and lift them out. Place the buns on a serving platter and slowly pour the glaze over the tops, letting it seep inside the buns and drip over the sides. Sprinkle the buns with the remaining chopped pecans. Store

PROOFING YEAST

For all recipes using dry yeast, you must dissolve the yeast in a warm liquid (not boiling hot) and stir in a teaspoon of sugar. The yeast should thicken and bubble within 10 minutes. If it doesn't, then your yeast is dead, and you should dump it and start again with fresh yeast.

covered at room temperature for up to four days or freeze for up to three months. Reheat to serve. ■

WHOLE GRAIN CARROT CAKE

Serves 12 to 15

This moist cake is made with a combination of dark and white whole-wheat flours. White whole-wheat flour is a welcome addition to the baker's pantry because it has the same nutritional value as darker whole-wheat flour but has a milder taste.

4 large eggs
1 cup (200g) sugar
1 cup (220g) light brown sugar, packed
1 cup (240ml) canola oil
½ cup (120ml) orange juice
2 teaspoons pure vanilla extract
1½ cups (190g) white whole-wheat flour
½ cup (65g) whole-wheat flour
1½ teaspoons baking powder
½ teaspoon salt
2 teaspoons cinnamon
3 cups peeled and grated carrot (not packed, from about 5 large carrots)
spray oil containing flour or spray oil plus 2 tablespoons flour for greasing and flouring pan

PREHEAT OVEN to 350°F (180°C). Grease and flour a 12-cup (2.8-liter) Bundt pan. Set it aside.

IN A LARGE BOWL, beat the eggs with the white and brown sugars with an electric mixer on medium speed for three minutes, or by hand with a whisk, until very thick. Add the oil, orange juice, and vanilla and mix on low speed to combine.

IN A MEDIUM BOWL, whisk together the white whole-wheat flour, whole-wheat flour, baking powder, salt, and cinnamon. Add half of this mixture to the bowl and mix on low speed to combine. Add the rest of the flour mixture and mix until combined.

USING THE SIDE OF A BOX GRATER, or other zester, grate the carrots into small threads, about ¾ inch (2cm) long. Add the grated carrots to the batter and mix well. Pour the mixture into the prepared Bundt pan.

BAKE for one hour, or until a skewer inserted in the cake comes out clean. Cool the cake in the pan for 10 minutes and then turn it out onto a wire rack to cool completely. Store covered at room temperature for up to four days or freeze for up to three months. ■

Desserts for High Holiday Entertaining

The following recipes are for entertaining during Rosh Hashanah and to serve your guests if you are hosting a break-fast following Yom Kippur. When preparing for a major holiday, I always make the soup and desserts first so that I'll have already prepared the first dish my guests taste at the meal and the last taste they enjoy before they leave. If you can impress them with these bookends, you do not have to wow them with everything in between.

QUINOA PUDDING WITH CARAMELIZED APPLES AND HONEY

Serves 6

This is a dessert that is truly good for you. Quinoa is a grainlike seed grown in South America that has a high protein content and contains iron and calcium. You can make this dessert sugar-free by omitting the brown and white sugars.

Pudding

1 cup (180g) quinoa, rinsed
2½ cups (600ml) water
½ teaspoon cinnamon, divided
¼ cup (55g) light brown sugar, packed
2 tablespoons honey

Apples

2 tablespoons canola oil
2 tablespoons sugar
2 teaspoons light brown sugar, packed
2 red apples, peeled and cut into ½-inch
    (1.25-cm) cubes
¼ teaspoon cinnamon
pinch ground nutmeg

Garnish

⅓ cup (40g) sliced almonds or other nuts,
    toasted at 325°F (160°C) for 20 minutes
⅓ cup (50g) raisins or pomegranate seeds,
    optional

PLACE QUINOA, water, ¼ teaspoon of the cinnamon and light brown sugar into a small heavy-bottomed saucepan and bring to a boil over medium-high heat. Reduce heat to low and cook covered for 20 minutes, or until most of the water has been absorbed, except for about ½ inch (1.25cm) of water at the bottom of the saucepan. If all the water is gone, the pudding will be too dry and you will need to add more honey to moisten it. Stir. Let the quinoa sit covered for 5 minutes.

WHILE THE QUINOA IS COOKING, heat the oil over medium-high heat in a medium frying pan. Add the sugar, brown sugar, apples, cinnamon, and nutmeg and cook for 4 minutes, until just fork-tender.

AFTER THE QUINOA HAS SAT for five minutes, add the remaining ¼ teaspoon cinnamon and honey and whisk in. Let the quinoa sit for another 5 minutes, covered.

TO SERVE, divide warm or room temperature quinoa into six bowls and top with about ¼ cup of the apples. Sprinkle 2 teaspoons toasted nuts over each pudding and add the raisins or pomegranate seeds, if desired. May be made three days in advance and stored covered in the fridge. ▪

MODERATE

NUT-FREE • PARVE

NANA'S HOLIDAY APPLE CAKE

Serves 20 (huge cake!)

This recipe is from my friend Annette Lerner, who takes baking for her family so seriously that she once flew her famous mandelbread from California to Washington, DC, on the same flight as the Washington Nationals (her family owns the baseball team) to get the cookies to her grandchildren. I have personally witnessed her at the ballpark handing out cookies from shoeboxes. This is an enormous cake, and you will need your largest Bundt or tube pan to bake it; I used one that was 8 inches (20cm) high and the cake rose all the way to the top.

Batter

2 cups (400g) sugar

4 large eggs

3 cups (375g) all-purpose flour

1 tablespoon baking powder

½ teaspoon salt

1 cup (240ml) canola oil

½ cup (120ml) orange juice

2 teaspoons pure vanilla extract

Apple Filling

¾ cup (150g) sugar

2 tablespoons cinnamon

5 medium or 4 large Granny Smith apples

PREHEAT OVEN to 350°F (180°C). Grease and flour a 12-cup (2.8-l) Bundt, tube, or angel food cake pan, with about 8-inch (20-cm) high sides.

To make the batter

PLACE THE SUGAR and eggs into a large mixing bowl and beat at high speed for about one minute, until creamy. In a separate bowl, mix together the flour, baking powder, and salt. Add one-third of the dry ingredients to the mixing bowl and mix on low speed. Add a third of the oil. Alternate the dry ingredients with the oil until both are all mixed in. Add the orange juice and vanilla and mix at medium speed for about 30 seconds.

To prepare the apples

IN A SMALL BOWL, combine the sugar and cinnamon. Scoop out ¼ cup of the mixture and set it aside. Peel and core the apples and then cut them into very thin slices. To julienne the apples, turn the stack of slices on its side so the slices are on top of each other and then slice the stack into thin sticks. Use your hands to gently toss the apples with the cinnamon-sugar. Use a silicone spatula or wooden spoon to fold the apples into the cake batter.

Assembling the cake

SPRINKLE half of the reserved cinnamon sugar onto the bottom of the prepared pan. Scoop the cake batter into the pan and sprinkle the remaining cinnamon and sugar on top of it. Bake the cake for 60 to 75 minutes, or until the top is browned. To test for doneness insert a skewer. If it comes out clean, the cake is done. Annette likes to start checking the cake after it bakes for about 50 minutes. Allow the cake to cool completely—for at least two hours—before turning it out of the pan onto a wire rack. Store covered at room temperature for up to three days or freeze for up to three months. ▪

CAKE TESTING TIP

Keep long wooden skewers handy to test large cakes for doneness. Toothpicks are too short to use for testing taller cakes.

MODERATE

NUT-FREE • PARVE • VEGAN

APRICOT AND BERRY STRUDEL

Serves 10

Apple strudel is a classic Jewish dessert. Over the past few decades, however, I noticed that very few people served strudel for holidays, which led me to believe that perhaps the recipe needed updating. In this version of the classic dessert, which I usually make with blackberries, dried apricots provide a chewy element while juicy blackberries provide just the right amount of gooeyness. You could also make this dessert with plums, or substitute dates or dried figs for the apricots. You will have enough filo to double the recipe and can easily double the filling to serve more people. Filo comes in 8 x 12-inch (20 x 30-cm) sheets—a welcome alternative to the filo that comes in a larger box and which requires trimming. The smaller sheets are easy to work with and were used to make the rolls pictured here.

1 cup (200g) dried apricots, chopped into
⅓-inch pieces
1½ cups (6 ounces; 170g) blackberries,
blueberries, or raspberries
3 tablespoons sugar
1 tablespoon cornstarch
1 pound (450g) filo dough (8 x 12-inch
(20 x 30-cm) sheets), thawed according
to package directions
spray oil

PREHEAT OVEN to 350°F (180°C). Line a 12 x 16-inch (30 x 40-cm) jelly roll pan or cookie sheet with parchment. Set aside. Keep a clean, damp dishtowel on hand.

PLACE THE CHOPPED APRICOTS and berries into a medium bowl. Add the sugar and cornstarch and toss lightly. Set aside.

PLACE A LARGE PIECE OF PARCHMENT paper on the counter. Take the filo out of its package and unroll. Separate one sheet and place on top of the parchment. Spray with the oil. Place a second sheet on top and spray again. Repeat with two more sheets. Cover the remaining filo with a piece of parchment or waxed paper and top with a clean, damp dishtowel.

PLACE HALF THE FILLING along the long end of the filo, 2 inches (5cm) from the edge. Fold the right and left sides (the short sides) in 1 inch (2.5cm). Roll the long end of the filo (with the filling), into a tight, long log. Place it on the baking sheet. Repeat to make another log.

BAKE THE STRUDEL for 40 minutes, or until it's lightly browned on top. Let the strudel cool and cut it into 2-inch (5cm) slices. Serve warm or at room temperature. Store covered at room temperature for up to two days. Reheat to serve. ▪

MULTIPLE STEP
NUT-FREE • PARVE

VANILLA AND CHOCOLATE 12-LAYER CAKE

Serves 20 to 24

I was very proud of my 6-layer chocolate ganache cake, but when I read about even taller layer cakes that women bake in the southern United States, I was up for the challenge. Once you know how to make a two-layer cake, then you can make a 12-layered one. I promise. It definitely takes more time, but it is not any harder and it serves an army of people. For me, the biggest challenge in creating this recipe was the icing. I wanted a traditional, Southern cooked icing with cocoa, but every one I tried had a grainy texture that no one liked. I went back to my favorite ganache, and with some adjustments created the creamy glaze I was seeking. I like to serve thin slices of this elegant, tall cake.

Cake

6 large eggs

3 cups (600g) sugar

1½ cups (360ml) canola oil

3¾ cups (470g) all-purpose flour

1 cup (240ml) soy milk

1 tablespoon baking powder

¼ teaspoon salt

2 teaspoons pure vanilla extract

spray oil containing flour or regular
spray oil plus 2 tablespoons flour

Chocolate Glaze

21 ounces (600g) semisweet or bittersweet
chocolate

2 teaspoons pure vanilla extract

1¼ cups (300ml) soy milk

2 tablespoons (28g) margarine

PREHEAT OVEN to 350°F (180°C). Grease and flour three 8-inch (20-cm) round pans (disposable ones work fine).

To prepare the cake

IN A LARGE MIXING BOWL, place the eggs, sugar, and oil and whisk until combined. Add the flour, soy milk, baking powder, salt, and vanilla and mix well. Divide the batter evenly among the three pans, about 2⅓ cups batter for each pan.

BAKE THE CAKES for 45 to 50 minutes, or until a toothpick inserted in the center comes out clean.

WHEN THE CAKES ARE BAKED, remove them from the oven and cool for 10 minutes. Turn the cakes out of the pans onto a cooling rack and let them cool completely while you prepare the glaze.

To make the glaze

BREAK THE CHOCOLATE into small pieces and melt them either over a double boiler, or place in

a microwave oven for one minute, remove and stir, heat 45 seconds and stir, heat 30 seconds and stir, and then heat for 15-second increments, stirring after each cycle, until melted. Whisk in the vanilla. Heat the soy milk until it's hot, but not boiling. Add it to the chocolate mixture a little at a time and whisk well after each addition. Add the margarine and whisk until very smooth.

Assembling the cake

SLICE each cake into four layers. To do this, place one cake on top of a piece of waxed paper. Use a long serrated knife to trim the top and sides of the cake so that they are straight. Mark on the side of the cake where you will slice the cake to make four even layers. Hold the knife in one hand and place the other hand palm down on top of the cake. First cut the slice in the middle to divide the cake in half, by slicing about 2 to 3 inches (5 to 8cm) into the cake while turning the cake with the other hand. Keep turning and slicing until you have sliced 2 to 3 inches (5 to 8cm) into the cake all around, but not all the way across the cake.

CAKE STORY

After I developed this recipe, some of my Maryland friends would stop by and, upon seeing the gigantic cake, state that I had made a "Smith Island Cake," which I had never heard of. It turns out that Smith Island, the only inhabited island in the Chesapeake Bay, is known for its 8- to 12-layer cakes that are made with different flavors. In 2008 it became the Official State Dessert of Maryland! The residents of Smith Island believe that the cake came over with Welsh settlers back in the 1600s. So here is a nod to my state.

AFTER YOU HAVE CUT 2 to 3 inches (5 to 8cm) in all around, place the knife into one cut part and pull it straight across the cake to join the cuts, to create an even slice. Leave the cut slice on top of the cake and repeat for the next slice of cake, and slice between the first cut and the top of the cake. After you have made the second cut, place a piece of waxed paper on top of the cake and turn the cake over so the bottom is facing up. Remove the waxed paper from the top and slice the cake between the middle slice and the top once again by slicing in a few inches while turning the cake with the other hand, and then joining the cuts by pulling the knife across the cake. You will have four layers. Keep the stack together and move it aside while you repeat for the other two cakes.

PLACE ONE of the top cake layers in the center of a platter or a cake-decorating turntable, with the top facing down. Tuck pieces of waxed paper under the cake all around to catch the drippings. Scoop up about 3 to 4 tablespoons of the chocolate glaze and dump it in the center of the cake layer. Use a silicone or metal flat-blade spatula to spread the glaze back and forth all the way to the edges of the cake layer. You will need only a thin layer of glaze for each cake layer; stop yourself from adding any more than you need to just cover each layer. Place a middle cake layer on top of the ganache and press gently so that it is even. Add 3 to 4 tablespoons of glaze to this layer and spread, and then add another cake layer. Repeat for the next ten layers, saving your best bottom slice to use as the top of the cake. Every few layers, bend down and look at the cake from the side; if it is uneven, use your hand to press down on the taller parts of the cake to even it out.

WHEN YOU ARE READY for the top layer, place it on the cake with the bottom (the smooth, not interior) side facing up. At this point, you may trim the sides to even them out if you like. Eat the scraps. Scoop up about half a cup of the remaining glaze and dump it on top of the cake. Use the spatula to spread and cover the entire top, allowing the glaze to drip down the sides. Add more glaze and make sure there are many parts of the cake sides that have the chocolate drizzles, but do not spread the glaze to completely cover the sides. Remove the pieces of waxed paper under the cake and enjoy. **STORE** covered at room temperature for up to five days or freeze for up to three months.

MULTIPLE STEP

NUT-FREE • PARVE

CHOCOLATE GANACHE LAYER CAKE SQUARES WITH FRUIT SAUCE

12-16 servings

A few years ago for Rosh Hashanah, I decided that after a multi-course, heavy meal, my guests would appreciate a lighter dessert. Instead of a grand dessert buffet with multiple desserts, I gave each person a plate with a slice of apple strudel and a square of this chocolate layer cake that was surrounded by a strawberry sauce.

Cake

1½ cups (190g) all-purpose flour
⅓ cup (25g) unsweetened cocoa
1¼ cups (250g) sugar
½ teaspoon baking soda
½ teaspoon baking powder
½ teaspoon salt
2 large eggs
⅓ cup (80ml) canola or vegetable oil
½ teaspoon pure vanilla extract
½ cup (120ml) water
½ cup (120ml) soy milk
spray oil containing flour or spray oil plus 2 tablespoons flour for greasing and flouring pan

Sugar Syrup

¼ cup (60ml) water
⅓ cup (65g) sugar

Ganache

10 ounces (280g) semisweet or bittersweet chocolate, plus extra for decorating cake, if desired
1 teaspoon pure vanilla extract
⅔ cup (160ml) soy milk
2 tablespoons (28g) margarine

Fruit Sauce

2 cups (240g) strawberries, raspberries, or blackberries
2 tablespoons confectioners' sugar
1 to 2 tablespoons hot water

To bake the cake

PREHEAT OVEN to 350°F (180°C). Grease and flour an 8-inch- (20-cm) square pan.

IN A LARGE BOWL, mix together the flour, cocoa, sugar, baking soda, baking powder, and salt. Add the eggs, oil, vanilla, water, and soy milk. Beat by hand with a whisk or an electric mixer on medium speed until combined, about one minute, scraping down the sides of the bowl as necessary. Scoop the batter into the prepared pan. Bake for 45 minutes, or until a skewer inserted into the cake comes out clean.

MEANWHILE, prepare the sugar syrup. Place the water and sugar into a small heavy saucepan over medium-high heat. Stir to dissolve the sugar and bring to a rolling boil. Boil for one minute. Remove from heat. Let sit at room temperature until you are ready to use. May be made 5 days in advance and stored, covered, at room temperature.

WHEN THE CAKE IS BAKED, remove it from the oven and let it cool in the pan for 10 minutes. Take the cake out of the pan, put it on a rack, and let it cool completely while you prepare the ganache.

To make the ganache

BREAK THE CHOCOLATE into small pieces and melt over a double-boiler or in the microwave oven, for 45 seconds and stir, heat for 30 seconds and stir, and then heat for 15 second intervals, until melted and smooth. Whisk in the vanilla. Heat the soy milk until hot, not boiling. Add it to the chocolate mixture a little at a time and whisk well after each addition. Add the margarine and whisk until very smooth. Cover with plastic wrap and place in the refrigerator for 15 minutes to thicken.

To assemble the cake

WHEN THE CAKE HAS COOLED, trim off the top to make it flat and trim the sides to make them straight (eat the scraps). Slice each cake across into three pieces so you will have three layers. (See page XV for directions on how to slice cake layers.)

SET THE CAKE BOTTOM ASIDE to use as the top layer. Place the top slice of the cake, top side down, on a serving plate or cookie sheet and put some pieces of waxed paper under the cake to catch the drippings. Using a pastry brush, dip into the sugar syrup and brush the top of the cake slice all around to moisten it. Scoop up a heaping ¾ cup (180ml) of the ganache and, using a silicone spatula, spread it evenly on that layer of cake. Add the next piece of cake, moisten it with syrup, and spread it with another heaping ¾ cup (180ml) of ganache. Place the cake bottom, bottom side up, on top of the ganache, but do not moisten it with the sugar syrup. As you assemble the cake, try to make it even by gently pressing it down if it is too tall on one side.

USE a long metal spatula to spread ganache on the top of the cake. Reserve 1 to 2 tablespoons of ganache to use for decorating the slices. Heat the blade of the metal spatula in very hot or boiling water and wipe lightly with a towel to dry it, and then immediately slide it around the top of the cake to make the ganache completely smooth.

PLACE THE CAKE in the fridge until serving. May be made three days in advance.

To make the fruit sauce

WASH AND TRIM the fruit and place it in a food processor with the confectioners' sugar and water. Purée and then strain out the seeds, if desired. Store covered in the fridge for up to three days.

To serve

HEAT a long knife and cut the cake into squares or rectangles. Spoon your favorite fruit sauce on the plate and then place a cake slice in the center. PLACE leftover ganache into a pastry bag fitted with a decorative tip and squeeze out stars, flowers, dots, or swirls on top of each slice. If the ganache gets too thick, reheat slightly and stir until creamy. You can also scrape extra chocolate with a vegetable peeler on top of the slices. STORE IN THE FRIDGE for up to five days. May be frozen for up to three months. ◼

MULTIPLE STEP

NUT-FREE • PARVE

OMBRÉ LAYER CAKE

Serves 16 to 20

The first time I heard the word ombré (which means shaded in French) was when celebrities started dyeing their long hair with different graduated colors, which inspired my daughter Emily to do the same. Then I saw my first ombré cakes—with different colored layers in graduated colors—and they were just beautiful. Rather than spending hours with many colors of icing and multiple pastry bags, doing intricately detailed decorations or cutting fondant into tiny shapes, here is a way to create a "wow" cake with a lot less effort. You can make this tea-flavored cake without coloring any of the layers, and it will taste great. The novelty really is the graduated

colors of the cake and icing. If you create a truly spectacular version of this cake, please send me your photos.

Cake

2 cups (400g) sugar
4 large eggs
1 cup (240ml) canola oil
1 tablespoon fresh lemon juice
1 teaspoon pure vanilla extract
2½ cups (315g) all-purpose flour
2 teaspoons baking powder
¼ teaspoon salt
1 English Breakfast tea bag steeped in ⅔ cup (160ml) boiling water
gel food coloring

Seven Minute Icing

1½ cups (300g) sugar
⅓ cup (80ml) warm water
3 large egg whites, at room temperature for one hour
1 tablespoon light corn syrup
dash salt
1 teaspoon pure vanilla extract

To make the cake

PREHEAT OVEN to 350°F (180°C). Grease and flour four 8-inch (20-cm) round baking pans; I use the disposable ones.

PLACE THE SUGAR, eggs, oil, lemon juice, and vanilla into a large mixing bowl and mix well. Add the flour, baking powder, and salt and mix well. Squeeze the tea bag into the cup, discard the tea bag, and add the brewed tea to the batter. Mix gently. Divide the batter among four mixing bowls; there should be about 2½ cups of batter for each bowl. COLOR EACH BOWL of batter a different shade of the same color. I set aside one bowl of batter to remain white and color only three bowls of batter. Add one drop of food coloring to one bowl, two drops to the second. and then three drops to the third. Mix each bowl. Add more color to the darkest batter to make it as dark as possible. Adjust the lighter colors by adding more coloring—only if necessary to make sure there is enough contrast between them. Keep in mind that you can always add more color, but it is impossible to remove the color once you've added it.

POUR EACH BOWL of batter into a prepared pan and bake for 30 to 35 minutes, or until a toothpick inserted in the cakes comes out clean. Let the cakes cool in the pans for 10 minutes and then turn them onto a wire rack to cool completely. Every once in a while, move the cakes around so they do not stick to the rack. The cakes may be made in advance, wrapped in plastic wrap, and stored at room temperature for up to two days or frozen for up to three months.

To make the icing

POUR A FEW inches of water into the bottom of a double boiler or a medium saucepan and bring to a boil, then reduce the heat to medium. Off the stove, put the sugar and ⅓ cup (80ml) warm water in the top of the double boiler or in a metal bowl that can sit on top of a saucepan without falling in. Whisk to dissolve the sugar. Add the egg whites, corn syrup, and salt, and beat for one minute with an electric mixer on medium-high speed. Place the top of the double boiler (or metal bowl) over the gently boiling water and beat with an electric mixer on high speed for a full 7 minutes. If the water starts to bubble too much, turn the heat

down. Remove the pan from the heat, add vanilla, and beat for another 30 seconds, until the frosting is thick and has soft peaks.

Assembling the layers

IF THE CAKES HAVE A DOME on top, trim the tops so they are flat. Eat the scraps. Stack the cakes and then trim the sides so they are straight. Separate the cake layers on pieces of waxed paper. Place the lightest-colored cake layer on a serving plate and tuck pieces of waxed paper underneath it to catch any drips of icing. Spread the layer with ¼ cup of white icing. Place the next darker-colored cake layer on top of the first layer and spread it with icing. Add the next darkest layer, spread it with icing; and then add the last, and darkest, layer to the stack of cakes, with the bottom side facing up. TAKE THE REMAINING ICING and divide it among four bowls. Leave one bowl white. Color the icing in each of the other bowls three graduated colors (I try to match the cake colors). Ice the outside of each cake layer with the opposite icing color, so that the white cake is surrounded by the darkest color icing, and so on. Use a metal flat-blade spatula to scoop up the darkest color icing, and ice a band of that color around the bottom white cake layer. Scoop up the next lightest icing and ice another band the height of the next cake layer. It is OK if the colors blend a little; this helps achieve the graduated color effect. Repeat until you get to the top. Spread the white icing over the top of the cake and onto the first inch or so (from the top down) on the sides of the cake. Heat the metal spatula with some boiling water, dry it, and then use it to smooth the sides and top of the cake, blending the colors to achieve the "ombré" effect. STORE in the fridge for up to four days or freeze for up to three months.

EASY

NUT-FREE • PARVE • VEGAN

APPLE PIZZA TART

Serves 15 to 20

This dessert is a large apple tart made with frozen puff pastry, but it looks like a pizza. It is extremely easy to make yet looks elegant. Make sure you slice the apples very thin. The recipe uses between 3 and 4 medium apples, depending on how thin you slice them and how much they overlap. Just eat any leftover pieces.

1 sheet frozen puff pastry (from a 17.3-ounce or 490g box)
2 tablespoons sugar
1 teaspoon cinnamon
3–4 medium red apples (Gala, Fuji)
⅓ cup (100g) apricot jam or preserves

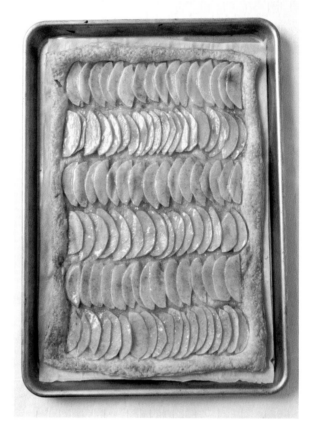

PREHEAT OVEN to 400°F (200°C). Thaw puff pastry at room temperature for 45 minutes. You will need a jelly roll pan, about 12 x 16 inches (30 x 40cm).

CUT OUT a piece of parchment paper large enough to fit just inside the pan. Place the trimmed parchment on your counter.

WHEN THE PASTRY IS THAWED, sprinkle a little flour on the parchment paper and unroll the pastry on top. Use a rolling pin to roll the pastry until it is the exact size of the parchment paper (trim the pastry if necessary). After every few rolls of your rolling pin, lift the dough and sprinkle a little flour underneath it. Slide the dough and parchment paper onto the jelly roll pan. Use a fork to dot the dough with holes, leaving a one-inch border clear, without any holes. Put the pan in the freezer while you prepare the apples so that the moment the apples are sliced, everything else is ready to go, and the apples will not turn brown.

IN A SMALL BOWL, combine the sugar and cinnamon. Peel and core the apples and slice into very

thin slices, thinner than ¼-inch (6mm). (I usually use only the larger slices for the tart and nosh on the smaller ones.) Remove the dough from the freezer. Sprinkle half of the cinnamon and sugar on the dough, leaving the border clear. Place the apple slices on the pastry overlapping in rows down the short side of the dough. I alternate the direction the apples are facing for each row. Sprinkle the apples with the remaining cinnamon and sugar. Bake for 25 to 30 minutes, or until the apples are soft and the pastry is golden.

HEAT THE APRICOT JAM in the microwave or on the stovetop and then use a sieve to strain out the large pieces. Use a pastry brush to brush the apple slices with the jam. Slide the pastry onto a cooling rack. Cut into squares or rectangles. Serve warm or at room temperature. Store covered at room temperature for up to two days.

MULTIPLE STEP

PARVE

RASPBERRY AND ROSE MACARON CAKE

Serves 8

Pierre Hermé is the most famous pastry chef in Paris. Every time I travel to Paris, I make sure to visit his Saint-Germain-Des-Prés shop and line up with the throngs of people who are also there to see his latest creations. For the last few years, Hermé's most famous dessert has been the Ispahan Macaron, a French macaron cookie filled with rose-flavored pastry cream, raspberry gel, and litchi fruit. Pierre calls it the pastry equivalent of a Chanel suit—the top of his line. If you can find litchi fruit, press pieces into the pastry cream. If not, the dessert is lovely with only raspberries. When you finish assembling the cake, you will not want to cut it because it is so beautiful; but you will be surprised by how easy it is to slice into wedges.

Macaron Cookie Layers

⅔ cup (180g) almond flour (grind 1½ cups slivered almonds in a coffee grinder)

1⅓ cups (160g) confectioners' sugar

3 large egg whites, at room temperature for 2 hours

¼ cup (50g) sugar

½ teaspoon raspberry extract, optional

pink or red gel food coloring

Rose Pastry Cream

¾ cup (180ml) soy milk

½ vanilla bean, split and seeds scraped, or 1 teaspoon pure vanilla extract

5 tablespoons sugar, divided

2 tablespoons (28g) margarine

3 large egg yolks

3 tablespoons all-purpose flour

1 teaspoon unflavored gelatin powder

2 teaspoons rose water, or more to taste

⅓ cup (80ml) dairy-free whipping cream

9 to 12 ounces (255 to 340g) fresh raspberries, or 6 ounces (170g) raspberries and ½ cup litchi fruit (about 8 litchis), cut in pieces.

Preparing the eggs

SEPARATE THE EGGS and let the whites sit out at room temperature for at least two hours. Meanwhile, prepare the pastry cream.

To make the pastry cream

IN A HEAVY SAUCEPAN, bring the soy milk, scraped seeds and vanilla bean pod, three tablespoons of the sugar, and margarine to a rolling boil. Whisk the mixture to separate the vanilla seeds so they do not clump up. In a medium bowl, use a whisk to beat the egg yolks with the remaining 2 tablespoons sugar. Add the flour and gelatin and whisk well. Strain half the soy milk mixture into the egg bowl and whisk. Strain the other half of the milk into the eggs and mix well. Discard the vanilla bean pod.

RETURN THE MIXTURE to the saucepan and cook on low heat for 3 to 4 minutes, whisking often. You will need a silicone spatula to mix the cream where the bottom and sides of the saucepan meet. Every 15 seconds, let the mixture sit without whisking until you see some bubbles; it should look like the mixture is breathing. In the meantime, rinse the mixing bowl. When the mixture looks like thick vanilla pudding, remove it from the heat and place it into a clean bowl. Let the mixture sit for 10 minutes and then cover it with plastic wrap and place it in the fridge until chilled for at least four hours or overnight. To use it sooner, place the bowl of pastry cream over a larger bowl filled with 2 to 3 cups of ice cubes and 2 cups of water, whisking occasionally, for 30 minutes, or until the cream is chilled. The cream can be made three days in advance and stored in the fridge.

To make the cookies

CUT a sheet of parchment paper to perfectly fit the bottom of a 12 x 16-inch (30 x 40-cm) jelly roll pan or cookie sheet. Use a pen to trace two 8-inch (20-cm) circles on the parchment paper (I use 8-inch (20-cm) round baking pans as "stencils"). Turn the paper over.

PLACE THE ALMOND FLOUR and confectioners' sugar into the bowl of a food processor fitted with a metal blade. Process for three full minutes. Sift the mixture into another bowl, discarding any large almond pieces.

IN THE BOWL OF A STAND MIXER, beat the egg whites until stiff. Reduce the speed to low, add the granulated sugar a tablespoon at a time, and then increase the speed to high for another three minutes. Add the raspberry extract, if using, and food coloring to achieve a bright pink color, and beat another 30 seconds. Add the almond and sugar mixture and mix on low speed to mostly combine and then finish mixing with a spatula; you do not want to mix the batter too much.

PLACE THE BATTER into a pastry bag fitted with a ¼-inch (6-mm) round tip. Squeeze a little batter under the corners of the parchment to "glue" the parchment to the cookie sheet. Starting in the center of each circle, squeeze out spirals going around and around until your batter fills the drawn circle. Repeat for the second circle. If you

have any batter left over, squeeze out some small, 1 to 1½-inch (2 to 2.5-cm), circles to make small macarons to use to decorate the cake. Let sit at room temperature 40 minutes.

PREHEAT OVEN to 300°F (150°C). Bake the cookies for 25 to 30 minutes, until they've puffed up and are solid when touched. Do not let the tops brown. Remove the cookies from the oven and let them cool completely. Do not remove the cookies

from the parchment until you are ready to assemble the cake.

To finish the rose cream

WHIP the whipping cream until stiff. Whisk the rose water into the pastry cream. Fold in the whipped cream in three parts. Place the cream in the fridge for 20 minutes.

To assemble the cake

FIRST REMOVE each cookie from the parchment by peeling the parchment off the cookie, not the cookie off the parchment, which can cause it to break. Place the less pretty of the two cookies on a serving platter. When the cream has chilled, scoop it up and place it in the center of the cookie and spread it around, leaving a 1-inch (2.5-cm) border without cream, and reserving a tablespoon or two of cream to decorate the top. Place raspberries standing up on the border and pack them tightly next to each other. Press the sides of the berries gently into the cream.

SCATTER either more raspberries or the chopped litchis (or both) over the rose cream and press them in until they are mostly covered by the cream. Gently place the second cookie on top of the cream and fruit, top side up. Dip the small macarons into the cream and attach them vertically on top of the cake or assemble a few mini macaron cookies (use any leftover cream for the filling between the cookies) and place them on top of the cake. You can also use rose petals for decoration. Store in the fridge for up to two days. ■

CHECKING MACARON COOKIES FOR DONENESS

It is hard to check the bottoms of larger macarons for doneness without breaking them. If in doubt, bake the larger macaron cookies for another two minutes. The dessert will work just as well if the cookie is too crisp, but it will fall apart if it is too gooey inside.

MODERATE

NUT-FREE • PARVE

APPLE AND HONEY CHALLAH ROLLS

Makes 24

Almost every year on Rosh Hashanah I host at least 25 people in my home. I give each guest his or her own small plate with a challah roll, apple slices, and a small bowl of honey to save some of the time that slips away when passing these essential holiday elements around the table. Perhaps I invented these challah rolls, which are filled with sautéed apples and honey, to further streamline the entire beginning of the meal? In any case, they are great with dinner or for breakfast. If you only want 12 rolls, you can shape half the dough into a braided or round challah and fill the large strands with the apple mixture. Bake the bread for about 30 minutes, or until it's golden brown.

Dough

½ ounce (2 envelopes; 14g) dry yeast
⅓ cup (80ml) warm water
⅔ cup (130g) plus 1 teaspoon sugar, divided
½ cup (120ml) plus 1 teaspoon canola oil, divided
1 tablespoon salt
1 cup (240ml) boiling water
½ cup (120ml) cold water
3 large eggs
1 teaspoon pure vanilla extract
2 teaspoons cinnamon
6¼ to 6½ cups (780 to 815g) bread flour

Apples

5 Gala or Fuji apples
2 tablespoons oil
⅓ cup (75g) light brown sugar, packed
1 tablespoon honey
2 teaspoons cinnamon, divided
2 pinches ground nutmeg

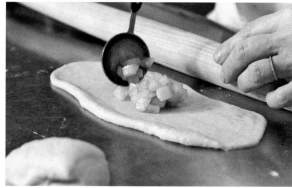

Glaze

reserved egg plus 2 teaspoons water
1 tablespoon honey

To prepare the dough

PLACE ⅓ cup (80ml) warm water into a liquid measuring cup. Add the yeast and teaspoon of sugar and mix. Let the mixture sit for 5 minutes, or until it thickens. Meanwhile, in a large mixing bowl, place ½ cup (120ml) of the oil, the salt, and ⅔ cup (130g) sugar. Whisk well. Add the boiling water and whisk to dissolve the salt and sugar. Add the cold water and mix again.

BEAT THE EGGS in a separate bowl and add them to the oil mixture, reserving one tablespoon to brush on the loaves. Cover the reserved tablespoon of egg and put it in the fridge. Add the vanilla and cinnamon to the bowl and whisk it in. Do not worry if the cinnamon does not dissolve; it will mix in later. When the yeast bubbles, add the yeast mixture to the bowl and stir.

ADD 6 cups (750g) of the flour, 1 cup (125g) at a time, mixing the flour in completely after each addition. (You can use the dough hook in a stand mixer.) Place the dough on a floured surface and knead until smooth, adding flour a little at a time from the remaining ½ cup (or more, as needed). The dough is done when you rub your palm across it and it feels soft. Shape the dough into a ball. Pour the remaining teaspoon of oil into the bowl;

rub the oil all around the bowl and on top of the dough. Place the dough into the oiled bowl and cover it with plastic wrap or a clean dishtowel. Let rise for one hour.

To prepare the apples

MEANWHILE, peel and core the apples and cut them into ¼-inch (6-mm) cubes. Heat the oil in a large frying pan over medium heat. When the oil is hot, add the brown sugar, 1 teaspoon cinnamon, nutmeg, and apples. Cook for 5 to 10 minutes, stirring often, until the apples are fork tender. You do not want them to be too soft. Add the remaining teaspoon of cinnamon and honey and stir. Transfer the mixture to another bowl and let it cool. If any liquid remains in the bowl, strain it out before filling the rolls.

To fill the rolls

COVER TWO COOKIE SHEETS with parchment paper or silicone baking mats.

WHEN THE DOUGH HAS RISEN, divide it into 24 pieces. Roll each piece into a ball and then roll it between your hands in order to make an 8-inch (20-cm) strand. Place it horizontally in front of you and use a rolling pin to roll the dough until it is about 4 inches (10 cm) wide. Add one heaping tablespoon of apple filling to the dough, and use your fingers to spread it along the dough the long way. Fold one long side of dough over the filling and then roll it up into a long, thin cigar shape. Pinch the edges closed, tucking in any apples that try to escape. Tie each strand into a knot, pulling an end through the top to look like a button, or shape into a spiral by coiling the strand around one end and tucking in the other end. Place on the prepared baking sheets and cover with plastic wrap. Let the dough rise for 30 minutes.

PREHEAT OVEN to 375°F (190°C). Add 2 teaspoons of water and 1 tablespoon of honey to the reserved egg and stir. Brush the tops of the rolls with the egg mixture.

BAKE THE ROLLS for 20 to 25 minutes, or until they're browned. Store covered at room temperature for up to three days or freeze for up to three months. ▨

HAFRASHAT CHALLAH

The mitzvah of taking challah recalls the portion of dough that Jews were commanded to give to the priests at the Temple. If you make a batch of challah dough out of less than 5 pounds (2.2 kg) of flour, tear off a piece of your dough and burn it without saying the blessing. If your batch uses 5 pounds (2.2 kg) of flour or more, separate the piece, say the blessing, and burn it in the oven. The blessing is: Baruch atah Adonai Elohaynu melech ha-olam, asher kidushanu b'mitzvotav vitzivanu lehafrish challah min ha-issa. Blessed are you, Lord our G-d, king of the universe, who has sanctified us with his commandments and commanded us to separate the challah from the dough.

Sukkot

Sukkot is our autumn holiday when, for eight days, we eat outside in huts to remind us of how the Israelites lived as they traveled through the desert from Egypt to Israel. The holiday reminds us that we are still reliant upon G-d's protection. Eating and (for some) sleeping in the sukkah also show us that we have the capacity to live simply, without all the fancy trappings of our lives and to recognize that happiness is not dependent on external circumstances.

A sukkah can be small or extremely large, as long as there are more than two solid walls, but the ceiling must not be opaque. We use bamboo poles or branches to cover most of the top of the sukkah. I have childhood memories of driving around with my father as he "collected" large weeds and branches from various locations to cover our sukkah.

In addition to the collective mitzvah of gathering in the sukkah, we also perform the individual mitzvah of the lulav and etrog. We say prayers over palm, myrtle, and willow branches and an etrog, a yellow citron fruit. Every year after Sukkot, my Dutch friend, Gidon van Emden, makes etrog vodka (his grandmother's recipe), which he shares with us every Purim.

Growing up in Long Beach, New York, we always had a sukkah, as did so many in our town. When I was a little girl, our sukkah was roughly 10 feet by 10 feet, a play fort in the backyard that barely fit the five of us. G-d bless my mother, who had to schlep the food through the house, outside, down the stairs and around the house to the garden to get to the fort. Today in Maryland we have a giant sukkah, that fits everyone we want to invite. When my husband, Andy, and I lived in Geneva, Switzerland, the community sukkah was on the roof of a Jewish-owned hotel, on the sixth floor. Everyone carried up food and dishes for

their family to have their meals. It was tiring, but there was a nice view of the lake on top.

In most places in the United States, by Sukkot, the weather has cooled, so this is the holiday when we typically transition to warm fall desserts. On this holiday, you have to plan meals that do not involve a multitude of dishes—so you have fewer things to bring outside—including one dessert that's big enough to feed everyone. The first two days of the holiday are festival days when we do not work and we have festive meals and fancy desserts. The remaining days are *chol ha-moed*. On those "intermediate days" of Sukkot, we are permitted to work and so we need appropriate snacks for them as well. To celebrate both the collective and individual mitzvot of Sukkot, I offer large desserts for sharing and smaller desserts.

The last two days of the holiday are Shmini Atzeret and Simchat Torah, both festival days, when we are commanded to refrain from work. In Israel, they are celebrated on one day. Shmini Atzeret features the prayer for rain. On Simchat Torah we celebrate the conclusion as well as the restart of the Torah-reading cycle. On Simchat Torah we sing and march and dance with Torah scrolls to show our love for the Torah. Rugelach and whoopee pies are great to have around to grab on the way out the door before you go to synagogue.

Sukkot Snacks

Tea Sandwich Cookies 44

Chocolate and Peanut Butter Whoopie Pies 46

Fruit Cobbler with Chickpea, Pecan, and Cardamom Topping 47

Sugar-Free Pumpkin Bread 48

Mocha and Whisky Chocolate Bread Pudding 48

Sticky Toffee Pudding 51

Desserts for Sukkot Entertaining

Everything Rugelach 52

Chocolate Pistachio Molten Cakes 54

Chestnut Mousse 55

Pear and Almond Pithivier Cake 57

Red Velvet Layer Cake with Vanilla and Chocolate Frostings 59

Salted Caramel Banana Tart Tatin 62

Whole Grain Challah 64

Sukkot Snacks

One very nice tradition that has developed in many communities is to have a "sukkah hop" during the holiday. Several people serve snacks and drinks in their sukkah and then others "hop"—walk or drive—from sukkah to sukkah (depending on whether it is *chag* or *chol hamoed*), and have a bite in each place. I remember doing this as a child and getting a different candy in each sukkah. As an adult, I have served fruit and desserts such as the ones in this chapter.

MODERATE

NUT-FREE • PARVE • VEGAN

TEA SANDWICH COOKIES

Makes 20

I am a huge fan of shortbread cookies, which can be made in advance of any holiday and frozen. For these tea sandwich cookies I like to use mini cookie cutters to cut out small shapes in the top cookie so you see the jam inside. You can even cut out two shapes from the top cookie and fill it with two different-colored jams.

2 bags Earl Grey or other black tea, divided

¼ cup boiling water

1 teaspoon sugar

1 cup (120g) confectioners' sugar

2 cups (250g) plus 2 tablespoons all-purpose flour, plus extra for dusting

1 cup (2 sticks; 226g) margarine, cut into tablespoons

½ cup (160g) orange marmalade or other tropical-flavored fruit jam (see page 82 for homemade Mango Passion Fruit Jam)

To make the cookies

PLACE ONE TEA BAG into ¼ cup (60ml) of boiling water, stir in the teaspoon of sugar, and let sit 5 minutes. Squeeze all the tea out of the bag to make the tea as strong as possible. Set aside.

PLACE THE CONFECTIONERS' SUGAR and flour into the bowl of a food processor fitted with a metal blade. Open up the second tea bag and add the tea leaves to the bowl. Mix for 10 seconds. Add the margarine and process for about 20 seconds until the dough looks like sand. Add four teaspoons of the brewed tea and process until the dough starts to come together and you see a large gap in the dough in the food processor bowl. Divide the dough in half. Flatten each piece of dough into a disc and wrap it in plastic wrap. Place the discs in the freezer overnight.

PREHEAT OVEN to 400°F (200°C). Remove dough from the freezer and thaw until you can just press it gently.

TAKE TWO PIECES of parchment paper and sprinkle a little flour on one of them. Place a disc of dough on top of one of the papers and then sprinkle a little more flour on top of the dough. Place the second piece of parchment on top of the dough and roll on top of the parchment to roll out the dough until it is ¼-inch (6-mm) thick. Every few rolls, peel back the top parchment and sprinkle a little more flour on the dough. Remove the top parchment and use it to line a cookie sheet. Line another cookie sheet with fresh parchment.

ROLLING COOKIES

Always roll shortbread cookies between two pieces of parchment paper so that you don't have to keep sprinkling excess flour on the dough, which can make it dry and less flavorful.

USE COOKIE CUTTERS to cut out cookies and use smaller cutters to cut out shapes from half of the cut cookies to serve as a window to the jam filling. Use a metal flat-blade spatula to lift the cookies and place them on the prepared cookie sheets. Reroll any scraps and cut more cookies. Repeat with the second disc of dough.

BAKE the cookies for 10 to 12 minutes, or until they begin to brown on the bottom. Check halfway through baking to see if the cookies in the back are browning faster than those in the front; if so, just turn the cookie sheet around. Slide the parchment off the cookie sheet onto a wire rack and let the cookies cool.

To assemble the cookies

MATCH UP pairs of cookies. Spread 1½ teaspoons of jam on the bottom of one cookie and top with a second cookie to create a sandwich. Use the cookies with the cutouts as the top cookies. Repeat with the remaining cookies. Let them sit for 30 minutes to firm up. Store covered at room temperature for up to three days or freeze for up to three months. ∎

CHOCOLATE AND PEANUT BUTTER WHOOPIE PIES

Makes 14 to 16

Whoopie pies are essentially a sandwich of two pieces of cake with a cream filling. They are completely North American in origin, and several states claim to be the birthplace of the pies. They likely originated in New England or among the Pennsylvania Amish community. My favorite explanation for the name is that Amish women would place them in their husbands' lunch pails as hidden treats. When the men discovered them, they would shout "whoopee!" If you like peanut butter and jelly sandwiches, you can add a shmear of strawberry jelly to your whoopee pies.

Cakes

⅓ cup (80ml) canola oil

1 cup (200g) sugar

2 large eggs

1 teaspoon pure vanilla extract

1½ cups (190g) all-purpose flour

1 teaspoon baking soda

½ teaspoon baking powder

¾ cup (180ml) soy milk

1 cup (80g) dark unsweetened cocoa

pinch of salt

Peanut Butter Filling

½ cup (120g) creamy peanut butter

⅓ cup (80g) soy cream cheese

⅓ cup (40g) confectioners' sugar

⅓ cup (80ml) dairy-free whipping cream

4 teaspoons strawberry or raspberry jam, optional

PREHEAT OVEN to 350°F (180°C). Line two cookie sheets with parchment paper or a silicone baking mat, or plan to bake the cakes in batches.

To make the cakes

PUT THE OIL, sugar, eggs, and vanilla into a large bowl and beat with an electric mixer on low speed until smooth. Add the flour, baking soda, and baking powder, and mix thoroughly. Cover the bowl with a towel to keep the flour from showering your kitchen floor. Add half the soy milk and mix. Add the cocoa and mix until incorporated. Scrape down the sides of the bowl. Add the remaining soy milk and mix on low speed until smooth.

DROP A TABLESPOON of batter onto the cookie sheet, and swirl it around with your finger or the back of a spoon to make it round. Leave 2 inches between each cake. Bake the cakes for 12 minutes, or until a toothpick inserted comes out clean. Use a spatula to immediately lift each cake off the cookie sheet and place it flat side down on a wire rack. Repeat for the second batch. As the cakes cool, move them around on the rack so they do not stick.

To make the peanut butter filling

IN A MEDIUM BOWL, place the peanut butter, cream cheese, and confectioners' sugar and beat with an electric mixer on medium speed until smooth. In a separate bowl, beat the whipping cream until thick. Gently fold the whipping cream into the peanut butter mixture. Cover and place in the fridge for 30 minutes.

To assemble the whoopie pies

PLACE HALF THE CAKES on a plate with the flat side facing up. Spoon a heaping tablespoon of the peanut butter filling into the center of the flat side of each cake. Top with another cake, flat side down, and press together gently to evenly spread the peanut butter filling, so you can see the filling from the sides; it should not ooze out. You can also spread ¼ teaspoon of jam on the second cake before sandwiching the two together to create a peanut butter and jelly whoopie pie. Repeat for the other cakes. Store covered in the fridge for up to three days or freeze for up to three months. ▪

Fancier whoopie pies

To make these little cakes look even prettier, fit a pastry bag with a large star tip and fill it with the peanut butter mousse. Squeeze the mousse onto the cakes so you see the ridges of the cream from the sides.

EASY

GLUTEN-FREE • PARVE • VEGAN

FRUIT COBBLER WITH **CHICKPEA, PECAN,** AND **CARDAMOM TOPPING**

Serves 20

This is a completely gluten-free dessert. I first learned about chickpea flour from my friend Amanda Goldstein whose brother owns the Lucini olive oil company that sells chickpea flour—and I challenged myself to come up with a dessert that uses this versatile ingredient.

Fruit

8 cups of fruit cut into ¾-inch (2-cm) cubes (about 8 plums and 4 peaches, or 5 large apples), or blueberries, raspberries, or blackberries—as long as the total amount of fruit is 8 cups

2 tablespoons honey

¼ cup (50g) potato starch

Crumb Topping

1½ cups (180g) pecan halves

½ cup (1 stick; 113g) margarine

1½ cups (165g) chickpea flour

1 cup (220g) light brown sugar, packed

½ teaspoon ground cardamom

PREHEAT OVEN to 375°F (190°C). Put the fruit in a 9 x 13-inch (23 x 33-cm) pan. Add the honey and potato starch and toss until the starch dissolves.

FINELY CHOP the pecans by hand or in a food processor. In a separate bowl, place the pecans, margarine, chickpea flour, brown sugar, and cardamom. Use your hands to crumble the mixture together. Spread it evenly over the fruit.

BAKE the cobbler for 40 minutes, or until the crumb topping browns and the fruit starts to bubble. Let it cool for 10 minutes. Store covered in the fridge for up to three days. Reheat to serve. ▪

PREHEAT OVEN to 350°F (180°C). Grease and flour a 12-inch (30-cm) loaf pan.

IN A LARGE BOWL, beat the oil, agave syrup, vanilla, and eggs for 30 seconds, or until mixed. Add the pumpkin purée and mix well. Add the white whole-wheat and spelt flours, baking powder, baking soda, cinnamon, ginger, nutmeg, cloves, and salt and mix well. Spoon the mixture into the prepared loaf pan and smooth the top. Lift the loaf pan two inches above the counter and drop it on the counter three times to remove any bubbles.

BAKE THE BREAD for 45 minutes, or until a skewer inserted in the center comes out clean. Let the bread cool for ten minutes and then turn it out onto a wire rack to cool completely. Store at room temperature for up to five days or freeze for up to three months. ▪

EASY

LOW SUGAR • NUT-FREE • PARVE

SUGAR-FREE PUMPKIN BREAD

Serves 12

This recipe uses agave syrup rather than sugar to sweeten the bread. Agave comes from the cactus plant and has a low glycemic index compared to other sweeteners; it does not cause wide fluctuations in blood sugar levels.

⅔ cup (160ml) canola oil

½ cup (120ml) agave syrup

2 teaspoons pure vanilla extract

3 large eggs

1¼ cups (300g) pumpkin purée (not pumpkin pie filling)

1½ cups (190g) white whole-wheat flour

½ cup (55g) spelt flour

1 teaspoon baking powder

1 teaspoon baking soda

1½ teaspoons cinnamon

1 teaspoon ground ginger

½ teaspoon ground nutmeg

½ teaspoon ground cloves

½ teaspoon salt

spray oil containing flour for greasing pan

EASY

NUT-FREE • PARVE

MOCHA AND WHISKY CHOCOLATE BREAD PUDDING

Serves 20

The only time I buy challah is when I make bread pudding (my family will not give up a homemade challah without a fight!). The challah cubes need to be stale and dry to soak up the chocolate custard. Let them sit out overnight in a pan or for at least 3 to 4 hours before use. Toss the cubes every once in a while to expose them to the air to help dry them out.

one large loaf stale challah, cut into ½-inch cubes

2½ cups (600ml) soy milk

10 ounces (280g) bittersweet chocolate, chopped into ½-inch (1.25-cm) pieces

1 tablespoon instant coffee granules

2 tablespoons Scotch Whisky

5 large eggs

¾ cup (150g) sugar

1 tablespoon unsweetened cocoa

2 teaspoons confectioners' sugar, for dusting,
  if desired

PREHEAT OVEN to 350°F (180°C). Put the cubed challah in an ungreased 11 x 14-inch (28 x 36-cm) pan. Bake them for 10 minutes, tossing twice. Let the cubes cool 15 minutes, and give them a toss every once in a while.

MEANWHILE, put the soy milk, chopped chocolate, and coffee in a small saucepan. Whisk the mixture over medium heat until it's smooth and the chocolate has melted. Remove it from the heat, add the whisky, and stir. Cool 15 minutes.

PLACE THE EGGS, sugar, and cocoa in a medium bowl and whisk well. When the chocolate mixture has cooled, pour ½ cup of the soy milk and chocolate mixture into the egg mixture and mix. Add the remaining soy milk and chocolate mixture in three parts, whisking well after each addition. Pour it over the bread cubes and stir well to thoroughly coat all of the challah cubes. Let them sit for 5 minutes to absorb the custard.

BAKE for 35 minutes, or until the pudding is set and does not jiggle.

TO SERVE, dust the pudding with confectioners' sugar, if desired, and cut it into squares. Serve warm or at room temperature. Store at room temperature for up to three days or freeze for up to three months. ■

EASY

NUT-FREE • PARVE

STICKY TOFFEE PUDDING

Serves 20

Some twenty years ago I had Shabbat dinner at the London home of my friend Rhonda Alexander-Abt's mother-in-law, Muriel Abt, and I tasted my first sticky pudding—a date cake that has a sweet topping that you pour on the cake. It is the classic English boarding school dessert because it feeds a crowd. The consistency of the topping is more like syrup than thick toffee, but it has a butterscotch taste. One friend said that it tastes like American breakfast pancakes and syrup.

Pudding

4 tablespoons (57g) soft margarine, plus
    1 tablespoon for greasing pan
1½ cups (7 ounces; 200g) pitted dates
1¼ cups (155g) flour, plus 1 teaspoon for
    sprinkling on dates
1 cup (240ml) boiling water
1 teaspoon baking soda
1 teaspoon pure vanilla extract
¾ cup (165g) dark brown sugar, packed
2 large eggs
1 teaspoon baking powder

Toffee Topping

½ cup (1 stick; 113g) margarine
½ cup (110g) light brown sugar, packed
⅓ cup (80ml) dairy-free whipping cream

PREHEAT OVEN to 350°F (180°C). Grease a 9 x 13-inch (23 x 33-cm) pan with 1 tablespoon of margarine and set it aside.

TOSS THE DATES in a small bowl with one teaspoon of flour to prevent the dates from sticking to your knife while you're chopping them. On a cutting board, use a large knife to chop the dates into ¼ to ½-inch (6mm to 1.25-cm) pieces. Put the dates back in the bowl and pour the boiling water on top. Add the baking soda and vanilla and stir. Set aside.

IN THE BOWL of a stand mixer or in a large bowl, beat the margarine and brown sugar on medium speed until creamed together. Add the eggs and beat for one minute, stopping to scrape down the bowl once, and beat until thick and creamy. Add ¼ cup (30g) flour and baking powder and mix on low speed. Add another ½ cup (65g) flour and mix until just mixed in. Add the last ½ cup (65g) flour and mix until just combined. Add the date-and-water mixture and mix well with a silicone spatula or wooden spoon.

POUR THE MIXTURE into the greased pan and bake for 20 to 22 minutes, or until a toothpick inserted in the center comes out clean. Check the cake for doneness, starting after about 19 minutes of baking—you want to remove the cake precisely when it is just baked and not a minute longer.

To prepare the topping

IN A SMALL SAUCEPAN, cook the margarine and brown sugar over medium heat until the margarine is melted, stirring often. Mix in the cream. Cook the mixture until it boils and continue cooking it for three more minutes. Reduce the heat to low and cook the mixture for another two minutes.

To finish the pudding

WHEN THE PUDDING IS BAKED, remove it from the oven and raise the oven temperature to broil. Use a lollipop stick or skewer to poke holes all over the cake. Pour the toffee over the top of the cake and put it in the oven for one minute, allowing the mixture to bubble.

TO SERVE, cut the warm pudding into squares or scoop it out of the pan with a spoon. Store covered at room temperature for up to five days or freeze for up to three months. Reheat to serve.

Desserts for Sukkot Entertaining

In America, we have four festival days during Sukkot (people in Israel celebrate only two) when we serve holiday meals. But we also may want to eat some exceptional desserts during the intermediate (*chol hamoed*) days, when people often invite family and friends. The following are recipes for entertaining to make the entire eight-day holiday feel special. Some of them you will want to repeat throughout fall and into the winter months.

MULTIPLE STEP

PARVE • VEGAN

EVERYTHING RUGELACH

Makes 60 to 70 pieces

As the name implies, this rugelach has everything in it. You can add more of the ingredients you like and less of those you don't like. I got the idea for the filling from Sandy Bobb, who showed me her family's revered strudel recipe, which has so many different ingredients in the filling. I guessed correctly that the filling would work for rugelach as well.

Dough
1 cup (2 sticks; 226g) margarine
8 ounces (230g) soy cream cheese, at room temperature for at least 30 minutes
2 cups plus 2 tablespoons (265g) all-purpose flour, plus extra for dusting
1 tablespoon confectioners' sugar
1 teaspoon pure vanilla extract

Filling
½ cup (160g) raspberry or other berry jam
½ cup (160g) apricot preserves
¼ cup (50g) sugar
2 teaspoons cinnamon

¼ cup (30g) walnut halves, chopped into ¼–½ inch (6mm to 1.25-cm) pieces
1 cup (120g) pecan halves, chopped into ¼–½ inch (6mm to 1.25-cm) pieces
2 tablespoons slivered almonds
2 tablespoons dry coconut flakes
⅓ cup (60g) mini chocolate chips
½ cup (80g) raisins or dried cranberries

To make the dough
IN THE BOWL OF A MIXER fitted with a paddle or a food processor fitted with a metal blade, mix the margarine, cream cheese, flour, confectioners' sugar. and vanilla until the dough just comes together. Divide the dough in half, wrap each piece in plastic wrap, and flatten. Freeze overnight. Let the dough thaw until you can press it in a little.

To assemble the rugelach
PREHEAT OVEN to 350°F (180°C). To roll out the dough, place a 10 x 15-inch (25 x 38-cm) sheet of parchment paper on the counter. Sprinkle it with flour and place one disc of dough on the parchment, sprinkle with more flour and then cover with a second sheet of parchment. With a rolling pin, roll over the parchment until the dough is 10 x 13 to 15 inches (25 x 33 to 38 cm). Peel back the top parchment a few times while rolling and sprinkle some more flour on the dough. Remove the top parchment and reserve it to cover the second disc of dough.

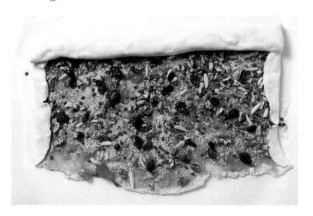

IN A SMALL BOWL, combine the raspberry and apricot jams. Use a silicone spatula to spread half of the jam mixture over the dough.

IN ANOTHER SMALL BOWL, combine the sugar and cinnamon. Sprinkle half of the cinnamon-sugar over the jam on the dough. Then sprinkle half of all the remaining ingredients on top. Fold the short sides of the dough 1 inch (2.5cm) in toward the center to keep the filling inside. Using the parchment to help you, roll up the long side, working slowly and rolling as tightly as you can. Make sure the seam ends up on the bottom. Slide the roll and parchment onto a cookie sheet. Repeat with the second piece of dough and place on the parchment a few inches away from the first roll.

BAKE the rolls of dough for 40 to 45 minutes, or until the tops begin to brown. Let them cool and then slice the rolls into one-inch pieces. You can freeze the slices or the rolls, slicing them when you're ready to serve.

STORE covered with plastic or in an airtight container at room temperature for up to five days or freeze for up to three months. ◾

MODERATE

PARVE

CHOCOLATE PISTACHIO MOLTEN CAKES

Serves 12

I created this dessert because I was so very tired of seeing chocolate molten or "lava cake" on every restaurant menu worldwide and as the dessert at every bar and bat mitzvah I have attended for the last decade. On my last trip to France I found a little cookbook that featured little cakes with many different flavored gooey centers. I knew it was time to bring that concept home and develop a twist on the classic molten cake. The pistachio filling will not ooze—it will remain creamy, surrounded by warm, gooey chocolate and moist chocolate cake.

Chocolate Cake

½ cup (1 stick; 113g) margarine

½ cup (65g) plus 1 tablespoon all-purpose flour, divided

1 tablespoon unsweetened cocoa

7 ounces (200g) semisweet or bittersweet chocolate, chopped or broken into 1-inch pieces

2 large eggs plus 2 yolks

½ cup (100g) sugar

Pistachio Filling

4 ounces (110g) white chocolate chips (a little less than ⅔ cup)

½ cup (60g) shelled unsalted pistachios, ground into a powder

YOU WILL NEED twelve 3-inch (8-cm) fluted molds or small ramekins. Melt 1 tablespoon of the margarine and use a pastry brush to grease the molds. In a shallow bowl, combine 1 tablespoon flour with the cocoa. Holding a mold over the bowl, spoon in 1 tablespoon of the flour and cocoa mixture. Make sure all the sides are covered with the mixture by tilting the mold all around and shaking it. Tap any excess into the bowl. Repeat with the other 11 molds and place them on a jelly roll pan. Set aside.

MELT THE CHOCOLATE with the remaining margarine over a double boiler, or heat them together in a microwave oven for 45 seconds, stir, then heat 30 seconds, and stir again, and then heat in 15-second increments, stirring after each cycle, until melted. Whisk well. While the chocolate and margarine are melting, use an electric mixer on low speed to mix the eggs, egg yolks, and sugar in a large bowl. Increase the speed to high and beat for five minutes. The mixture will look creamy. Add the remaining ½ cup (65g) flour and beat on low speed until just combined. Gently whisk in the melted chocolate and margarine mixture.

DIVIDE THE BATTER among the prepared molds, a little less than ⅓ cup for each. Place the molds in the fridge for ½ hour or up to 4 hours.

MELT the white chocolate chips either slowly over a double boiler, or heat them in a microwave oven in 30 seconds increments, stirring between cycles, until they've melted. Add the ground pistachio nuts to the chocolate and mix well. Place the mixture in the fridge for 15 minutes or until it is mostly hard; it should still be a little soft, so you can shape it into balls. Divide the mixture into

12 clumps and roll them into balls. Place them on a waxed-paper lined pan. If you are making the molten cakes after they chill for 30 to 60 minutes, let the pistachio balls sit at room temperature. Otherwise chill the pistachio balls in the fridge until ready to bake the cakes.

PREHEAT OVEN to 350°F (180°C). Place one pistachio ball into the middle of each mold and press down so that the balls are mostly submerged in the chocolate batter. Bake the cakes on top of the jelly roll pan for 9 to 10 minutes, just until the top looks mostly set. Remove the cakes from the oven and let them rest for one minute. To release the cakes, turn over the molds and tap them gently on a platter. Serve the cakes immediately, if possible. To serve later, line a cookie sheet with parchment paper and tap the cakes onto the parchment. Store covered in the refrigerator for up to three days. May be reheated. ▪

MOLTEN CAKE MOLDS

Teflon-coated fluted molds make it easy to pop out the cakes.

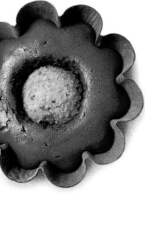

MODERATE

GLUTEN-FREE • PARVE

CHESTNUT MOUSSE

Serves 8

A few years ago, several kosher companies started selling roasted and peeled chestnuts, and I have enjoyed snacking on them. When I was growing up, my father would roast chestnuts under the broiler. Note that this recipe contains raw eggs.

10 ounces (about 1¾ cups; 280g), roasted and
   peeled chestnuts, plus 8 more for garnish
3 tablespoons confectioners' sugar
4 large eggs, separated
3 tablespoons sugar
½ cup (120ml) dairy-free whipping cream

PLACE the chestnuts and confectioners' sugar into the bowl of a food processor fitted with a metal blade and process for one minute, stopping to scrape down the bowl twice. You should have a thick paste. Add the egg yolks, one at a time, mixing them in and scraping down the bowl before each addition. Scoop the mixture into a large bowl.
IN A SEPARATE BOWL, beat the egg whites with an electric mixer on medium-high speed until they form soft peaks. Reduce the speed to low and add the sugar, one tablespoon at a time, incorporating it completely before each addition. Increase speed to high and beat another minute. Use a whisk to mix half of the egg whites into the chestnut mixture. Add the remaining egg whites and mix them in.
RINSE the bowl and beaters. Pour the whipping cream into the bowl and whip until the cream is stiff. Gently fold the cream into the chestnut mixture.
DIVIDE THE CHESTNUT MOUSSE among eight small bowls or glasses. Cover them with plastic wrap and refrigerate for at least four hours. Top the mousse with roughly chopped chestnut pieces and serve. Store covered in the fridge for up to three days. ▪

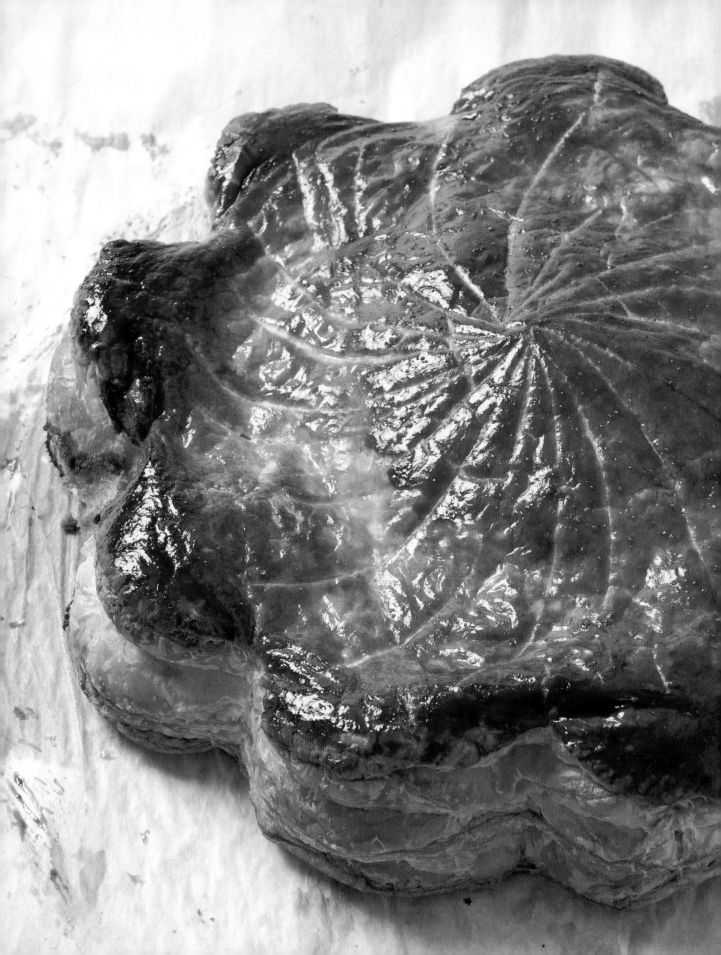

PEAR AND ALMOND PITHIVIER CAKE

Serves 8 to 12

This French dessert (pronounced *pitivyay*) has two layers of puff pastry that sandwich almond cream. I have added vanilla and thyme-poached pears to the filling. The name comes from the town in France where the dessert originated.

1 package frozen puff pastry (2 sheets from a 17.3-ounce or 490g box)

Poached Pears
4 cups (960ml) water
1 cup (200g) sugar
1 tablespoon pure vanilla extract
bunch thyme stems (about 10)
2 firm pears
juice from ½ lemon

Almond Cream
4 tablespoons (57g) margarine
⅓ cup (65g) sugar
½ cup (60g) almond flour
1 tablespoon all-purpose flour
1 large egg
1 teaspoon pure vanilla extract

Glaze
1 large egg, beaten
2 teaspoons sugar to sprinkle on top

THAW the puff pastry at room temperature for at least 45 minutes.

To poach the pears
PUT THE WATER, sugar, vanilla, and thyme branches in a medium saucepan and bring to a boil. Meanwhile, squeeze the lemon juice into a shallow bowl.

Slice off the stem and very bottom of each pear and peel the pears. Halve them from stem to bottom. With a measuring spoon or melon-baller, scoop out the core of the pear, including the vein that runs from top to bottom; then put each half into the lemon juice and rub it all over to coat the fruit.

WHEN THE SYRUP has boiled, reduce the heat so the liquid simmers and add the pear halves. Cook for 20 to 25 minutes, or until the tip of a sharp knife slides easily into the inside of one of the pear halves. Let the fruit cool in the saucepan. The pears may be made two days in advance and stored covered in the fridge with some of the poaching liquid.

To prepare the almond cream
IN A MEDIUM BOWL, beat the margarine with an electric mixer on high speed until soft. Add the sugar, almond flour, and flour and beat until creamy. Add the egg and vanilla. Increase the speed to high and beat for one minute, until the mixture is light and airy. Cover the cream and leave it in the fridge for up to three days, until you're ready to assemble the cake.

To prepare the puff pastry
YOU WILL NEED two dinner plates or round baking pans, one that is about 8 inches (20cm) in diameter and one that is 10 inches (25cm) in diameter. Place a piece of parchment on the counter and sprinkle it with some flour. Unroll one sheet of puff pastry and use a rolling pin to smooth out the lines until it is larger than a 10-inch (25-cm) plate. Put the plate over the pastry and run a knife around the plate to cut out a 10-inch (25-cm) circle. Discard the trimmings. Take an 8-inch (20-cm) pan or plate and press it on top of the pastry to mark a smaller circle in the center of the pastry circle, or use a dull knife to score the circle without cutting through it. Set it aside.

ON ANOTHER PIECE of parchment paper, roll out

the second sheet of pastry the same way you rolled out the first one. Make sure to lift the dough off the parchment from time to time and sprinkle some flour underneath it so that it doesn't stick to the parchment. Place a 10-inch (25-cm) plate on top and cut out another 10-inch (25-cm) circle.

To assemble the cake

REMOVE the almond cream from the fridge. Lift the pear halves out of the syrup and place them on paper towels to dry. Slice the pears the long way into ¼-inch (6-mm) slices.

BRUSH THE BEATEN EGG on the 2-inch (5-cm) border made between the scored circle and the outer edge of the puff pastry. Using a silicone spatula, spread the almond cream on the circle inside of the egg-brushed border (not on the border). Try to spread it as evenly as possible. Place the pear slices cut side down on top of the almond cream, overlapping if necessary to use up most of them. With your hand under the parchment, gently flip the second pastry circle over on top of the almond cream. Peel off the parchment and stretch the dough so that you can press the edges of the two pastry sheets together to seal the top and bottom pieces. Pinch to seal tightly. Place your 8-inch (20-cm) plate or pan on top of the pastry, and use the back of a knife to score but not cut a circle around the filled center so you have a border around the part that contains the cream filling. Use a knife to cut a scalloped pattern on the border, being careful not to cut the two pastry sheets where the filling is.

USE A KNIFE to mark but not cut a pattern on top of the pastry, by holding the tip of the back of the knife in the center and marking curves from the center to the inside border. Brush the cake with the beaten egg. Reserve the egg to brush the top again before baking. Place the pan with the cake into the freezer for 20 minutes.

PREHEAT OVEN to 450°F (230°C).

REMOVE THE COOKIE SHEET from the freezer and brush the dough again with the beaten egg. Sprinkle the top with two teaspoons of sugar. Bake for 15 minutes. Reduce the temperature to 400°F (200°C) and bake another 25 to 30 minutes, or until browned. Serve slices warm or at room temperature. Store covered in plastic at room temperature for up to three days. ▪

MULTIPLE STEP

NUT-FREE • PARVE

RED VELVET LAYER CAKE WITH VANILLA AND CHOCOLATE FROSTINGS

Serves 16 to 20

This cake will feed everyone in your neighborhood who stops by to visit your sukkah. If you want a smaller cake, you can make two three-layer cakes and freeze one for another occasion. I find that red food coloring makes red velvet cake too cherry-red; if you mix the red coloring with burgundy or maroon coloring, you can achieve a darker red.

Cake

¾ cup (180ml) soy milk

1 tablespoon fresh lemon juice

2½ cups (315g) all-purpose flour

3 tablespoons unsweetened cocoa

2 cups (400g) sugar

1 teaspoon baking powder

1 teaspoon baking soda

½ teaspoon salt

3 large eggs

1 teaspoon pure vanilla extract

1 cup (240ml) canola oil

1 teaspoon white vinegar

2 teaspoons red gel food coloring

1 teaspoon burgundy gel food coloring

Vanilla Cream Cheese Frosting

8 ounces (230g) soy cream cheese

2 teaspoons pure vanilla extract

4 cups (480g) confectioners' sugar

1 tablespoon soy milk

Chocolate Frosting

10 ounces (280g) semisweet or bittersweet
   chocolate, plus extra for decorating cake, if
   desired

1 teaspoon pure vanilla extract

⅔ cup (160ml) soy milk

2 tablespoons (28g) margarine

To make the cakes

FIRST, measure the soy milk and add the lemon juice. Let it sit for 5 minutes. This creates a buttermilk substitute.

PREHEAT OVEN to 350°F (180°C). Grease and flour two 8-inch (20-cm) round pans. Set aside.

IN A LARGE BOWL, thoroughly mix the flour, cocoa, sugar, baking powder, baking soda, and salt. Add the eggs, vanilla, oil, soy milk, and vinegar and mix again. Add the food colorings and mix well for one minute to achieve a dark red color, adding more color if necessary. Divide the batter between the two pans.

BAKE THE CAKES for 40 to 45 minutes, or until a skewer inserted in the cakes comes out clean. Let the cakes cool in the pans for ten minutes and then turn them onto a wire rack to cool completely. The cakes may be made three days in advance, wrapped in plastic wrap, and stored at room temperature, or frozen for up to three months.

To make the chocolate frosting

BREAK THE CHOCOLATE into small pieces and melt it over a double boiler, or heat in a microwave oven for 45 seconds, remove and stir, heat again for 30 seconds and stir, and heat for 15 seconds more, and stir, until melted. Whisk in the vanilla. Heat the soy milk until hot, not boiling. Add it to

the chocolate mixture a little at a time and whisk well after each addition. Add the margarine and whisk until very smooth. Cover the mixture with plastic wrap and leave it in the fridge for 15 minutes. The chocolate frosting may be made two days in advance but will need to be reheated and stirred until creamy and spreadable.

To make the vanilla frosting

IN A LARGE BOWL, beat the cream cheese and vanilla with an electric mixer at high speed until smooth. Add the confectioners' sugar in three parts, mixing each addition completely before adding the next one. Add the soy milk and beat for 30 seconds, or until the frosting looks creamy. The vanilla frosting may be made two days in advance and stored covered in the fridge.

To assemble the cake

WHEN THE CAKES have cooled, slice each of them horizontally into three thin layers. (refer to the cake-slicing instructions on page XV). After slicing both cakes, you should have a total of six layers. Set aside one of the cake bottoms to use as the top of the cake. Place the other cake bottom, bottom side down, on your serving plate and place some pieces of waxed paper underneath to catch the drippings. If you want the top of the cake to be chocolate, then the first frosting layer should be vanilla, and vice versa.

USE A SILICONE SPATULA to spread ⅓ cup of the vanilla frosting back and forth from the middle to the edge of the layer of cake. Add the next piece of cake and spread ⅓ to ½ cup of the chocolate frosting. Top with a slice of cake and then the white frosting followed by a cake slice and the chocolate frosting followed by cake. Continue building the cake, alternating white and chocolate frostings between cake layers. Place the reserved cake bottom on top, bottom side up. If the cake is too tall on one side, you can even it out by gently pressing down on it.

YOU WILL HAVE ENOUGH of each frosting to decide which flavor you want to use on top and which you want on the sides. Use a long metal flat-blade spatula to ice the top and sides. Try to reserve 1 to 2 tablespoons of each frosting to decorate the cake. Heat the blade of the metal spatula in very hot or boiling water and wipe lightly with a towel and then immediately slide around the sides and top of the cake to make them completely smooth; you may need to reheat the blade and repeat this step a few times. Store the cake at room temperature for up to five days or freeze it for up to three months. ▪

MODERATE

NUT-FREE • PARVE • VEGAN

SALTED CARAMEL BANANA TART TATIN

Serves 12

Tart tatin is typically an upside-down apple cake made in an 8 to 10-inch round pan. As I have a big family and everyone drops by on holidays, I decided to make this banana version in a 9 x 13-inch (23 x 33-cm) pan to have more servings. It is tasty warm or at room temperature, but best served right out of the oven. You can also make this as a dairy recipe and serve it with vanilla ice cream.

1 sheet frozen puff pastry (from a 17.3-ounce or 490g box)
1 cup (200g) sugar
1 tablespoon water
3 tablespoons (42g) margarine
½ cup (120ml) dairy-free whipping cream
1¼ teaspoons kosher salt, divided
5 large just ripe (not overripe) bananas
all-purpose flour for dusting
spray oil or margarine for greasing pan

PREHEAT OVEN to 400°F (200°C). Thaw puff pastry at room temperature for 45 minutes. Use spray oil or some margarine to grease a 9 x 13-inch (23 x 33-cm) pan. Cut out a piece of parchment paper that is large enough to cover the bottom of the pan as well as the sides, making sure that the paper on the sides extends over the top of the pan by a couple of inches. Press the parchment paper into the pan, making sure it sticks to the bottom, corners, and sides. Set it aside.

IN A MEDIUM SAUCEPAN, cook the sugar and water over medium-high heat for several minutes without stirring until the edges start to color. Stir occasionally until all the sugar granules have melted and the caramel turns amber. This should take about five minutes. Add the margarine and whipping cream and stir. The mixture will bubble up and congeal, then dissolve again as you stir it. Add a teaspoon of the salt and mix well. Cook another two minutes on low heat, stirring often. Remove the pan from the heat and let it sit as you prepare the bananas. Peel the bananas and slice them in half the long way.

POUR THE CARAMEL into the prepared pan and tilt it to cover the entire pan. Arrange the sliced bananas, cut side down, diagonally across the pan, nesting them closely together. You can cut some of the halves into smaller pieces to fill any gaps.

PUT A PIECE OF PARCHMENT paper a few inches larger than the pan on your counter and sprinkle some flour on it. Place a sheet of puff pastry on the parchment with the creases parallel to the longer side. With a rolling pin, roll the pastry sheet out to about an inch larger than the bottom of the pan (pastry dough shrinks when it's baked). Lift the pastry off the parchment a few times and sprinkle a little flour underneath it so the pastry does not stick. Trim the pastry dough to make the sides straight.

TURN THE PARCHMENT PAPER and pastry on top of the bananas. Press the dough into the pan corners and up the sides of the pan. Peel off the parchment paper. Use a sharp knife to poke about 20 holes all over the pastry to allow air to escape.

BAKE the pastry for 25 to 28 minutes, or until the top is golden. Let it cool for 15 minutes and then place a rectangular platter or plate over the pan. Flip the tatin onto the platter. Remove the parchment paper. Sprinkle the tatin with the remaining ¼ teaspoon kosher salt. Serve warm. Store covered in the fridge for up to two days. Reheat to serve. ■

MODERATE

PARVE

WHOLE GRAIN CHALLAH

Makes 1 large or 2 medium challahs

It took me a long time to develop an entirely whole-wheat challah that was soft enough and tasty enough to satisfy my four children. This recipe was designed to make one large challah because I like to offer both this one and my classic challah at festive meals. You can always double the batch of whole grain challah if you wish.

¼ ounce (1 envelope; 7g) dry yeast

⅓ cup (80ml) warm water

½ cup (100g) plus 2 teaspoons sugar, divided

½ cup (120ml) canola oil, plus one teaspoon for greasing bowl

2 teaspoons salt

½ cup (120ml) boiling water

¼ cup (60ml) cold water

1½ cups (190g) white whole-wheat flour plus extra for dusting

1 cup (110g) spelt flour

1 cup (130g) whole-wheat flour (not stone-ground)

2 large eggs, beaten

DISSOLVE THE YEAST in the ⅓ cup (80ml) warm water and mix in two teaspoons sugar. Let the mixture sit for ten minutes, or until it thickens.

IN A LARGE BOWL, whisk together the ½ cup oil, salt and sugar. Add the boiling water and whisk again to dissolve the sugar and salt. Add the cold water and mix. In a medium bowl, whisk together the white whole-wheat, the whole-wheat, and the spelt flours.

BEAT THE EGGS in a small bowl and add them to the oil mixture, reserving 1 tablespoon to brush on top of the challah, and whisk them in. Add the yeast mixture and mix it in well. Add one cup of the flour mixture and whisk it into the liquids. Add another cup of the flour mixture and use a wooden spoon, silicone spatula, or the dough hook of a stand mixer to mix it in. Add the remaining flour and mix it in. To get all of the dough out of the bowl, scrape your fingers down the sides and gather the dough into a ball. Put the dough on a surface dusted with some white whole-wheat flour. Add more white whole-wheat flour to the dough, a little at a time, and knead it into the dough until it holds together as a ball and is mostly smooth. It can be a little sticky.

WASH THE BOWL. Add the remaining teaspoon of oil to the bowl and rub it around. Return the dough to the bowl, rub some oil on top of it and cover the bowl with a clean dishtowel or plastic wrap. Let the dough rise for 1½ hours.

TO BRAID THE DOUGH into one large loaf or two medium loaves: Divide each portion of dough into three equal balls and then roll each of them into a long strand. Flour hands as needed. Place the three strands in front of you vertically, about 3 inches (8cm) apart. Gently press the top ends together. Pull one outside strand into the center between the other two strands. Take the outside strand from the other side and place that between the other two strands. Go to the other side and pull that strand into the center of the other two. You want to pull the dough a little each time to braid it tightly. Keep alternating sides until you reach the bottom. Braid as far down as you can and then press the ends of the strands together, tuck under the loaf, and press tightly.

TURN THE LOAF around so the end you just completed braiding is on top. Undo the strands that you loosely pressed together when you started braiding. Now you will braid underneath: Take the outside strand that looks like it is on top of the other three and pull it under and in between the other two. Take the opposite outside strand and pull it under the other two. Repeat until you can braid no more, press the ends together, and tuck underneath, pressing tightly. Repeat with the other piece of dough if braiding a second challah. Place the loaf or loaves on a baking sheet and let rise for one hour.

PREHEAT OVEN to 375°F (190°C). Brush the top and sides of the dough with the reserved egg mixed with 1 to 2 teaspoons water.

BAKE for 30 to 35 minutes, or until the bread is golden. ▪

CLASSIC CHALLAH

Makes 2 large or 3 medium challahs

½ ounce (2 envelopes; 14g) active dry yeast
1 teaspoon sugar, to activate the yeast
⅓ cup (80ml) warm water
½ cup (120ml) plus 1 teaspoon canola or
    vegetable oil, divided
1 tablespoon salt
¾ cup (150g) sugar
1 cup (240ml) boiling water
½ cup (120ml) cold water
3 large eggs
6½–7 cups (815–875g) bread flour

IN A MEASURING CUP, dissolve the yeast in the warm water. Add the teaspoon of sugar and mix. Let sit for 10 minutes, or until it thickens. In a large bowl, whisk together ½ cup (120ml) of the oil, the salt, and ¾ cup (150g) sugar. Add the boiling water and whisk again to dissolve the salt and sugar. Add the cold water and mix again.

BEAT THE EGGS in a separate bowl and add to the oil mixture, reserving 1 tablespoon to brush on the loaves. When the yeast bubbles, add the yeast mixture to the bowl and stir.

ADD 6 cups of the flour, 1 cup at a time, mixing the flour in completely after each addition. Place the dough on a floured surface and knead until smooth, adding flour a little at a time from the remaining cup of flour. The dough is done when you rub your palm across the dough and it feels soft. Shape the dough into a ball.

ADD the remaining 1 teaspoon of oil to the bowl and rub all around the bowl and on top of the dough. Place the dough into the oiled bowl and cover with plastic wrap or a towel. Let rise 1 hour.

DIVIDE THE DOUGH into 2 or 3 balls, depending whether you are making 2 or 3 loaves. Divide each ball into three pieces. Roll the pieces into long strands and then braid them. Place on a parchment-lined cookie sheet and let rise 45 minutes.

PREHEAT OVEN to 375°F (190°C). Brush the tops and sides of the loaves with the reserved beaten egg mixed with a teaspoon of water.

BAKE for 35 minutes, or until the bread is golden. ▪

Chanukah

In December 1999, while others were obsessing about the millennium, I was in the hospital on bed rest for three full weeks awaiting the safe birth of my twin boys, Jake and Joey. This coincided with the entire holiday of Chanukah and sadly I could not be home with my two older children, Emily and Sam. The nanny brought them to visit me almost every day, and the kids brought me some Chanukah pictures they'd drawn to decorate the walls. I had a menorah in my room and I lit candles every night, saying a prayer for my babies, who were born healthy at 36½ weeks—Joey was 5 pounds 5 ounces, and Jake 7 pounds 1 ounce, which is pretty much a miracle in the world of twins.

On Chanukah we celebrate the miracle that a small amount of oil lit the Temple menorah for eight nights. It occurred shortly after the Jews defeated the Syrian Greeks, who had tried to convert the Jews to Hellenism. King Antiochus had imposed harsh decrees forbidding Jewish worship and also had desecrated the Temple and its Torah scrolls. A small band of Jews, the Maccabees, revolted to save the Jews and preserve their Jewishness. After they liberated Jerusalem, the Maccabees cleared the Temple of idols. They fashioned a new menorah, but only found one pitcher of oil to light it. It was only enough oil to keep the menorah lit for just one day, yet miraculously it lasted for eight days.

Chanukah, which means "dedication," is also called the Festival of Lights because of this miracle. We are commanded to light candles for eight nights. On the first night we light one candle and then add another candle on each consecutive night. On Chanukah we play with a dreidel (a spinning top) that has the Hebrew letters *nun*, *gimel*, *hay,* and *shin*, which stand for words that mean "a great miracle happened there." The custom is to give Chanukah *gelt*, or money, to children, although in the United States, most people exchange gifts.

Chanukah is a holiday that represents the strength of Jewish survival. Even today, when we can express our Judaism freely, Chanukah should remind us that we must not take that for granted. Today, it may be argued, the challenges to our observance of Judaism are internal rather than external. We must continue to search for the spark to ignite our own deeper commitment to Judaism. Chanukah also teaches us that you do not have to wait for all your resources before you start a project. The Maccabees found a small amount of oil in the Temple and they knew it would only light the Menorah for one day. Rather than abandon their efforts because they were unlikely to accomplish much, they lit the menorah, and the oil lasted for eight nights. If a project is important enough, it is worth taking the first step, even if the outcome is uncertain.

At every baking demonstration event someone tells me that they simply do not bake. They claim baking is too precise, that they do not have the right equipment, and that it takes too much time. My friend Ellen Kessler bought my book at *The Kosher Baker* launch and said that she was buying the book to be nice to me, but she was not planning to bake. A week later she sent me a message that she had baked one recipe and her family was thrilled. I have taught baking classes to people in their eighties who had no prior baking experience. Start small, like the drop of oil, and you might find that your efforts achieve greater results than you ever thought possible.

To celebrate the miracle of the oil, the tradition on Chanukah is to eat fried desserts such as doughnuts, called by their Hebrew name, *sufganiyot*. Over the last few years, I have expanded the Chanukah doughnut repertoire by introducing new and modern doughnut flavors such as pumpkin and citrus, as well as some that are topped like cupcakes, and they all can be found here. I also include desserts made with olive oil, for another way to connect with the miracle of the holiday.

Clockwise from upper right: Whole-Wheat Jelly Doughnuts, Chocolate Ganache Glazed Doughnuts, Vanilla Doughnut Holes, Pumpkin Doughnuts

Easy Chanukah Desserts

Fancier Chanukah Desserts

Easy Chanukah Desserts

Every Chanukah I find myself making a fresh batch of potato latkes almost every night, mostly because there are never any leftovers, and also because I prefer them crispy. While latke-making is not difficult, it takes time and results in a sink full of dishes. Therefore, on nights when you make latkes, you need easy dessert recipes that do not demand an arsenal of equipment.

MODERATE
NUT-FREE • PARVE

DECORATED COOKIES WITH **ROYAL ICING**

Makes 36 2- to 3-inch (5- to 8-cm) cookies, more if smaller

Cookie decorating is a fun activity to do with friends, family, and children. Make the dough a week before the holiday so you are ready when your helpers arrive. The dough may be made with butter. Cut and decorate the cookies as you like. The tiny Chanukah-themed cookie cutters I use for this recipe can be ordered from my friends at www.thekoshercook.com.

Shortbread

1 cup (120g) confectioners' sugar

2 cups plus 2 tablespoons (265g) all-purpose flour, plus extra for dusting

1 cup (2 sticks; 226g) margarine, cut into tablespoons

Royal Icing

2 large egg whites

½ teaspoon pure vanilla extract

3¼ cups (390g) confectioners' sugar

boiling water

food coloring

To make the shortbread

PLACE THE CONFECTIONERS' SUGAR and flour into the bowl of a food processor fitted with a metal blade. Mix for 10 seconds. Add the margarine and process until the dough starts to come together and you see a large gap in the dough in the food processor bowl.

DIVIDE THE DOUGH in half, wrap each piece loosely in plastic wrap and flatten into discs. Place the dough in the freezer overnight.

PREHEAT OVEN to 400°F (200°C). Remove the dough from the freezer and thaw just until you can press it in gently.

PLACE ONE DISC of dough on top of a piece of parchment paper that has been sprinkled with flour, and sprinkle a little more flour on top of the disc. Place a second piece of parchment on top of the dough and roll on top of the parchment until the dough is ¼-inch (6-mm) thick. Every few rolls, peel back the top parchment and sprinkle a little more flour on the dough. Remove the top parchment and use it to line a cookie sheet. Line another cookie sheet with fresh parchment.

USE COOKIE CUTTERS to cut out cookies in any shape. Use a metal flat blade spatula to place the cookies on the prepared cookie sheets. Reroll any scraps and cut more cookies. Repeat with the second disc of dough.

BAKE for 10 to 12 minutes, or until the cookies begin to brown on the bottom. Check halfway through baking to see if the cookies in the back are browning faster than those in the front; if they are, just turn the cookie sheet around. Slide the parchment off the cookie sheet onto a wire rack and let cool.

To make the icing

PLACE THE EGG WHITES and vanilla into a mixing bowl and beat with an electric mixer on medium-low speed until foamy, about one minute. Add the confectioners' sugar, 1 cup at a time, mixing on low speed and scraping down the bowl often. Once all the sugar has been added, beat at high speed for five minutes, or until thick and shiny. Add teaspoons of boiling water until you have a consistency that you can spread. If the icing gets too loose, add some confectioners' sugar; if it's too thick, add more drops of water.

DIVIDE ICING into bowls and color with food coloring as desired. You can use a small metal spatula or knife to ice the cookies. For a more professional look, place the icing in a pastry bag fitted with a small round tip. First ice a border on the cookies and then squeeze more icing into the center, to cover. Let the icing dry at room temperature for 20 minutes. Store cookies with or without icing in an airtight container for up to five days or freeze for up to three months. ■

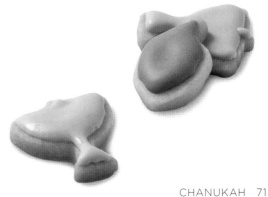

GINGERBREAD COOKIES

Makes 30 3-inch (8-cm) cookies

I thought this recipe would be easy to develop, but after two different friends tested the recipe and both pronounced it not spicy enough, I worked hard to create a full-flavored gingerbread cookie. The *aleph-bet* cookie cutters shown here are from www.thekoshercook.com.

Dough
¾ cup (1½ sticks; 170g) margarine
¾ cup (165g) dark brown sugar, packed
1 large egg
½ cup (120ml) unsulfured blackstrap molasses
1 teaspoon pure vanilla extract
3 cups (375g) all-purpose flour
1 teaspoon baking soda
¼ teaspoon salt
1 tablespoon cinnamon
4 teaspoons ground ginger
1 teaspoon ground nutmeg
½ teaspoon ground cloves
¼ teaspoon ground allspice

Glaze
½ cup (60g) confectioners' sugar
1 tablespoon boiling water

To make the dough
PLACE THE MARGARINE and brown sugar into a large bowl. Beat with an electric mixer or by hand with a wooden spoon until creamy. Add the egg, molasses, and vanilla and beat until mixed in. Add two cups (250g) of the flour, baking soda, salt, cinnamon, ginger, nutmeg, cloves, and allspice and mix with a spatula or wooden spoon; if you are using an electric mixer, mix carefully so the flour does not dust your face. Add the last cup (125g) of flour and mix until combined. The dough

will be gooey. Place two large pieces of plastic wrap on your counter. Scoop up and place half of the dough on one piece of plastic and the remaining half on the other. For each half of the dough, fold the plastic over the dough and then flatten it into a pancake, about ½ to 1-inch (1.25- to 2.5-cm) thick. Freeze overnight.

PREHEAT OVEN to 350°F (180°C). Remove one disc of dough from the freezer and let it sit for five minutes; you want to roll it out while it is just barely soft enough to roll. You will need to bake in batches. Take two pieces of parchment and sprinkle a little flour on one, place dough on top and then dust with a little more flour. Place the second piece of parchment on top of the dough and roll on top of the parchment to roll out the dough until it is a little thicker than ¼-inch (6-mm) thick; do not roll too thin. Every few rolls, peel back the top parchment and sprinkle a little more flour on the dough from about 10 inches (25cm) high, so you do not get big white spots on the dough. Remove the top parchment and use it to line a cookie sheet. Line another cookie sheet with fresh parchment.

USE COOKIE CUTTERS to cut out cookies and then use a metal flat-blade spatula to lift the cookies and place them on the prepared cookie sheets. Use a pastry brush on the cookies to dust off any excess flour. Reroll any scraps and cut more

COOKIE TIPS

Make sure to roll the dough when it is still cold and hard. For very chewy cookies bake for 9 minutes; for medium chewy, 10 minutes; and for crisper cookies, 11 minutes.

cookies, adding a little flour each time, taking care not to roll the scraps too thin. If the dough becomes too soft and gets stuck to the bottom parchment, put it in the freezer until it hardens slightly. Repeat with the second disc of dough.

BAKE for 9 to 11 minutes, or until the cookies are set. When they are done, you should be able to press into them slightly. Slide the parchment off the cookie sheet onto a wire rack and let the cookies cool for one minute and then use a spatula to lift the cookies onto the rack.

To make the glaze

PUT THE CONFECTIONERS' SUGAR into a small bowl. Add the boiling water and whisk well. Let the mixture sit for five minutes and then drizzle on the cookies. Once the glaze has dried, store the cookies in an airtight container for up to six days or freeze for up to three months. ▇

EASY

PARVE

ALMOND AND OLIVE OIL CAKE

Serves 8 to 12

The use of olive oil in cakes dates back farther than the Chanukah story itself. Olive oil was used in baked offerings at the Temple. This is a super easy teatime cake that reminds me of simple cakes I have eaten in Italy. If you are feeling decadent, serve this with whipped cream.

¾ cup (90g) sliced almonds (with or without skins)
1 cup (200g) sugar
3 large eggs
½ cup (120ml) extra virgin olive oil
1 cup (125g) all-purpose flour
½ cup (60g) ground almonds
1½ teaspoons baking powder

¼ teaspoon salt
1 teaspoon almond extract
½ teaspoon orange zest (from one orange)

spray oil containing flour

PREHEAT OVEN to 350°F (180°C). Trace an 8-inch (20-cm) round pan on parchment paper and cut it out with scissors. Grease and flour the pan, press in the parchment circle; and grease and flour the top of the parchment and sides of the pan. Sprinkle and spread the sliced almonds on the bottom of the pan to cover it.

IN A MEDIUM BOWL, beat the sugar, eggs, and olive oil for about one minute at medium speed until creamy. Add the flour, ground almonds, baking powder, salt, almond extract, and orange zest and beat until combined. Pour the mixture over the sliced nuts. Bake for 35 minutes, or until a skewer inserted in the middle of the cake comes out clean.

LET THE CAKE COOL in the pan for 10 minutes and then run a knife around the sides. Turn the cake onto a wire rack and let it cool. Serve the cake almond side up. Store it covered at room temperature for up to four days or freeze for up to three months. ▇

LINE PANS WITH PARCHMENT

For extra insurance against any cake sticking to any size pan, line the pan bottom with parchment paper cut to fit the bottom of the pan. Grease the pan, press in the trimmed parchment, and then grease again.

EASY

NUT-FREE • PARVE

CHEWY CHOCOLATE OLIVE OIL COOKIES

Makes 3 dozen

These very dark chocolate cookies are baked with olive oil to recall the Chanukah miracle.

⅔ cup (160ml) extra virgin olive oil
1 cup (200g) sugar
1 cup (220g) light brown sugar, packed
4 large eggs
2 teaspoons pure vanilla extract
2 cups (250g) all-purpose flour
1 cup (80g) dark unsweetened cocoa
2 teaspoons baking powder
½ teaspoon salt
1 cup (170g) chocolate chips

IN A LARGE BOWL, use an electric mixer on medium speed to beat together the olive oil, sugar, and brown sugar, scraping down the bowl a few times, until the mixture comes together into small clumps and looks like crystals. Turn the mixer to low speed and, with the mixer on, add the eggs one at a time, and beat well after each addition. Stop the machine and scrape down the bowl as needed. Add the vanilla and whisk again. Add the flour, cocoa, baking powder, and salt and mix well with a wooden spoon or silicone spatula. Add the chocolate chips and mix to distribute.

CHILL THE DOUGH in the fridge for one hour.

PREHEAT OVEN to 400°F (200°C). Line three baking sheets with parchment paper, or bake in batches. Cover and refrigerate the dough between batches. Drop heaping tablespoons of the dough onto the prepared baking sheets, about two inches apart.

BAKE the cookies for 12 to 14 minutes until they are mostly set, but the centers are still soft; when you press the centers, your finger should be able to press halfway down into the cookie. Use a spatula to immediately lift the cookies onto a wire rack and let them cool. Store the cookies at room temperature in an airtight container for up to five days or freeze for up to three months. ▨

EASY

NUT-FREE • PARVE

APPLE LATKES

Makes 20

These pancakes look just like potato latkes. You can serve them either as a dessert or a side dish during Chanukah.

½ cup (65g) all-purpose flour, plus one
  tablespoon, if batter is very wet
2 tablespoons sugar
¼ teaspoon cinnamon
¼ teaspoon ground nutmeg
1 teaspoon baking powder
3 apples (Fuji, Gala, or Granny Smith)
1 tablespoon fresh lemon juice
2 large eggs
2 tablespoons confectioners' sugar for dusting

PLACE A PAPER BAG over a cookie sheet to use for draining the latkes after frying them. Heat ¼ inch (6mm) of oil in a large frying pan over medium-high heat.

PLACE THE FLOUR, sugar, cinnamon, nutmeg, and baking powder into a large bowl and stir. Beat the eggs in a small bowl. Set aside. Peel and core the apples and grate them on the large holes of a box grater or the large holes of a food processor blade. Add the shredded apples to the bowl with the dry ingredients. Sprinkle with the lemon juice, add the beaten eggs and mix.

THE OIL IS READY for frying when it feels very hot when you place your hand two inches above the pan. Scoop up a heaping tablespoon of the apple mixture and gently drop it into the pan, using the back of the tablespoon to flatten it. Fry the latkes for 1½ to 2 minutes per side, until golden. Drain them on the paper bag and let them cool for about 15 minutes.

IF THE BATTER gets very watery halfway through the frying, add a tablespoon of flour to the mixture and mix it in.

USE A SIEVE to dust the latkes with confectioners' sugar. These are best eaten fresh but can be reheated in the oven. Store them in the fridge for up to three days or freeze them for up the three months. To reheat, place frozen latkes onto a cookie sheet and bake them in a 400°F (200°C) oven until crisp. ■

Fancier Chanukah Desserts

When you have an eight-day holiday, you can find the time to prepare a special dessert that you only make once a year. After years of making plain doughnuts filled with red jam, I decided that it was time to mess around with the dough flavors to create new and memorable Chanukah desserts. Your family and friends will also be impressed with homemade funnel cake and churros.

MULTIPLE STEP

NUT-FREE • PARVE

VANILLA DOUGHNUT HOLES

Makes 50

Doughnuts, along with potato latkes, are the most traditional Chanukah foods. Like latkes, doughnuts are best eaten the day they are made, but even on the second day you can get good results by re-warming them. To make doughnuts look festive, roll them in colored sugar.

¼ ounce (1 envelope; 7g) dry yeast

¼ cup (60ml) warm water

½ cup (100g) plus 1 teaspoon sugar, divided

½ cup (120ml) soy milk

2 tablespoons (28g) margarine, at room temperature for at least 15 minutes

1 large egg

2 teaspoons pure vanilla extract

¼ teaspoon salt

2¼–2½ cups (280–315g) all-purpose flour, plus extra for dusting

½ cup (100g) plain or colored sugar for dusting doughnuts

canola oil for frying

IN A LARGE BOWL, place the yeast, warm water, and one teaspoon of the sugar and stir. Let the mixture sit for 10 minutes, or until thick. Add the remaining sugar, soy milk, margarine, egg, vanilla, salt, and 1½ cups (190g) flour and mix—either with a wooden spoon or with a dough hook in a stand mixer—on low speed. Add ½ cup (65g) more flour

DOUGHNUT MAKING SUCCESS

No matter how many commercial dough-nuts you have enjoyed in your life, nothing compares to homemade doughnuts. If made properly, fresh doughnuts are never greasy and have a soft bread-like interior. To make healthier doughnuts, any of the dough-nuts featured here can be *baked* in a 350°F (180°C) oven for 20 minutes, rather than fried.

Equipment
* Round cookie cutters, different sizes
* Rolling pin
* Heavy medium saucepan that can hold 1½ inches (4cm) of oil with space for the oil to bubble up
* Candy thermometer—there is no way to fry properly without maintaining oil temperature between 365°F and 375°F (185°C and 190°C)
* Chopsticks or silicone spatula for gently turning the doughnuts
* Slotted spoon to lift doughnuts out of the oil
* Wire rack
* Aluminum-foil covered cookie sheet to put under the wire rack

Methodology
If the oil is the proper temperature, frying seals the outside layer of the doughnut and prevents the oil from seeping in. If the tem-perature of the oil is too low, it cannot form an exterior seal, resulting in greasy dough-nuts that have absorbed too much oil. If the oil is too hot, the outside will burn before the inside is fully cooked and your doughnuts will be gooey and raw inside. Check the oil tem-perature between batches and adjust heat if necessary.

Tips
* Best oil for frying: canola, safflower, or peanut
* Do not crowd your doughnuts; it causes the oil temperature to drop. Fry no more than six to eight doughnut holes at a time and no more than four or five larger doughnuts in one batch.
* While frying doughnuts, stay put and watch them. They can go from perfect to burnt in moments.

and mix in. Add ¼ (30g) cup flour and mix in. If the dough remains sticky, add more flour, a tablespoon at a time, until the dough becomes smooth. Cover the bowl with a clean dishtowel and let the dough rise for one hour in a warm place. I use a warming drawer (see Note) on a low setting (about 200°F/90°C), or you can turn your oven on to its lowest setting, place the bowl in the oven, and then turn off the oven.

AFTER ONE HOUR, punch down the dough by folding it over a few times and reshaping it into a ball. Re-cover the dough and let it rise for 10 minutes.

DUST A COOKIE SHEET with flour. Sprinkle some flour on the counter or on parchment paper and use a rolling pin to roll the dough out until it's about ½-inch (1.25-cm) thick. Using a small round cookie cutter about 1 to 1½ inches (2.5 to 4cm) in diameter, cut out small circles very close to each other and place them on the cookie sheet. Reroll any scraps. Cover the doughnuts with the towel. Place the cookie sheet back in the oven (warm but turned off) or warming drawer. Let the doughnuts rise for 30 minutes.

HEAT 1½ inches (4cm) of oil in a medium saucepan for a few minutes and use a candy thermometer to see when the oil stays between 365°F and 375°F (185°C to 190°C); adjust the flame to keep the oil in that temperature range. Cover a cookie sheet with foil. Place a wire rack on top of the cookie sheet and set it near the stovetop.

WHEN THE OIL IS READY, add the doughnut holes to the oil one at a time, top-side down, putting an edge in first and then sliding in the rest of the doughnut; if you drop the doughnuts into the pan an inch or higher from the oil it can splatter and burn your fingers. You can fry up to eight doughnut holes at a time. Cook for 45 to 60 seconds. Use tongs or chopsticks to turn the doughnut holes over and cook them another 45 to 60 seconds, or until golden. Lift with a slotted spoon and place on the wire rack to cool. Repeat with the remaining doughnuts.

PLACE THE SUGAR in a shallow bowl and roll the doughnut holes in the sugar to coat. Store covered at room temperature for up to one day and reheat to serve. ▪

NOTE: A warming drawer can be built right into your kitchen cabinet. It is ideal for keeping cooked food hot, warming plates, and even proofing bread dough.

MULTIPLE STEP

NUT-FREE · PARVE

PUMPKIN DOUGHNUTS

Makes 15

Pumpkin purée and classic pumpkin pie spices give these doughnuts a soft, comforting texture and taste.

¼ ounce (1 envelope; 7g) dry yeast

¼ cup (60ml) warm water

¼ cup (50g) plus 1 teaspoon sugar, divided

2 tablespoons light brown sugar, packed

⅓ cup (80ml) soy milk

2 tablespoons (28g) margarine, at room temperature for at least 15 minutes

1 large egg

½ cup (120g) pumpkin purée (not pumpkin pie filling)

½ teaspoon salt

½ teaspoon cinnamon

¼ teaspoon ground nutmeg

½ teaspoon pure vanilla extract

3–3¼ cups (375–405g) all-purpose flour, plus extra for dusting

canola oil for frying

¼ cup (30g) confectioners' sugar for dusting

IN A LARGE BOWL, place the yeast, warm water, and one teaspoon of sugar and stir. Let the mixture sit for 10 minutes, or until thick.

oven on to its lowest setting, wait until it reaches that temperature, place the bowl in the oven, and then turn off the oven.

PUNCH DOWN THE DOUGH by folding it over a few times and reshaping it into a ball. Then re-cover the dough and let it rise for 10 minutes.

DUST A COOKIE SHEET with some flour. Sprinkle some flour on your counter or on a piece of parchment paper and roll the dough out until it's about ½ inch (1.25cm) thick. Use a 2½-inch (6cm) round cookie cutter or drinking glass to cut out circles and place them on the prepared cookie sheet. Reroll any scraps. Cover the doughnuts with the towel. Place the cookie sheet back in the oven (warm but turned off) or warming drawer. Let the doughnuts rise for 45 minutes.

HEAT 1½ inches (4cm) of oil in a medium saucepan for a few minutes and use a candy thermometer to see when the temperature stays between 365°F and 375°F (185°C and 190°C); adjust the flame so the oil stays in that temperature range.

COVER A COOKIE SHEET with foil. Place a wire rack on top of it and set it near your stovetop. Gently slide no more than four doughnuts, top side down, into the oil and fry for 1½ minutes. Turn the doughnuts over and cook another 1½ minutes. Remove with a slotted spoon, letting excess oil drip off, and place on a wire rack to cool. Repeat for the remaining doughnuts. Dust with the confectioners' sugar and serve. Store covered at room temperature for up to one day and reheat to serve. ■

ADD THE REMAINING SUGAR, brown sugar, soy milk, margarine, egg, pumpkin purée, salt, cinnamon, nutmeg, vanilla, and 2 cups (250g) of the flour to the bowl and mix on low speed with either a dough hook in a stand mixer or a wooden spoon. Add another cup (125g) of flour and mix well. Add more flour, a tablespoon at a time, and mix it in until the dough becomes smooth, scraping down the sides of the bowl each time before adding more flour.

COVER THE DOUGH with a clean dishtowel and let it rise for one hour in a warm place. I use a warming drawer on a low setting, or you can turn your

USE A THERMOMETER WHEN FRYING

The consequences of using oil that is either too cool or too hot will be food and desserts that are inedible.

CHOCOLATE GANACHE GLAZED DOUGHNUTS

Makes 10 to 12

When I was contemplating new flavors for doughnuts, the cupcake craze came to mind, particularly chocolate ganache cupcakes. You can dip these doughnuts into the ganache, but you can also double the filling recipe and squeeze some inside the center of each doughnut as well.

Dough

½ ounce (2 envelopes; 14g) dry yeast

¼ cup (60ml) warm water

½ cup (50g) plus 1 teaspoon sugar, divided

⅓ cup (80ml) soy milk

2 tablespoons (28g) margarine, at room temperature for at least 15 minutes

1 large egg

¼ teaspoon salt

1 teaspoon pure vanilla extract

½ cup (40g) unsweetened cocoa

1¾–2 cups (220–250g) all-purpose flour, plus extra for dusting

canola oil for frying

Ganache

5 ounces (140g) bittersweet chocolate

¼ cup (60ml) soy milk

1 tablespoon confectioners' sugar

1 tablespoon (14g) margarine

To prepare the dough

IN A LARGE BOWL, place the yeast, warm water and 1 teaspoon sugar and stir. Let the mixture sit for 10 minutes, or until thick.

ADD THE REMAINING SUGAR, soy milk, margarine, egg, salt, vanilla, cocoa, and 1 cup (125g) flour and mix on low speed either with a dough hook in a stand mixer or with a wooden spoon. Add another ¼ cup (30g) flour and mix well. Scrape down the sides of the bowl. Add another ¼ cup (30g) flour and mix again. If the dough is still sticky, add more flour, if needed, a tablespoon at a time, and mix it into the dough until it becomes smooth. Each time you add flour to the dough, make sure you mix it in thoroughly, so that it's well integrated. You don't want to see any white patches of flour before you add more to the dough.

COVER THE DOUGH with a clean dishtowel and let rise for one hour in a warm place. I use a warming drawer on a low setting, or you can turn your oven on to its lowest setting, wait until the oven reaches that temperature, place the bowl in the oven, and turn off the oven.

PUNCH DOWN THE DOUGH by folding it over a few times and reshaping it into a ball. Then re-cover the dough and let it rise for 10 minutes.

DUST A COOKIE SHEET with some flour. Sprinkle some flour on your counter or a piece of parchment and roll the dough out until it's about ½ inch (1.25cm) thick. Use a 3-inch (8-cm) round cookie cutter or drinking glass to cut out circles and place them on the prepared cookie sheets. Reroll any scraps. Cover the doughnuts with the towel. Place the cookie sheet back in the oven (warm but turned off) or warming drawer. Let the doughnuts rise for 45 minutes.

HEAT 1½ inches (4cm) of oil in a medium saucepan for a few minutes and use a candy thermometer to see when the temperature stays between 365°F and 375°F (185°C and 190°C); adjust the flame until the oil stays in that temperature range.

COVER A COOKIE SHEET with foil. Place a wire rack on top and set it down near your stovetop. Add the doughnuts, no more than five at a time, top side down into the oil and cook for 1½ minutes. Use tongs or chopsticks to turn the doughnut over and cook another 1½ minutes. Remove the doughnuts with a slotted spoon, letting any excess oil drip off, and place them on the wire rack to cool. Repeat for the remaining doughnuts.

BREAK THE CHOCOLATE into small pieces and melt it in a double boiler or in the microwave oven for 45 seconds, then stir; heat again for 30 seconds and stir. Heat for another 15 seconds and stir until melted. Heat the soy milk until it's hot, not boiling. Whisk it into the chocolate mixture a little at a time and then whisk it again after each addition. Add the confectioners' sugar and mix. Add the margarine and whisk well. If the chocolate ganache hardens, heat it in the microwave for a few seconds and stir.

To glaze the doughnuts

DIP THE SMOOTHEST SIDE of the doughnut into the ganache and swoosh it around a few times for a generous coating. Eat the doughnuts immediately or store them covered at room temperature for up to one day. Reheat to serve. ■

MULTIPLE STEP

NUT-FREE • PARVE

TROPICAL DOUGHNUTS

Makes 12 to 14

These are lime-flavored doughnuts filled with tropical jam. It is best to fill them with orange, apricot, mango, and other similar flavors. For a unique filling, use my recipe for mango passion fruit jam. The only hard part is finding fresh passion fruit. Not everyone can pick it right off the tree like my nephew Yonatan can, in Kadima, Israel.

Dough

¼ ounce (1 envelope; 7g) dry yeast
¼ cup (60ml) warm water
½ cup (50g) plus 1 teaspoon sugar, divided
⅓ cup (80ml) soy milk
2 tablespoons (28g) margarine
1 large egg
¼ teaspoon salt
2 teaspoons lime zest (from 1 lime)
1 teaspoon fresh lime juice
2¾–3 cups (345–375g) all-purpose flour, plus extra for dusting
canola oil for frying

Mango Passion Fruit Jam

⅔ cup (130g) sugar
¾ cup (170g) mango purée (from two mangoes)
pulp and seeds from 1 large or 2 small passion fruits

¼ cup (50g) sugar for rolling doughnuts (optional)

To prepare the dough

IN A LARGE BOWL, place the yeast, warm water, and 1 teaspoon of the sugar and stir. Let the mixture sit for 10 minutes, or until thick.

ADD THE REMAINING SUGAR, soy milk, margarine, egg, salt, zest and juice, and 1½ cups (190g) flour and mix on low speed, either with a dough hook in a stand mixer or a wooden spoon. Add another ½ cup (65g) of the flour and mix it in. Scrape down the sides of the bowl. Add another ¼ cup (30g) of flour and mix it in, and then another ¼ cup (30g) of the flour, adding more by the tablespoon until the dough becomes smooth and not sticky. Thoroughly mix in the flour before you add more.

COVER THE DOUGH with a clean dishtowel and let it rise for one hour in a warm place. I use a warming drawer on a low setting, or you can turn your oven on to its lowest setting, wait until the oven reaches that temperature, place the bowl in the oven, and then turn off the oven.

PUNCH DOWN THE DOUGH by folding it over a few times and reshaping it into a ball. Then re-cover the dough and let it rise for 10 minutes. Dust a cookie sheet with flour. Sprinkle some flour on your counter or on a piece of parchment and roll the dough out until it's ½ inch (1.25cm) thick. Use a 3-inch (8-cm) round cookie cutter or drinking glass to cut out circles and place them on the prepared cookie sheet. Reroll any scraps. Cover the doughnuts with the towel. Place the cookie sheet back in a warm place. Let the doughnuts rise for 45 minutes.

HEAT 1½ inches (4cm) of oil in a medium saucepan for a few minutes and use a candy thermometer to see when the temperature stays between 365°F and 375°F (185°C and 190°C); adjust the flame until the oil stays in that temperature range.

COVER A COOKIE SHEET with foil. Place a wire rack on top of it and set it down near your stovetop. Add the doughnuts to the oil, no more than five at a time, top side down, and cook 1½ minutes. Use tongs or chopsticks to turn the doughnuts over and cook another 1½ minutes. Remove with a slotted spoon, letting any excess oil drip off, and place on the wire rack to cool. Repeat for the remaining doughnuts.

To make the jam

PLACE THE MANGO PURÉE, passion fruit pulp and seeds, and sugar into a small saucepan and bring to a boil. Simmer for 20 minutes. Let cool for 15 minutes. Transfer to a bowl and refrigerate for at least one hour.

Filling the doughnuts

USE A KNIFE or skewer to puncture a hole in the side of each doughnut, moving the knife or skewer around inside to make a space for the jam. Place ½ cup of the jam (160g) in a pastry bag fitted with a small, round tip (about ¼ inch/6mm) and squeeze some jam into the hole; you will feel the doughnut get heavier. Add more jam to the pastry bag as needed. Roll each filled doughnut in the remaining ¼ cup (50g) of sugar to cover it completely and serve. Store the doughnuts covered at room temperature for up to one day. Reheat to serve. ▪

MULTIPLE STEP

LOW SUGAR • NUT-FREE • PARVE

WHOLE-WHEAT JELLY DOUGHNUTS

Makes 16

These doughnuts have less sugar and more whole-wheat flour than the traditional recipe, and I fill them with low-sugar jam. To reduce the sugar even more, skip the sugar-dusting.

Dough

¼ ounce (1 envelope; 7g) dry yeast
¼ cup (60ml) warm water
¼ cup (50g) plus 1 teaspoon sugar, divided
½ cup (120ml) soy milk

3 tablespoons canola oil, plus extra for frying

1 large egg

1 teaspoon pure vanilla extract

¼ teaspoon salt

1½ cups (190g) white whole-wheat flour

1½ cups (190g) all-purpose flour, plus extra for dusting

Filling

½ cup (160g) low-sugar jam

¼ cup (50g) sugar, plus ½ teaspoon cinnamon for dusting, optional

To prepare the dough

IN A LARGE BOWL, place the yeast, warm water, and 1 teaspoon of sugar and stir. Let the mixture sit for 10 minutes, or until thick. Add the remaining sugar, soy milk, oil, egg, vanilla, salt, and 1 cup (125g) of the white whole-wheat flour and 1 cup (125g) of the all-purpose flour. Mix on low speed, either with a dough hook in a stand mixer or a wooden spoon. Add ½ cup (65g) of the white whole-wheat flour and ¼ cup (30g) of the all-purpose flour and mix into the dough. Add ¼ cup (30g) all-purpose flour and mix in. If the dough remains sticky, add more all-purpose flour, a tablespoon at a time, until the dough becomes smooth.

COVER THE DOUGH with a clean dishtowel and let it rise for one hour in a warm place. I use a warming drawer on a low setting, or you can turn your oven on to its lowest setting, wait until the oven reaches that temperature, place the bowl in the oven, and then turn off the oven.

PUNCH DOWN THE DOUGH by folding it over a few times and reshaping it into a ball. Then re-cover the dough and let it rise for 10 minutes. Dust a cookie sheet with some flour. Sprinkle some flour on your counter or on a piece of parchment and roll the dough out until it's ½ inch (1.25cm) thick. Use a 3-inch (8-cm) round cookie cutter or drinking glass to cut out circles and place them on the prepared cookie sheets. Reroll any scraps. Cover

the doughnuts with the towel. Place the cookie sheet back in a warm place. Let the doughnuts rise for 45 minutes.

HEAT 1½ inches (4cm) of oil in a medium saucepan for a few minutes and use a candy thermometer to see when the temperature stays between 365°F and 375°F (185°C and 190°C); adjust the flame until the oil stays in that temperature range.

COVER A COOKIE SHEET with foil. Place a wire rack on top of it and set it down near your stovetop. Add the doughnuts to the oil, no more than five at a time, top side down, and cook 1½ minutes. Use tongs or chopsticks to turn the doughnuts over and cook another 1½ minutes. Remove with a slotted spoon, letting any excess oil drip off, and place on the wire rack to cool. Repeat for the remaining doughnuts.

Filling the doughnuts

USE A KNIFE or skewer to puncture a hole in the side of each doughnut, moving the knife or skewer around inside to make a space for the jam. Place the jam in a pastry bag fitted with a small, round tip (about ¼-inch/6-mm) and squeeze some jam into the hole; you will feel the doughnut get heavier. Add more jam as needed. If desired, combine the ¼ cup (50g) sugar and cinnamon in a shallow bowl, dip one side of each filled doughnut in the mixture, and serve.

STORE COVERED at room temperature for up to one day and reheat to serve. ▪

ROLLING DOUGH SCRAPS

To reroll doughnut scraps, gather them together and knead the pieces back into a uniform ball. Roll out with only a little flour on the surface and cut out more doughnuts.

MODERATE

NUT-FREE • PARVE

CHURROS

Makes 35

Churros are long, thin-ridged Spanish dough-nuts made out of choux pastry, the dough used for éclairs and profiteroles. In Cuba and Brazil, churros are filled, just as we fill *sufganiyot*. Here they are rolled in cinnamon sugar, the way they are eaten as street food in many Latin American countries.

Dough

1 cup (240ml) water
¼ cup (60ml) canola oil, plus extra for frying
1 tablespoon sugar
1 teaspoon pure vanilla extract
¼ teaspoon salt
1 cup (125g) all-purpose flour
3 large eggs

Cinnamon Sugar

⅓ cup (65g) sugar
2 teaspoons cinnamon

8 ounces (230g) melted chocolate for dipping,
   if desired

Preparing the dough

PLACE THE WATER, oil, sugar, vanilla, and salt into a small saucepan and stir over medium heat to dissolve the sugar. Bring to a rolling boil. Reduce heat to low and add the flour.

USE A WOODEN SPOON to mix the dough over the heat until the flour is completely mixed in and the dough comes together into a ball, about 30 seconds. Remove this mixture from the heat and scoop it into a medium bowl. Spread the dough around the bowl and press the dough up the sides of the bowl and let sit for about two minutes to help it cool down.

ADD THE EGGS one at a time, mixing well after each addition. You will need to mix vigorously to incorporate the eggs. Press the dough into the sides of the bowl with the spoon to mash the eggs into the dough. The dough will clump up, but after more stirring it will come together. Put the dough in a pastry bag fitted with a large star tip or a round tip with points, with about a ⅓-inch (8-mm) opening; I use Ateco #864.

IN A SHALLOW BOWL, combine the sugar and cinnamon. Set aside.

HEAT 1½ inches (4cm) of oil in a medium saucepan over medium-high heat until the temperature holds at 375°F (190°C). Place a wire rack over an aluminum foil-covered baking sheet. Hold the pastry bag an inch or two over the hot oil by reaching a little into the saucepan. With the pastry bag in one hand and a knife or kitchen scissors in the other, quickly squeeze out a 3- to 4-inch-long (8- to 10-cm) strip of dough and then use the knife or scissors to cut it off and let the dough drop into the hot oil. Repeat five more times. Cook no more than six strips of dough at a time.

AFTER ONE MINUTE, separate any churros that are stuck together. Fry for a total of four to five minutes, turning them over after about two minutes, until they're golden. Use a slotted spoon to lift the churros onto the rack to cool slightly for a minute, or until you can handle them. Roll the churros in the cinnamon sugar and serve. Do not wait until the churros are completely cool before rolling them in the sugar; the residual oil helps the cinnamon sugar stick to the churros. These are best eaten the day they are made. Serve with melted chocolate. Store covered at room temperature for up to two days or freeze for up to three months. Reheat to serve. ▪

OLIVE OIL CHALLAH AND CHALLAH DOUGHNUTS

*Makes 2 medium challahs
and 22 small doughnuts*

This recipe allows you to make your challah and dessert at the same time. You will have enough dough for two challahs for the Shabbat of Chanukah and a batch of doughnuts.

Dough

½ ounce (2 envelopes; 14g) dry yeast

⅓ cup (80ml) warm water

⅔ cup (130g) plus 2 teaspoons sugar, divided

½ cup (120ml) plus 2 teaspoons extra virgin olive oil, divided

1 tablespoon salt

1 cup (240ml) boiling water

½ cup (120ml) cold water

3 large eggs

6–6¼ cups (750–780g) bread flour

½ teaspoon chopped fresh rosemary leaves for the challahs

canola oil for frying

¼ cup (30g) confectioners' sugar for dusting doughnuts

To make the dough for both the challahs and the doughnuts

IN A CUP, dissolve the yeast in the ⅓ cup (80ml) warm water. Add the teaspoon sugar and stir. Set aside for 10 minutes, or until thick.

IN A LARGE BOWL, whisk together ½ cup (120ml) olive oil, salt, and ⅔ cup (130g) sugar. Add the boiling water and whisk to dissolve the salt and sugar. Add the cold water and whisk again. In a small bowl beat the eggs. Add the eggs to the oil mixture, reserving one tablespoon of beaten eggs to brush on the loaves. When the yeast mixture bubbles, add it to the bowl and stir. Cover the reserved eggs and place in the fridge.

ADD 6 CUPS (750g) of the flour, 1 cup (125g) at a time, mixing the flour in completely after each addition. Place the dough on a floured surface and knead until smooth, adding a little more flour if the dough remains sticky. The dough is ready when you rub your palm across the dough and it feels soft. Shape the dough into a ball.

ADD THE REMAINING teaspoon of olive oil to the bowl and rub it all around the bowl and on top of the dough. Place the dough into the oiled bowl and cover it with plastic. Let the dough rise for one hour.

DIVIDE THE DOUGH into three balls. Set aside one ball for the doughnuts. Braid the other two balls to make two challahs (see page 64 for instructions) and place them on a parchment-covered baking sheet. Let rise for 45 minutes.

PREHEAT OVEN to 375°F (190°C). Add the remaining teaspoon of oil to the reserved beaten eggs and stir. Brush the tops of the challahs and sprinkle them with the chopped rosemary. Bake the loaves for 30 to 35 minutes, or until browned. Cool and store wrapped in foil at room temperature for up to two days or freeze for up to three months.

To make the doughnuts

ROLL OUT the remaining ball of dough on a floured surface until it's about ½-inch (1.25cm) thick. Cut the dough into 2 to 3-inch (5 to 8-cm) circles and place them on a cookie sheet dusted with flour. Cover the cookie sheet with a clean dishtowel and let the dough rise in a warm place for 45 minutes.

HEAT 1½ inches (4cm) of oil in a medium saucepan for a few minutes and use a candy thermometer to see when the temperature stays between 365°F and 375°F (185°C and 190°C); adjust the flame until the oil stays in that temperature range.

COVER A COOKIE SHEET with foil. Place a wire rack on top and put it near your stovetop. Carefully add the doughnuts to the oil, top side down, and fry for 1½ minutes. Fry no more than five at a time. Using tongs or chopsticks turn the doughnuts over and cook another 1½ minutes, or until golden. Use a slotted spoon to lift them out of the saucepan, allowing the excess oil to drip off, and place on a wire rack to cool. Repeat for the remaining doughnuts. Use a sieve to dust the doughnuts with confectioners' sugar. Store covered at room temperature for up to one day and reheat to serve. ■

MODERATE

DAIRY • NUT-FREE • PARVE

FUNNEL CAKE

Makes 14

This dessert will remind you of trips to the beach and the boardwalk. I was surprised to discover how easy it is to make. You will notice that these funnel cakes are smaller than the ones you remember, and are really all you need of this fried treat. Just like making crêpes, you'll get the hang of making funnel cakes after the first one or two. In this recipe, I give you three different ways to squirt the batter into the oil; my favorite method is to use a plastic squirt bottle with the tip snipped off so the opening is about ¼ to ⅓-inch (6 to 8-mm) wide.

2 large eggs

1½ cups (360ml) soy milk or milk

2 teaspoons pure vanilla extract

2 tablespoons water

¼ cup (50g) sugar

2 cups (250g) all-purpose flour

1 teaspoon baking powder

½ teaspoon salt

⅓ cup (40g) confectioners' sugar, for dusting cakes

PLACE THE EGGS, soy milk or milk, vanilla, and water into a large bowl and whisk together. Add the sugar, flour, baking powder, and salt and whisk well. This dough may be made one day in advance and stored, covered, in the fridge.

PLACE A PIECE of aluminum foil under a wire cooling rack set next to the stovetop.

HEAT 1½ inches (4cm) of oil in a medium saucepan- for a few minutes and use a candy thermometer to see when the temperature stays between 365°F and 370°F (185°C and 188°C); adjust the flame until the oil stays in that temperature range. Place the batter into a squirt bottle with a ⅓ inch (8mm) hole, a pastry bag with a ½ inch (1.25cm) round tip, or use a funnel (the classic way) and place about ⅓ cup batter in the funnel for each cake. If you're using a pastry bag, tilt the tip of the bag upward and rest it in a large cup so that the batter does not drip out. If you're using a funnel, once the oil is hot, place your finger under the hole and then fill it with the batter. Whatever method you use, the idea is to swirl the batter around and around into the saucepan to create the desired spirals and avoid squirting too much batter in one spot.

WHEN THE CORRECT OIL TEMPERATURE is achieved, squirt the batter in a steady stream into the saucepan in a spiral motion until you have made about eight to ten circles about 4 inches (10cm) wide altogether. Cook no more than three or four funnel cakes at a time, depending on the size of your pan; you need space between each cake. Cook for 1½ to 1¾ minutes, or until golden; you will see the color of the bottom through the top of the lacy cake, and when browned, the cake is ready to be turned over. Use a slotted spoon to turn them over and cook another 1½ minutes, or until golden. Gently lift each cake out of the saucepan and place it on a wire rack, allowing the excess oil to drip off. Let cool slightly.

WHEN ALL THE CAKES have been cooked, sift confectioners' sugar generously on top. Store at room temperature for up to one day. You can reheat funnel cakes in a toaster oven for two minutes, or until crisp. Add more sugar on top. ■

Tu B'Shvat

Tu B'Shvat, which literally means the fifteenth of the Jewish month of Shvat, celebrates the new year for trees. It generally corresponds with the months of January or February. During the Temple period, Tu B'Shvat was when people brought the first fruits of their harvest to offer to the priests. The holiday is also an opportunity for Jews in the Diaspora to connect with the actual *land* of Israel. These days, Tu B'Shvat has an added significance, namely, raising awareness about the importance of preserving the environment.

The tradition is to plant trees, both outside and inside Israel, and to eat from the Seven Species of grains and fruit that are highlighted in the Torah as prized products of the *land* of Israel: wheat, barley, grapes, olives, figs, pomegranates, and dates. We also eat almonds, which ripen in Israel around the time of Tu B'Shvat.

When I was growing up in New York, every year on Tu B'Shvat we received snack bags with dried fruit and pods from the carob tree, *bokser* in Yiddish. I recall how I thought it would break my teeth to eat the carob pods. It never did.

MODERATE

PARVE

TU B'SHVAT BABKA

Serves 15

A few years ago, my friend Leah Hadad invited a group of women to her home for a Tu B'Shvat luncheon. I went and enjoyed a lovely meal that culminated in Leah's Tu B'Shvat babka. In 2012, Leah's company, Tribes-A-Dozen, launched a packaged challah bread mix called "Voila! Hallah!" that makes challah-baking super easy. Leah's hope is that people who are afraid to bake challah from scratch will use her mix to bake homemade challah for their families. This recipe uses Leah's Traditional mix, but you can also use your favorite challah dough recipe and set aside enough dough for one medium-size challah and then use that for this delicious babka.

Dough

1 box Voilà! Hallah Traditional Egg Bread Mix, or any challah dough (see recipe on page 88 for Olive Oil Challah, or pages 64–65 for Whole Grain Challah or Classic Challah), enough for one medium loaf of challah (21 ounces; 600g)
½ cup (120ml) lukewarm soy milk
¼ cup (60ml) oil, plus ½ teaspoon for greasing bowl
1 large egg plus 1 yolk (reserve white for glaze)

Filling

½ cup (60g) blanched slivered almonds
½ cup (140g) canned whole berry cranberry sauce
½ cup (160g) orange marmalade
2 tablespoons vanilla sugar
½ cup (25g) dry unsweetened coconut flakes

Glaze

reserved egg white
1 teaspoon vanilla sugar
1 tablespoon coconut flakes

spray oil containing flour

To make the dough

IF YOU ARE USING Voilà! Hallah Traditional Egg Bread Mix, place the mix and yeast packet into the bowl of a stand mixer. Add the warm soy milk and stir to combine. Add the oil, egg, and yolk and mix on medium-low speed for 10 minutes, scraping down the bowl a few times. The dough will be a little sticky. Use your hands to rub the ½ teaspoon oil around a clean bowl. Use your oiled hands to form the dough into a ball and place it in the oiled

bowl. Turn the ball of dough once to coat it with oil. Then cover it with a towel or plastic wrap and place the dough in a warm place to rise for 45 minutes. (If you're making the bread from a recipe—not a box—mix the dough according to the directions and let rise 45 minutes.)

To prepare the filling

MEANWHILE, place the almonds, cranberry sauce, and orange marmalade into the bowl of a food processor and process until the nuts are chopped. Add the vanilla sugar and mix it in. Set it aside.

GREASE a 12-inch (30-cm) loaf pan with spray oil containing flour. Set it aside.

To assemble the babka

DUST YOUR COUNTER with some flour and use a rolling pin to roll out the dough into a 16 x 18-inch (40 x 46-cm) rectangle. Spread the filling evenly over the dough and sprinkle the coconut on top.

Roll up the long side of the dough into a long rope. Fold the rope in half so that the two ends meet each other. Hold the rounded corner with one hand and the two ends together in the other hand. Then twist the two ends around each other a few times. Pinch the two loose ends together and tuck them under the loaf so the loaf is even in thickness. Place the loaf in the prepared loaf pan and let it rise for 15 minutes.

PREHEAT OVEN to 375°F (190°C).

To make the glaze

IN A SMALL BOWL, combine the egg white and vanilla sugar and brush it over the loaf. Sprinkle the loaf with the tablespoon of coconut flakes.

BAKE THE BABKA for 45 minutes, or until golden. Let it cool in the pan for ten minutes and then turn it out onto a wire rack. Store covered at room temperature for up to five days or freeze for up to three months. ▪

Purim

Purim is usually celebrated in March and is another holiday that commemorates the survival of the Jewish people. It comes with a rather dramatic story. While the Jews were scattered under Persian rule, the reigning king, Ahasuerus, rejected his queen and decided to replace her by staging a beauty contest. Esther, the cousin of Mordechai, who was himself the leader of the Jews, was brought to the palace and chosen to be the new queen. At the same time, the king promoted the evil Haman to prime minister. Haman issued a decree that people should rise up against the Jews because Mordechai would not bow down to him. Mordechai appealed to Esther to beg clemency from the king. When Esther told the king that she and her people would be killed by the decree of the evil Haman, the king ordered Haman killed. As the king could not rescind Haman's decree, because he had given his official ring to Haman, making the order irrevocable, Ahasuerus empowered the Jews to mobilize and defend themselves. They defeated their enemies, and Esther and Mordechai established the holiday of Purim.

One of the ways we celebrate our survival from potential tragedy is with humor. We put on Purim *spiels*, comedic plays that enact the Purim story. We dress in costumes and are commanded to drink and make merry. Indeed, Purim is the most whimsical holiday of the Jewish calendar.

The story of Purim is in the book *Megillat Esther*, the biblical Book of Esther. Interestingly, the Megillah (scroll) is the first place in the Bible where the word *Jew* appears, specifically in reference to Mordechai. In the Purim story, all the Jews who were scattered throughout the Persian kingdom were willing to fight for their survival, rather than abandon their faith. We came together, as we would many times later on in history, to fight for our right to live as Jews.

Although the word *Jew* is notable in the Megillah, mention of G-d is noticeably absent. The Purim narrative lacks an obvious miracle like the ones in the Chanukah and Passover stories. On Purim, we eat triangular shaped cookies called hamantaschen that are filled with jam, poppy seeds, prunes, or chocolate. The filling is mostly hidden, and only when we break open the cookie do we experience the flavor inside. Just like the filling in the hamantaschen, the role of G-d in the Purim story is hidden. The story, albeit dramatic, is really a series of mundane events: a beauty contest, a few parties, palace intrigue, and a parade. Only when we look back at all of the events do we see that the series of "coincidences" that together saved the Jews could only have come from the hand of G-d. Just as with hamantaschen, the true significance of the holiday unfolds. We should always look for the hidden and deeper meaning of our experiences in life as a way to acknowledge the unseen forces in the world.

One of the major ways we celebrate this holiday is to give gift baskets and bags that contain fruit and sweets (called *mishloach manot*) to friends and family. The giving of gifts celebrates our survival, an acknowledgment that we are still here. People start baking weeks in advance to create elaborate cookies and candies and craft original packaging to make impressive gifts. We eat and give hamantaschen, a deliciously edible reference to the three-pointed hat believed to have been worn by Haman.

Here, I've also included whimsical snacks such as *mazel* cookies (you know them as fortune cookies), decorated brownies, and fun-flavored truffles so you can enjoy and share some fun treats during Purim.

Hamantaschen asssortment.
From top: Raspberry, Vanilla Bean, Chocolate Chip,
Low-Sugar, Green Tea, Gluten-Free

Hamantaschen

Purim Cookies and Candies

Hamantaschen

Hamantaschen are typically vanilla or orange flavored and filled with poppy seed or prune filling, which is probably why they have never received much attention in the wider culinary world. Last year I did a blog posting called a "Rainbow of Hamantaschen" with pink raspberry, green pistachio, and brown chocolate hamantaschen; I knew it was time to update the traditional cookie, and my fans agreed. Have fun mixing and matching the doughs and fillings in this chapter to create your own signature hamantaschen.

NOTE: You will notice that some of my hamantaschen recipes contain baking powder and some do not—In those that contain baking powder, I was after a puffier, lighter dough; in recipes without baking powder, I wanted a crisper, cookie-type crust that keeps its shape.

HAMANTASCHEN BAKING TIPS

* The best way to mix the flour into the dough is to use your hands
* Chill dough before rolling it out
* While rolling the dough, sprinkle flour from above to avoid clumps of flour on the dough
* Roll dough between two pieces of parchment paper
* Do not overfill the center of the cookies
* Pinch the corners tightly
* Bake until the cookies are just starting to brown

MODERATE

NUT-FREE • PARVE

VANILLA BEAN HAMANTASCHEN

Makes 3 dozen

This is a variation on a recipe from my husband Andy's grandmother Celia Shoyer, from Romania. I like to fill this dough with raspberry jam, but feel free to use any filling you like.

Dough

3 large eggs
1 cup (200g) sugar
½ cup (120ml) canola or vegetable oil
seeds of one vanilla bean
2 teaspoons pure vanilla extract
3 cups (375g) all-purpose flour, plus extra for dusting
1 teaspoon baking powder
dash salt

Filling

1 cup (320g) raspberry or other jam

IN A LARGE BOWL, mix together the eggs, sugar, oil, vanilla bean seeds, and vanilla. Add the flour, baking powder, and salt and mix until the dough comes together. Cover the bowl with plastic wrap and leave in the fridge for one hour to firm up.

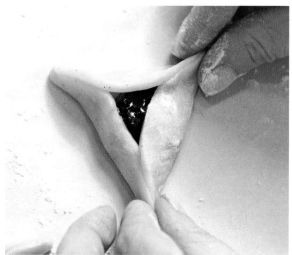

PREHEAT OVEN to 350°F (180°C). Line two or three large cookie sheets with parchment paper or silicone baking mats, or plan to bake in batches. Divide the dough in half.

TAKE ANOTHER TWO PIECES of parchment and sprinkle flour on one, place one dough half on top, and then sprinkle a little more flour on top of the dough. Place the second piece of parchment on top of the dough and roll on top of the parchment until the dough is about ¼-inch (6-mm) thick. Every few rolls, peel back the top parchment and sprinkle a little more flour on the dough.

USE a 2- to 3-inch (5- to 8-cm) drinking glass or round cookie cutter to cut the dough into circles. Use a metal flat-blade spatula to lift up the circle of dough and place it on another part of the flour-sprinkled parchment paper. Place up to 1 teaspoon of jam in the center of the dough circle and then fold the three sides in toward the middle to form a triangle, leaving a small opening in the center. Pinch the three sides together very tightly. Place the triangle on the prepared cookie sheet. Repeat with the remaining dough and scraps, making sure to sprinkle a little flour under and over the dough before you roll.

BAKE for 14 to 16 minutes, or until the bottoms are lightly browned but the tops are still light. Slide the parchment paper onto wire racks to cool the cookies. Store in an airtight container at room temperature for up to five days or freeze for up to three months. ■

MODERATE

NUT-FREE • PARVE

CHOCOLATE CHIP HAMANTASCHEN

Makes 3 dozen

These hamantaschen are made with chopped chocolate in the dough as well as in the filling and taste like your favorite chocolate chip cookies. This also means that they are best eaten straight out of the oven.

Dough

3 large eggs

1 cup (200g) sugar

½ cup (120ml) canola or vegetable oil

1 teaspoon pure vanilla extract

3 cups (375g) all-purpose flour, plus extra for dusting

dash salt

3 ounces (85g) semisweet or bittersweet chocolate, chopped into small pieces, no larger than ¼-inch (6mm; this is very important!)

Filling

6½ ounces (185g) semisweet or bittersweet chocolate cut into ½-inch (1.25-cm) squares OR

1½ cups chocolate chips

IN A LARGE BOWL, mix together the eggs, sugar, oil, and vanilla. Add the flour and salt and mix until the dough comes together. Add the chopped chocolate and mix in gently. Cover the bowl with plastic wrap and leave in the fridge for one hour to firm up.

PREHEAT OVEN to 350°F (180°C). Line two or three large cookie sheets with parchment paper or silicone baking mats, or plan to bake in batches. Divide the dough in half.

TAKE ANOTHER TWO PIECES of parchment and sprinkle flour on one, place one dough half on top, and then sprinkle a little more flour on top of the dough. Place the second piece of parchment on top of the dough and roll on top of the parchment until the dough is about ¼-inch (6-mm) thick. Every few rolls, peel back the top parchment and sprinkle a little more flour on the dough.

USE a 2- to 3-inch (5- to 8-cm) drinking glass or round cookie cutter to cut the dough into circles. Use a metal flat-blade spatula to lift up the circle of dough and place it on another part of the flour-sprinkled parchment paper. Place one ½-inch (1.25-cm) square of chocolate or 7 chocolate chips into the center and then fold the three sides in toward the middle to form a triangle, leaving a small opening in the center. Pinch the three sides together very tightly. Place on the prepared cookie sheets. Repeat with the remaining dough and roll and cut any dough scraps, making sure to sprinkle a little flour under and over the dough before you roll.

BAKE for 14 to 16 minutes, or until the bottoms are lightly browned but the tops are still light. Slide the parchment paper onto wire racks to cool the

CHILL NOW, ROLL LATER

If you do not have the time to roll out all of the hamantaschen dough at one time, cover the dough with plastic wrap and place in the fridge to assemble later or the next day.

cookies, but make sure to taste the cookies while the center is still gooey. Store in an airtight container at room temperature for up to five days or freeze for up to three months. ∎

MODERATE

NUT-FREE • PARVE

RASPBERRY HAMANTASCHEN

Makes 3 dozen

The flavor of these hamantaschen combines both fresh raspberries and raspberry jam.

Dough

3 large eggs

1 cup (200g) sugar

½ cup (120ml) canola or vegetable oil

1 teaspoon pure vanilla extract

1 teaspoon raspberry extract, optional

4-5 drops red food coloring

3 cups (375g) all-purpose flour, plus extra for dusting parchment and dough

dash salt

Filling

1 cup (320g) seedless raspberry jam

6 ounces (170g) fresh raspberries

IN A LARGE BOWL, mix together the eggs, sugar, oil, vanilla, raspberry extract, and few drops of red food coloring. Add the flour and salt and mix until the dough comes together. Cover the bowl with plastic wrap and leave it in the fridge for one hour to firm up.

PREHEAT OVEN to 350°F (180°C). Line two or three large cookie sheets with parchment or silicone baking mats, or plan to bake in batches. Divide the dough in half.

TAKE ANOTHER TWO PIECES of parchment and sprinkle flour on one, place one dough half on top, and then sprinkle a little more flour on top of the dough. Place the second piece of parchment on top of the dough and roll on top of the parchment until the dough is ¼-inch (6-mm) thick. Every few rolls, peel back the top parchment and sprinkle a little more flour on the dough.

USE a 2- to 3-inch (5- to 8-cm) drinking glass or round cookie cutter to cut the dough into circles. Use a metal flat-blade spatula to lift up the circle of dough and place it on another part of the flour-sprinkled parchment paper. Place one teaspoon of raspberry jam and one fresh raspberry in the center of the dough circle and then fold the three sides in toward the middle to form a triangle, leaving a small opening in the center. Pinch the three sides together very tightly. Place on the prepared cookie sheets. Repeat with the remaining dough and roll and cut any dough scraps, making sure to sprinkle a little flour under and over the dough before you roll.

BAKE for 14 to 16 minutes, or until the bottoms are

PINCH CORNERS AGAIN

After you have assembled all of your hamantaschen cookies, tightly pinch the edges a second time before they go into the oven.

lightly browned but the tops are still light. Slide the parchment paper onto wire racks to cool the cookies. Store in an airtight container at room temperature for up to five days or freeze for up to three months. ■

MODERATE

GLUTEN-FREE • NUT-FREE • PARVE

GLUTEN-FREE HAMANTASCHEN

Makes 40

I had experimented with gluten-free flour mixes without success until I tried King Arthur brand, a combination of white rice flour, tapioca starch, potato starch, and brown rice flour. These hamantaschen are whiter in appearance than typical hamantaschen. In addition, you need to bake them until they are browner on the bottom than other ones in this chapter. Wait until they cool before eating them because they are too crumbly when they're still warm; they are much better after they harden up.

Dough

3 large eggs

1 cup (200g) sugar

½ cup (120ml) canola or vegetable oil

2 teaspoons pure vanilla extract

1 teaspoon baking powder

1 teaspoon xanthan gum

3½ cups (560g) or 24-ounce package of gluten-free flour mix, plus extra for dusting

Filling

1 cup (320g) fruit jam or preserves, canned apricot or poppy seed pie filling

IN A LARGE BOWL, whisk together the eggs, sugar, oil, and vanilla and mix well. Add the baking powder, xanthan gum, and flour mix and use a wooden spoon to mix until the dough comes together. Cover the bowl with plastic wrap and leave in the fridge for one hour to firm up.

PREHEAT OVEN to 350°F (180°C). Line two large cookie sheets with parchment paper or silicone baking mats, or plan to bake in batches. Divide the dough in half.

TAKE TWO PIECES of parchment paper and sprinkle some gluten-free flour mix on one, place one dough half on top, and then sprinkle a little more of the mix on top of the dough. Place the second piece of parchment on top of the dough and roll on top of the parchment until the dough is ¼-inch (6-mm) thick or thinner. These cookies come out best when rolled thin. Every few rolls, peel back the top parchment and sprinkle a little more flour on the dough.

USE a 2- to 3-inch (5- to 8-cm) drinking glass or round cookie cutter to cut the dough into circles. Use a metal flat-blade spatula to lift up the circle of dough and place it on another part of the flour-sprinkled parchment paper. Place up to 1 teaspoon of jam in the center of the dough circle and then fold the three sides in toward the middle to form a triangle, leaving a small opening in the center. Pinch the three sides together very tightly. Place on the prepared cookie sheets. Repeat with the

remaining dough and roll and cut any dough scraps, making sure to sprinkle a little flour under and over the dough before you roll.

BAKE for 18 to 22 minutes, or until the bottoms are browned. Let the cookies cool completely on the cookie sheet. Store in an airtight container at room temperature for up to five days or freeze for up to three months. ▪

MODERATE

PARVE

PISTACHIO HAMANTASCHEN

Makes 3 dozen

These hamantaschen have ground pistachio nuts in the dough as well as in the filling. You can also fill the cookies with ½-inch pieces of chocolate.

Dough

3 large eggs

1 cup (200g) sugar

½ cup (120ml) canola or vegetable oil

1 teaspoon pure vanilla extract

1 teaspoon orange juice

4-5 drops green food coloring

2½ cups (315g) all-purpose flour, plus extra for dusting parchment and dough

½ cup (60g) shelled pistachio nuts, ground fine in a food processor or coffee grinder

1 teaspoon baking powder

dash salt

Filling

½ cup (120g) pistachio paste (or combine ½ cup (60g) shelled pistachio nuts, ground fine, one egg white, and ½ cup (50g) sugar)

IN A LARGE BOWL, mix together the eggs, sugar, oil, vanilla, orange juice, and few drops of green food coloring. Add the flour, ground pistachio nuts, baking powder, and salt and mix. Cover the dough with plastic wrap and leave in the fridge for one hour to firm up.

PREHEAT OVEN to 350°F (180°C). Line two or three large cookie sheets with parchment or silicone baking mats, or plan to bake in batches. Divide the dough in half.

TAKE ANOTHER TWO PIECES of parchment and sprinkle flour on one, place one dough half on top, and then sprinkle a little more flour on top of the dough. Place the second piece of parchment on top of the dough and roll on top of the parchment until the dough is about ¼-inch (6-mm) thick. Every few rolls, peel back the top parchment and sprinkle a little more flour on the dough.

USE a 2- to 3-inch (5- to 8-cm) drinking glass or round cookie cutter to cut the dough into circles. Use a metal flat-blade spatula to lift up the circle of dough and place it on another part of the flour-sprinkled parchment paper. Place one teaspoon of pistachio paste in the center of the dough circle and then fold the three sides in toward the middle to form a triangle, leaving a small opening in the center. Pinch the three sides together very tightly. Place on the prepared cookie sheets. Repeat with the remaining dough and roll and cut any dough scraps, making sure to sprinkle a little flour under and over the dough before you roll.

BAKE for 14 to 16 minutes, or until the bottoms are lightly browned but the tops are still light. Slide the parchment onto wire racks to cool the cookies. Store in an airtight container at room

USE THE GREENEST PISTACHIO NUTS

For prettier hamantaschen, look for shelled pistachio nuts that are more green than yellow.

temperature for up to five days or freeze for up to three months. ▪

NUT-FREE • PARVE

GREEN TEA HAMANTASCHEN

Makes 3 dozen

When I was visiting Paris in 2011, I saw macarons, chocolate candies, and even cakes made with green tea powder (matcha). Green tea is an antioxidant and believed to reduce the risks of cancer and heart disease, so this is a hamantasch that is also good for you. I fill these with apricot jam, but you can substitute any flavor you like. You can find kosher-certified green tea powder (matcha) online.

Dough

3 large eggs
1 cup (200g) sugar
½ cup (120ml) canola or vegetable oil
1 teaspoon fresh lemon juice
2 teaspoons green tea powder
3 cups (375g) all-purpose flour, plus extra for dusting
dash salt

Filling

1 cup (320g) apricot preserves

IN A LARGE BOWL, mix together the eggs, sugar, oil, and lemon juice and mix well. Add the green tea powder and mix well. Add the flour and salt and mix until the dough comes together. Cover the dough with plastic wrap and leave it in the fridge for one hour to firm up.

PREHEAT OVEN to 350ºF (180°C). Line two or three large cookie sheets with parchment or silicone baking mats, or plan to bake in batches. Divide the dough in half.

TAKE ANOTHER TWO PIECES of parchment paper and sprinkle flour on one, place one dough half on top, and then sprinkle a little more flour on top of the dough. Place the second piece of parchment on top of the dough and roll on top of the parchment until the dough is about ¼-inch (6-mm) thick. Every few rolls, peel back the top parchment and sprinkle a little more flour on he dough.

USE a 2- to 3-inch (5- to 8-cm) drinking glass or round cookie cutter to cut the dough into circles. Use a metal flat-blade spatula to lift up the circle of dough and place it on another part of the flour-sprinkled parchment paper. Place up to 1 teaspoon of jam in the center of the dough circle and then fold the three sides in toward the middle to form a triangle, leaving a small opening in the center. Pinch the three sides together very tightly. Place on the prepared cookie sheets. Repeat with the remaining dough and roll and cut any dough scraps, making sure to sprinkle a little flour under and over the dough before you roll.

BAKE for 14 to 16 minutes, or until the bottoms are lightly browned but the tops are still light. Slide the parchment onto wire racks to cool the cookies. Store in an airtight container at room temperature for up to five days or freeze for up to three months. ▪

RED VELVET HAMANTASCHEN

Makes 3 dozen

I use a combination of red and maroon-colored gel food coloring to achieve the dark red that is typical of red velvet cake. If the dough starts to get too gooey from the food coloring, mix a tablespoon of flour into the dough.

Dough

3 large eggs

1 cup (200g) sugar

½ cup (120ml) canola or vegetable oil

1 teaspoon pure vanilla extract

1½ teaspoons red gel food coloring

1 teaspoon maroon gel food coloring

3 cups (375g) all-purpose flour, plus extra for dusting

1 tablespoon unsweetened cocoa

dash salt

Filling

6½ ounces (185g) semisweet or bittersweet chocolate cut into ½-inch (1.25-cm) squares, OR

1¼ cups chocolate chips, OR

1½ cups white chocolate chips

IN A LARGE BOWL, mix together the eggs, sugar, oil, and vanilla and mix well. Add the red and maroon food coloring and mix well. Add the flour, cocoa, and salt and mix until the dough comes together. Cover the dough with plastic wrap and leave it in the fridge for one hour to firm up.

PREHEAT OVEN to 350°F (180°C). Line two or three large cookie sheets with parchment paper or silicone baking mats, or plan to bake in batches. Divide the dough in half.

TAKE ANOTHER TWO PIECES of parchment and sprinkle flour on one, place one dough half on top, and then sprinkle a little more flour on top of the dough. Place the second piece of parchment paper on top of the dough and roll on top of the parchment until the dough is about ¼-inch (6-mm) thick. Every few rolls, peel back the top parchment and sprinkle a little more flour on the dough.

USE a 2- to 3-inch (5- to 8-cm) drinking glass or round cookie cutter to cut the dough into circles. Use a metal flat-blade spatula to lift up the circle of dough and place it on another part of the flour-sprinkled parchment paper. Place one teaspoon or 6 to 7 dark or white chocolate chips, or one ½-inch (1.25-cm) chocolate chunk, in the center of the dough circle and then fold the three sides in toward the middle to form a triangle, leaving a small opening in the center. Pinch the three sides together very tightly. Place on the prepared cookie sheets. Repeat with the remaining dough and roll and cut any dough scraps, making sure to sprinkle a little flour under and over the dough before you roll.

BAKE for 14 to 16 minutes, or until the cookies are set and are no longer stuck to the pan; you cannot tell if they are browned because of the red color. Slide the parchment paper onto wire racks to cool the cookies. Store in an airtight container at room temperature for up to five days or freeze for up to three months. ▪

LOW-SUGAR HAMANTASCHEN

Makes 20

Unable to come up with completely sugar-free hamantaschen that I was satisfied with, I developed this recipe. I substituted white whole-wheat flour for white flour, which is healthier, especially for people on a low-sugar diet, and also reduced the amount of sugar in the dough.

Dough

1 ¼ cups (155g) white whole-wheat flour, plus extra for dusting

2 tablespoons sugar

1 teaspoon baking powder

¼ teaspoon salt

4 tablespoons (57g) margarine, frozen for 20 minutes

4 tablespoons (48g) solid vegetable shortening, frozen for 20 minutes

1 large egg

1 tablespoon cold water

Filling

½ cup (160g) low-sugar or sugar-free jam or preserves

PLACE THE FLOUR, sugar, baking powder, and salt into the bowl of a food processor fitted with a metal blade and mix for a few seconds until mixed. Add the chilled margarine and shortening and mix for 20 seconds, or until the mixture looks like sand. Add the egg and cold water and mix just until the mixture comes together. Wrap the dough in plastic and flatten. Place the dough in the freezer for about 45 minutes or overnight. When you're ready to bake, remove the dough from the freezer and thaw it until you can press it gently.

PREHEAT OVEN to 350°F (180°C). Line one or two large cookie sheets with parchment paper or silicone baking mats, or plan to bake in batches.

TAKE ANOTHER TWO PIECES of parchment paper and sprinkle flour on one, place one dough half on top, and then sprinkle a little more flour on top of the dough. Place the second piece of parchment on top of the dough and roll on top of the parchment until the dough is about ¼-inch (6-mm) thick. Every few rolls, peel back the top parchment and sprinkle a little more flour on the dough. Do not roll the dough too thin.

USE a 2- to 3-inch (5- to 8-cm) drinking glass or round cookie cutter to cut the dough into circles.

Use a metal flat-blade spatula to lift up the circle of dough and place it on another part of the flour-sprinkled parchment paper. Place up to 1 teaspoon of jam in the center and then fold the three sides in toward the middle to form a triangle, leaving a small opening in the center. Pinch the three sides together very tightly. Place on the prepared cookie sheets. Repeat with the remaining dough and roll and cut any dough scraps, making sure to sprinkle a little flour under and over the dough before you roll.

BAKE for 18 to 20 minutes, or until the bottoms are browned but the tops are still light. Slide the parchment onto wire racks to cool the cookies. Store in an airtight container at room temperature for up to five days or freeze for up to three months. ▪

SPRINKLING FLOUR

Remember to use white whole-wheat flour for sprinkling when rolling out the dough.

Purim Cookies and Candies

Over the years, my family has received every kind of *mishloach manot*, the gift packages we exchange on Purim; gifts have ranged from a paper bag containing two hamantaschen and a clementine to a large fancy basket containing several varieties of packaged cookies and candies, dried fruits, and even wine. I prefer the homemade packages and always appreciate it when someone puts in the extra effort to use a pretty box and add other personal touches. In this section, I want to supply you with recipes for cookies and candies that would make fun, colorful, but still tasty gift boxes.

EASY

NUT-FREE • PARVE

DECORATED BROWNIE BITES

Makes 96 one-inch bites

These are great treats to fill your *mishloach manot*. You can decorate them with colored sugars, sprinkles, nonpareils, crushed candies, or nuts.

10 ounces (280g) bittersweet chocolate

½ cup (120ml) canola oil, plus 2 teaspoons for greasing pan

1½ cups (300g) sugar

⅓ cup (80ml) soy milk

3 large eggs

2 teaspoons pure vanilla extract

½ teaspoon salt

¾ teaspoon baking powder

⅓ cup (25g) unsweetened cocoa

1¼ cups (155g) all-purpose flour

at least 3 different colored sugars, sprinkles, nonpareils, crushed candies, or ground nuts

PREHEAT OVEN to 350°F (180°C). Use 1 teaspoon oil to grease a 9 x 13-inch (23 x 33-cm) baking pan. Line with parchment paper, allowing some to extend up and over the sides. Grease top and sides with the other teaspoon of oil.

BREAK OR CHOP the chocolate into small pieces and melt it, either over a double boiler or in the microwave oven for 45 seconds, stir, heat for 30 seconds, stir, and heat another 15 seconds if needed, until completely melted.

WHEN THE CHOCOLATE is melted, add the oil and sugar and whisk well. Add the soy milk, eggs, and vanilla, and whisk again. Add the salt, baking powder and cocoa and mix. Finally, add the flour in four parts and whisk well each time. Scoop the mixture into the pan and spread it evenly.

BAKE for 30 minutes, or until the top looks dry and a toothpick inserted in the center comes out looking a little gooey. Cool for 30 minutes and then freeze for a minimum of one hour.

PLACE the decorations into small shallow bowls. Pull up the parchment paper to lift the brownie out of the pan. Trim ½ inch (1.25cm) from the sides and cut the short side of the brownie into long ¾- to 1-inch (2- to 2.5-cm) wide strips. Cut each strip into small squares.

TO DECORATE, press the top or bottom of each brownie into the desired decoration. Store in an airtight container at room temperature for up to three days or freeze them for up to three months. ■

PURIM COSTUMES

On Purim, the custom is to wear costumes, and I love seeing my children dressed up. Sometimes I dress up myself. After my children made it clear that wearing my chef's coat was unacceptable, I have been a Spanish dancer and a Philadelphia Eagles quarterback.

LICORICE OR ROOT BEER CHOCOLATE TRUFFLES

Makes 24 to 30

Here are two fun variations on chocolate truffles that would make great additions to your Purim gift boxes. Below are a few options for coatings, but you can also roll the truffles in colored sugars, crushed candies, or powdered nuts.

10 ounces (280g) semisweet or bittersweet chocolate

½ cup (120ml) dairy-free whipping cream

2 teaspoons anise/licorice extract OR 1 tablespoon root beer extract

2 tablespoons confectioners' sugar to dust licorice truffles, if you're making them

2 tablespoons unsweetened cocoa or 2 tablespoons vanilla sugar to dust root beer truffles, if you're making them

FOR EACH RECIPE, line a jelly roll pan with parchment or waxed paper. Set it aside.

BREAK OR CHOP the chocolate into small pieces and melt it either by heating it over a double boiler or in the microwave oven for one minute, stir, heat for 45 seconds, stir and then heat for another 30 seconds and stir until smooth. Heat the cream until it's very hot but not boiling. Whisk the hot cream into the melted chocolate in four parts. Add the desired extract (licorice or root beer) and whisk well. Pour the mixture into the lined pan and use a silicone spatula to spread it around evenly, about ⅓-inch (8-mm) thick. Place the pan in the freezer for at least 25 minutes. If you leave the pan in the freezer for longer than that, let it sit out a few minutes before you start scraping up the chocolate to form the balls.

SLIDE THE PARCHMENT or waxed paper off the pan. Line the pan with a new sheet of parchment or waxed paper. Scoop up teaspoons (or more for larger candies) of the chocolate and roll it into balls. It is helpful to wear plastic gloves for this. If the mixture gets too soft, put it back in the freezer to firm up. Put the balls on the lined pan and freeze for at least 10 minutes.

PLACE THE CONFECTIONERS' SUGAR, cocoa, or vanilla sugar into a medium bowl and roll the truffles, about six to eight at a time, in the desired coating. You can also swirl the truffles around in the bowl until they are evenly covered. Place them in a sieve over the bowl to shake off any extra coating. Store the truffles in an airtight container in the refrigerator for up to five days or freeze them for up to three months. Store each truffle in a mini candy paper cup.

YOU CAN ADD two to three teaspoons of any flavoring or liqueur to the ganache (chocolate and cream mixture) to create your own signature candies. ◾

EASY

GLUTEN-FREE • NUT-FREE • PARVE

PEPPERMINT CANDIES

Makes 24 to 28

This recipe for my version of thin mint chocolate candies packs a strong burst of mint flavor. I usually cut the candies into squares, but you can cut them into any shape you like or simply break them into shards. Please note that these peppermint candies have raw egg white in the filling.

11 ounces (310g) bittersweet or very dark chocolate, divided

1½ large egg whites, cold from the fridge (see instructions below for measuring)

2 teaspoons peppermint extract

2 cups (240g) confectioners' sugar

½ teaspoon oil for greasing pan

GREASE a 9 x 13-inch (23 x 33-cm) pan with the oil and press in a piece of parchment or waxed paper large enough to cover the bottom and about an inch up the sides of the pan. Make sure to press the parchment into the corners. Set aside.

CHOP OR BREAK five ounces of the chocolate into ½-inch (1.25-cm) pieces and place them in a heat-proof bowl. Melt the chocolate over a double boiler or in a microwave oven for 45 seconds, stir, heat another 30 seconds, stir, and then heat another 15 seconds, if needed, until completely melted. Whisk until smooth. Pour the melted chocolate into the prepared pan and use a silicone spatula to spread it all over the bottom, as evenly as possible. Put the pan into the fridge for 20 minutes, or until the chocolate feels hard to the touch. Do not wash the chocolate bowl; put the remaining chocolate in it and set it aside.

PUT ONE EGG WHITE into a large mixing bowl or the bowl of a stand mixer. Put the second egg white into a small bowl and mix it with a fork to break up the white. Scoop out one tablespoon of the mixed egg white and add it to the mixing bowl with the other white. (Instead of discarding the remaining white, reserve it for up to three days for your next omelet!) Beat the whites on medium speed for 15 seconds, or until foamy. Add the peppermint extract and mix again for a few seconds; it will not mix in perfectly. Add the confectioners' sugar in four parts, first mixing on low speed to incorporate the sugar and then increasing the speed to medium to mix well before the next addition. Scrape down the bowl often. You should have a thick but pourable cream.

WHEN THE CHOCOLATE HAS HARDENED, remove it from the fridge and spoon the peppermint cream on top of it. Use a clean spatula to spread the peppermint cream back and forth from the center of the pan to cover the chocolate with an even layer of cream. Put the cream-covered chocolate back in the fridge for 45 minutes to harden.

ONCE THE PEPPERMINT CREAM HAS HARDENED, leave the candy in the fridge while melting the remaining six ounces of chocolate. Stir until smooth. Remove the candy from the fridge and pour the melted chocolate all over the top of the cream and, working quickly, spread the chocolate to cover the cream. Don't worry about getting all the chocolate out of the bowl and onto the peppermint cream before you begin spreading; instead, start spreading as soon as most of the chocolate has been scooped out. You can use the remaining chocolate at the end to cover any bare parts.

PLACE THE CANDY back in the fridge for one hour, or until the chocolate is completely set. The candy will harden best if it's left to chill overnight. Remove it from the fridge and lift the parchment and candy out of the pan. Use a sharp knife to cut it into squares or other shapes. Store the candies, covered, in the fridge for up to five days or freeze for up to three months. Thaw in the fridge. ▪

MAZEL COOKIES
(FORTUNE COOKIES)

Makes 18 to 22

These fortune cookies are really fun to make. You can put any message you like inside—a note from you and your family, a simple *chag sameach* (happy holiday) greeting, or a blessing. At your Purim *seudah* (festive meal), a cookie can be used as a place card holder—with the name popping out—or it can be filled with a special or funny message for each guest. I would advise making just two cookies at a time in the first batch, so you learn how to fold them, and then make no more than four to six cookies at a time so they do not harden before you can fold them properly. If you have tight-fitting plastic gloves, they will protect your fingertips as you shape the hot cookies. To lift the cookies off the pan, you will definitely want to use a wide metal flat-blade spatula—like the ones used to plaster walls. I've also included a dark chocolate variation for this recipe, below.

2 large egg whites
½ cup plus 1 tablespoon (113g) sugar
½ teaspoon pure vanilla extract
1 teaspoon orange juice
3 tablespoons canola oil
½ cup (65g) all-purpose flour
¼ teaspoon salt

PREHEAT OVEN to 375°F (190°C). Cover a cookie sheet with a silicone baking mat or grease the cookie sheet with a little spray oil. You can also use parchment paper that is greased with a little canola oil. You will need a glass bowl, a measuring cup, or a mug for shaping the cookies over the rim and a muffin pan to help them hold their shape. Cut out about sixteen small typed or handwritten notes to put in the cookies.

PUT THE EGG WHITES and sugar in a large mixing bowl and beat with an electric mixer on medium-low speed for one minute, or until creamy. Add the vanilla, orange juice, and oil and mix again until combined. Add the flour and salt and mix well until you have a creamy batter, scraping down the bowl to incorporate all of the flour.

SCOOP UP two heaping teaspoons of batter and place them on the prepared cookie sheet. Repeat, spacing each little pile of batter at least four inches (10cm) apart. It is more efficient, however, to scoop up and drop four piles of batter one after the other onto the cookie sheet. Use the back of a measuring spoon or a teaspoon to swirl and spread the batter into a 3½-inch (9-cm) wide circular cookie.

BAKE the cookies for 7 to 8 minutes, or until they are browned from about half an-inch (1.25-cm) in from the outside edge. Remove the cookies from the oven. You will need to work quickly. Use a metal spatula to lift a cookie off the pan (removing the darker ones first) and turn it over onto the counter. Place a note in the center. Working quickly, fold the cookie in half so the browned edges meet and then with the browned edges facing up, bend the middle of the cookie over the rim of the bowl or cup. Count to five. Place the cookie on its side into the muffin cup and quickly repeat with the other baked cookies on the tray—and with the other batches.

STORE THE COOKIES in an airtight container at room temperature for up to five days or freeze them for up to three months. ▧

Dark Chocolate Variation

Substitute:

2 teaspoons pure vanilla extract for the
    ½ teaspoon vanilla and 2 teaspoons orange
    juice

⅓ cup (40g) all-purpose flour plus 3 tablespoons
    dark cocoa for the ½ cup of flour

HERE'S AN EASY WAY to tell when the chocolate cookies are done: When you press the top after about 8 minutes of baking, no batter should get on your fingers and the cookie should feel a little rubbery.

SILICONE MAT WORKS BEST

This is a recipe where a silicone baking mat (a Silpat) works better than either parchment paper or a greased baking pan. Using a Silpat helps you spread the batter faster, facilitates lifting the cookies off the pan, and makes the cookies a little cooler so they are easier to handle and shape.

MULTIPLE STEP

GLUTEN-FREE • NUT-FREE • PARVE • VEGAN

HOMEMADE MARSHMALLOWS

Makes 35

Because homemade marshmallows are so fluffy and can be made in different flavors, they win over people who have never enjoyed packaged marshmallows. Here are two variations on the classic marshmallow: coconut and raspberry swirl. These can also be made during Passover.

Coconut Marshmallows

1½ cups (75g) dry coconut flakes

3 envelopes (2 tablespoons or ¾ ounce; 21g total) unflavored gelatin powder

¾ cup (180ml) cold water, divided

2 cups (400g) sugar

⅔ cup (225g) honey

1 teaspoon pure vanilla extract

¼ teaspoon salt

¾ cup (180ml) coconut milk (the thick creamy kind)

½ teaspoon canola oil for greasing the pan

PREHEAT OVEN to 350°F (180°C). Place the coconut flakes on a parchment-covered jelly roll pan and bake for 8 to 10 minutes, or until the flakes are golden. Shake the pan once or twice so that all the flakes get toasted evenly. Set aside.

PLACE THE GELATIN POWDER into the bowl of a stand mixer. Pour ½ cup (120ml) cold water over the powder, do not stir, and let the mixture sit for 10 minutes. This is called "blooming the gelatin."

PLACE THE SUGAR, honey, vanilla, salt, and remaining ¼ cup (60ml) water into a small saucepan over medium-high heat. Bring the mixture to a boil, stirring occasionally, and cook until it reaches 250°F (120°C) on a candy thermometer. The mixture will get foamy and bubble up, almost to the top of the saucepan; just keep cooking until you reach the 250°F (120°C) temperature, and turn down the heat if necessary, to prevent boiling over.

USE THE WHISK attachment on low speed to stir the gelatin. While the mixer is going, slowly pour the hot honey mixture down the side of the bowl into the gelatin—not onto the wire whisk. When all of it has been poured in, cover the machine with a clean dishtowel and turn the speed up to medium-high. Beat the mixture for a full 12 minutes, until it gets very thick; it will fill the mixing bowl.

MEANWHILE, rub the bottom and sides of a 9 x 13-inch (23 x 33-cm) pan with a ½ teaspoon canola oil. Press a piece of parchment paper into the pan. The paper should be large enough to cover the bottom and sides. Spread ½ cup of the toasted coconut on the bottom of the pan so that it is covered evenly. Place the remaining toasted coconut into a shallow bowl and cover it. Set it aside.

WHEN THE MARSHMALLOW CREAM IS READY, use a silicone spatula to gently fold the coconut milk into the marshmallow cream. It is best to add the coconut milk in three parts. Scoop the mixture into the coconut-covered pan and spread it evenly. Let the pan sit uncovered overnight.

COVER a large piece of parchment paper with a heaping ½ cup (30g) of the toasted coconut flakes. Use the edges of the parchment to lift the marshmallow out of the pan and turn it over onto the coconut-covered parchment. Carefully peel off the bottom parchment paper. Use scissors, a pizza cutter, sharp knife, or cookie cutter to cut the marshmallow into squares or any shape you like (eat the scraps). Roll the marshmallows all around in the remaining toasted coconut. Let them sit uncovered at room temperature to dry for a few hours, and then cover them overnight. Store the marshmallows in an airtight container for up to two weeks or freeze them for up to three months. ■

Raspberry Swirl Marshmallows

12 ounces (340g) fresh raspberries

¾ cup (90g) plus 3 tablespoons confectioners' sugar, divided

3 envelopes (2 tablespoons or ¾ ounce; 21g) unflavored gelatin powder

¾ cup (180ml) cold water, divided

2 cups (400g) sugar

⅔ cup (225g) honey

1 teaspoon pure vanilla extract

¼ teaspoon salt

½ teaspoon canola oil for greasing the pan

PLACE THE GELATIN POWDER into the bowl of a stand mixer. Pour ½ cup (120ml) cold water over the powder, do not stir, and let sit 10 minutes.

PLACE THE SUGAR, honey, vanilla, salt, and ¼ cup (60ml) water into a small saucepan over medium-high heat. Bring the mixture to a boil, stirring occasionally, and cook until it reaches 250°F (120°C) on a candy thermometer. The mixture will get foamy and bubble up, almost to the top of the saucepan; just keep cooking until you reach the 250°F (120°C) temperature, and turn down the heat if necessary, to prevent boiling over.

USE THE WHISK ATTACHMENT on low speed to stir the gelatin. While the mixer is going, slowly pour the hot honey mixture down the side of the bowl into the gelatin—not onto the wire whisk. When all of it has been poured in, cover the machine with a clean dishtowel and turn the speed up to medium-high. Beat the mixture for a full 12 minutes, until it gets very thick.

MEANWHILE, rub the bottom and sides of a 9 x 13-inch (23 x 33-cm) pan with ½ teaspoon canola oil. Press a piece of parchment paper into the pan. The paper should be large enough to cover the bottom and sides. Using a sieve, dust the bottom of the pan with ¼ cup (30g) confectioner's sugar.

PLACE THE RASPBERRIES and three tablespoons of confectioner's sugar into the bowl of a food processor and process until completely puréed, scraping down the bowl several times. Strain the mixture into another bowl and discard the seeds. Set it aside.

USE A SILICONE SPATULA to gently fold the raspberry purée into the cream mixture. You can mix it in completely for all pink marshmallows or mix it in partway to create a marbled effect. Scoop the mixture onto the sugar-coated parchment and spread it around evenly, and into the corners. Let the mixture sit uncovered overnight.

BEFORE YOU LIFT the marshmallows out of the pan, prepare a piece of parchment paper larger than the 9 x 13-inch (23 x 33-cm) pan, and use a sieve to shake ¼ cup (30g) confectioner's sugar on top of it. Use the edges of the parchment in the pan to lift the marshmallow out of the pan and turn it over onto the sugar-covered parchment. Peel off the bottom parchment paper. Put the remaining confectioner's sugar in a shallow bowl. Cut the marshmallows into the shapes you desire and then roll them around in the sugar. Let them sit uncovered at room temperature to dry for a few hours, and then cover them overnight. Store the marshmallows in an airtight container for up to two weeks or freeze them for up to three months. ■

MULTIPLE STEP

TIE-DYED MINI BLACK AND **WHITE COOKIES**

Makes 70

These tie-dyed cookies are my whimsical Purim version of classic chocolate and vanilla black and white cookies. You can make any design you like (I provide a few options below). Have fun!

Cookie
½ cup (100g) sugar
¼ cup (60ml) canola oil
2 large eggs
1½ teaspoons pure vanilla extract
1 teaspoon fresh lemon juice (from ½ lemon)
⅓ cup (80ml) soy milk
1½ cups (190g) all-purpose flour
½ teaspoon baking powder
dash salt

Icing
2 cups (240g) confectioners' sugar
2 teaspoons pure vanilla extract
1 teaspoon fresh lemon juice
several colors of gel food coloring

To make the cookies
PREHEAT OVEN to 325°F (160°C).

PUT THE SUGAR, oil, eggs, vanilla, and lemon juice into a large bowl and beat for about 30 seconds with an electric mixer on medium speed until the ingredients are combined. Add the soy milk and mix in. Add the flour, baking powder, and salt and mix until combined.

COVER THREE COOKIE SHEETS with parchment paper, or plan to bake in batches. With a measuring teaspoon or melon-baller, drop heaping teaspoons of batter onto the cookie sheet, about 1½ inches (4cm) apart. Try to keep the shape of the cookies round.

BAKE THE COOKIES for 15 to 17 minutes, or until they feel solid when the top is pressed. The color should remain light; only the outside edges of the bottoms should look lightly browned if you lift up one cookie. If the cookies are stuck to the pan, they need a little more baking time. Remove the pan from the oven and slide the parchment onto a wire rack. When the pan has cooled, use a spatula to lift the cookies off the parchment, or peel the parchment off the cookies, and place them on the cooling rack. The cookies may be made one day in advance and stored covered at room temperature.

To make the icing
PUT THE CONFECTIONERS' SUGAR in a medium bowl. Add two tablespoons of boiling water, vanilla, and lemon juice and whisk vigorously. If the mixture is too thick to spread, add another ½ teaspoon (or more) of boiling water and whisk well until you have a thick but still pourable consistency. The icing will thicken as you ice the cookies and you will need to add another ½ teaspoon of boiling water to get the icing back to a spreadable consistency. If the white icing gets too loose, whisk in a teaspoon of confectioners' sugar.

To decorate the cookies
THERE ARE SEVERAL WAYS to decorate the cookies:
* Divide the icing among three or more bowls and color each with gel food coloring as desired. Spread about ¾ of a teaspoon on the flat side of each cookie. You can also ice half the cookie with one color and half with another color.
* Squeeze some drops of gel coloring onto a paper plate or waxed paper. Have a toothpick ready for each color. Ice about four cookies at a time with white icing. Use toothpicks to place tiny dots or short lines of different colors on the icing and then use a toothpick to create a marbled effect.

LET THE COOKIES SET for 15 minutes. Store them covered at room temperature for up to three days, or freeze the cookies for up to three months. ■

Passover

The eight-day spring holiday of Passover celebrates the liberation of the Israelites from slavery in Egypt. We gather at a Seder, a festive meal, where we retell the story of the Exodus. We read aloud how our ancestors came to Egypt, their suffering under Pharaoh, how G-d punished the Egyptians with Ten Plagues yet spared the Jews, and the miracle of the parting of the Red Sea. The Seder is full of rituals; among many other customs, we drink four cups of wine as a symbol of freedom, eat bitter herbs and other foods to remind us of our oppression as slaves, and children ask the Four Questions about our Seder customs. During the second part of the Seder, we celebrate our freedom and gratitude to G-d with lively songs. It is a holiday that celebrates the solidarity of the Jewish people. Families convene all over the world to remind themselves that they are fortunate to be part of a people who survived Egyptian slavery. Passover highlights that we are still here, together as a nation and free.

Most Jewish holidays revolve around food, but at Passover, food is not just for eating. Passover foods are edible symbols that connect Jews from all generations to the actual events commemorated by the holiday. When the Israelites departed Egypt, they had no time to allow their bread dough to rise. As a result, we eat unleavened cracker-like matzoh for eight days and avoid any food made from wheat because wheat combined with water causes the wheat to ferment and possibly leaven. Over the centuries, rabbis expanded this prohibition to include four additional grains: oats, rye, barley, and spelt. Any food that contains these ingredients, or has come in direct contact with them, is deemed chametz and is forbidden to be consumed during the holiday. Ashkenazi (Eastern European) Jews do not eat any grain that can be used to make bread, including corn and rice, or legumes that could be confused with grains. In addition, the restriction extends to other legumes that might be ground in mills that handle flour, increasing the risk that a bag of rice or legumes could contain forbidden grains. Sephardic (Middle Eastern) communities are more liberal, allowing the eating of rice and all legumes.

The prohibition against chametz has evolved into a process of completely changing over our kitchens. Because our dishes and utensils have come in contact with chametz all year long, we use separate equipment designated solely for Passover use. We clean our kitchens thoroughly to remove any traces of chametz. It is spring cleaning to the power of one hundred.

Once the cleaning and the changing of the dishes have been completed, the cooking and baking start. Working around the restrictions of Passover, most bakers feel more enslaved than liberated. And the processed, packaged Passover desserts that begin to appear on supermarket shelves many months before Passover are usually old before you use them and are not very good. And as very few kosher bakeries bake Passover desserts, it is the time of year when it makes a really big difference to be a good home baker.

I am here to give you your Passover baking freedom by supplying you with an arsenal of recipes. I'll let you know the kind of baking equipment you will need, at the minimum, to bake during Passover. And I'll give you all the tools you'll need to create desserts that are so delicious, you'll feel joyous and look forward to Passover baking every year! You may even surprise yourself by finding recipes in this chapter that you'll want to bake all year round. The time of Passover baking slavery is past. Your baking exodus has arrived.

Passover Snacks

Desserts for Passover Entertaining

PASSOVER BAKING EQUIPMENT

The restriction against chametz (leavened food or any food that could come in contact with leavened products) applies to utensils and cooking and baking equipment as well. That means that anything you use during the rest of the year that comes in contact with chametz may not be used, unless it is thoroughly cleaned and heated to purge any chametz that it may have absorbed. The rules are extremely strict about what can be koshered for Passover. You are permitted to kasher stainless steel baking pans if the pan is one piece of metal and has no crevices, but many baking items are excluded, including anything made out of glass, plastic, ceramic, and any utensils or pieces of equipment that cannot be fully cleaned. A good example would be food processor disks; it is impossible to clean thoroughly between the blade and the base. In addition, your oven must be thoroughly cleaned, either through a long self-cleaning cycle or, if cleaned manually, it must be left unused for 24 hours after cleaning. Check with your rabbinic authority for specific guidance regarding this and all the rules above.

Because the rules for Passover are so stringent, kosher households typically maintain a completely separate set of pots, dishes, and utensils reserved for use only during Passover. Yes, it is a crowded kitchen with yet another set of milk and meat everything. Many people use disposable baking pans during the holiday, which work adequately for most recipes, but cookies do not bake as well on them. Because you only want to buy and store precisely what you truly need, here is a list of the essential items you will need to bake all the recipes in this chapter:

* Hand mixer
* Food processor
* Large, medium, and small mixing bowls
* Liquid and dry measuring cups
* Measuring spoons
* Silicone spatulas
* Hand whisk
* One 9-inch (23-cm) pie pan (disposable OK)
* 12-cup (2.8-l) Bundt pan
* jelly roll pan
* 2 flat cookie sheets
* 2 8-inch (20-cm) round pans (disposable OK)
* 8-inch (20-cm) square pan (disposable OK)
* 9 x 13 inch (23 x 33 cm) pan
* Pastry bag and decorative tips, ¼-inch (6-mm) and ½-inch (1.25-cm) round and two others, such as a small star tip and another tip that makes flower shapes
* Candy thermometer
* Box grater
* 12-cup muffin tin (disposable OK)
* 12-cup mini muffin tin
* 12-inch (30-cm) loaf pan
* Zester
* Metal flat-blade spatula
* Large glass bowl
* Parchment paper or silicone baking mats

PASSOVER-FRIENDLY RECIPES IN OTHER CHAPTERS

* Quinoa Pudding with Caramelized Apples and Honey (page 24)
* Raspberry and Rose Macaron Cake (substitute almond milk for soy milk and potato starch for the flour) (page 36)
* Chestnut Mousse (page 55)
* Apple Latkes (substitute potato starch for the flour) (page 76)
* Coconut and Raspberry Swirl Marshmallows (pages 112–113)
* Low Sugar Cheesecake Muffins (substitute sugar-free Passover cookies for the crust and potato starch for the flour) (page 194)

THE PASSOVER BAKING PANTRY

An entire "Kosher for Passover" industry has responded to the stringent rules that apply to holiday baking by making ingredients such as confectioners' sugar without cornstarch and even kosher for Passover baking powder. Like all kosher food, any processed food consumed during Passover must have the "Kosher for Passover" designation and must have rabbinical certification. There are exceptions, such as unprocessed nuts. The list changes, so you should check with the kosher certification board that you follow to see the guidelines each year.

Passover products are very expensive, and you should try to buy only what you need. I keep my shopping lists and receipts from year to year and post them somewhere in my kitchen throughout the week of Passover. I add the baking ingredients I buy during the week to the list, and at the end of the holiday I mark down what I used and what I did not. If you buy two boxes of potato starch and only use up one, make a note of that on the list so that you'll know for the following year to buy less.

Here's my list of essential Passover baking ingredients:

BROWN SUGAR The major brands are kosher for Passover, but check first.

CONFECTIONERS' SUGAR A mixture of superfine sugar and cornstarch, to help keep the sugar from clumping. Regular confectioners' sugar is not kosher for Passover. The Passover version contains potato starch to replace the cornstarch. I have found that it works as well as the cornstarch version.

BAKING POWDER Baking powder for Passover surprises people who believe that anything that causes leavening is prohibited. In fact, only yeast-based leaveners, which depend on fermentation, are prohibited.

VANILLA EXTRACT Pure vanilla extract is forbidden during Passover because it contains alcohol, which is fermented. For many years, kosher bakers made their own vanilla sugar by placing a vanilla bean in a jar with granulated sugar and used that to add vanilla flavor to Passover desserts. Commercial vanilla sugar still appears on the shelves every Passover. Today you can find "imitation vanilla extract" during the holiday— it's not as bad as it sounds and works pretty well.

APRICOT AND RASPBERRY JAM Several brands of good quality jam have kosher for Passover certification.

CITRUS I use a lot of fresh orange, lemon, and lime juice in my baking and often use the zest as well. If you do not use zest during Passover because of the risk of exposure of the peel to chametz, add 1 to 2 teaspoons more juice to a recipe that calls for zest. To properly zest citrus, use a Microplane zester or box grater with small holes. Grate just the colored outer part. You should rub no more than twice in the same spot; once you hit the white, move on to another part of the fruit.

THE TEN PLAGUES OF PASSOVER BAKING

1. No flour
2. No yeast
3. No pure vanilla extract
4. No soy milk
5. Inferior parve margarine
6. No filo and puff pastry shortcuts
7. No good quality dairy-free whipping cream
8. Dealing with the density of matzoh cake meal
9. Fewer baking pans to work with
10. The need for a hen and a chicken coop in the backyard (one year I went through 26 dozen eggs)

UNFLAVORED KOSHER GELATIN POWDER You can find several brands of unflavored gelatin powder to use in creams and other desserts. Follow package or recipe instructions on how to "bloom," or activate, the gelatin to achieve a smooth consistency in your jelled dessert.

UNSWEETENED COCOA Several brands are marked kosher for Passover.

MARGARINE Some years, stores have only sold dairy-free Passover margarine in one-pound blocks. It is best to cut the solid pounds into four quarter-pound "sticks" and wrap them in plastic wrap before refrigerating so you have easier sizes to work with. To melt margarine you can use a small saucepan and heat over low heat on the stovetop until melted. To melt in the microwave oven, place the margarine into a heatproof bowl. For a stick of margarine, heat for one minute, or longer if needed. For amounts less than one stick, heat for 30 to 45 seconds.

VEGETABLE OIL Vegetable, cottonseed, olive, and nut oils are available for cooking and baking during Passover. I have found that vegetable oil is the best oil to use for cakes and other desserts during Passover.

EGGS Use *large* eggs. Please do not substitute any other size. Crack each egg into a separate bowl and discard it if there is a blood spot.

WHIPPING CREAM There are several brands that can be stored in the freezer. Thaw completely in the fridge and remember to shake well before using. It can be used as a substitute for sweetened condensed milk.

BITTERSWEET OR SEMISWEET CHOCOLATE Many of the parve chocolate brands I use all year are also kosher for Passover. They are not always classified by percentage of cocoa mass, the way other premium bar chocolates are, but both semisweet and bittersweet chocolate work very well in the chocolate desserts in this chapter. Parve baking

SUBSTITUTION RULES FOR CONVERTING RECIPES

This chapter contains many baking recipes that have already been converted for Passover use. If you want to convert your favorite recipes into Passover-friendly versions, use the chart below for ingredient substitutions, and if you come up with anything truly great, please let me know by email.

* 1 cup (125g) flour = ¾ cup (120g) potato starch plus ¼ cup (33g) matzoh cake meal
* 1 tablespoon flour = ½ tablespoon potato starch
* 1 tablespoon cornstarch = 1 tablespoon potato starch
* 1 cup (120g) confectioners' sugar = 1 cup (200g) minus 1 tablespoon granulated

sugar plus 1 tablespoon potato starch pulsed in a food processor or blender until it becomes a very fine powder

* ½ cup (120ml) corn syrup = ⅔ cup (130g) granulated sugar plus ½ cup (120ml) water boiled for 2 to 3 minutes or until it starts to thicken and left to cool. Store in a jar or container. I have also used equivalent amounts of honey as a corn syrup substitute.
* 1 cup vanilla sugar = 1 cup (200g) granulated sugar plus 1 split vanilla bean left to sit for 24 hours in a tightly covered jar
* 1 teaspoon cream of tartar = 1½ teaspoons lemon juice or 1½ teaspoons vinegar

chocolate is pricey and you will use a lot of it during the holiday, so comparison-shop for the best deals in stores and online.

To melt chocolate, you can use the top part of a double boiler or a microwave oven. A double boiler is a specially designed saucepan that has a top bowl that fits snugly over a saucepan. You heat water in the saucepan over medium heat and, as the water simmers, it melts the chocolate. You can create a makeshift double boiler by placing 2 to 3 inches (5 to 8 cm) of water in a medium saucepan and resting a medium metal bowl containing the chopped chocolate on top. The bowl should be big enough to just sit on top of the saucepan, not inside it; nor should it extend far over the sides of the pan. Stir the chocolate occasionally. To melt chocolate in a microwave oven, place the chopped chocolate into a microwave-safe bowl. Heat it for one minute and then remove the bowl from the microwave and stir the chocolate. Heat it for another 45 seconds; then remove and stir it well, trying to mix the unmelted chocolate into the melted part. Repeat as needed for 30 seconds and then in 15-second intervals, stirring for at least 30 seconds in between each cycle, until the chocolate is melted and smooth. Do not heat for 2 minutes straight, thinking it will speed up the process; this is likely to burn the chocolate.

CHOCOLATE CHIPS Unfortunately, the quality of parve chips available during Passover is not as good as the chocolate chips available all year round, so I sometimes create my own by chopping bars of semisweet chocolate into chip-size pieces.

MATZOH CAKE MEAL Matzoh cake meal is matzoh that has been ground finely into a soft powder that can be used in combination with potato starch to replace flour in recipes. If too much of it is used in a recipe, it can make Passover desserts taste dry and a little pasty.

POTATO STARCH Potato starch is a great kosher for Passover product that can be used like cornstarch—and as a flour substitute—when mixed with matzoh cake meal.

GLUTEN-FREE CAKE MEAL This is a new and welcome addition to the Passover pantry. It is made out of a combination of tapioca and potato starch. Note that it contains egg products.

MATZOH FARFEL Farfel are half-inch or smaller-size pieces of matzoh that I use in desserts to add extra crunch. You can buy boxes of it in stores or make your own by breaking apart whole matzoh with your hands. You can also put matzoh into a freezer bag and then bang it with a heavy saucepan to break it into ½-inch (1.25-cm) pieces. Farfel comes in both regular and whole-wheat versions.

ALMOND FLOUR Nut flours are a great, healthy alternative to matzoh cake meal and are used in many recipes in this book. I especially like almond flour because it is lower in fat than other nut flours and it has a mild flavor, which makes it versatile. You can buy almond flour already ground, with or without skins, or make your own using a coffee grinder or food processor to mill the nuts into a powder. If you are grinding slivered nuts, about eight ounces (230g) is the equivalent of two cups of almond flour. A quarter pound (115g) of whole nuts yields one cup of almond flour. Always taste nuts for freshness before grinding them to make sure the nut flour will be of the best quality.

GROUND HAZELNUTS Hazelnuts may be ground to make flour the same way you grind almonds

COMMON BAKING INGREDIENTS NOT AVAILABLE FOR PASSOVER

* Baking soda
* Dairy-free cream cheese or sour cream made from soy
* Solid vegetable shortening

*Clockwise from upper left: Pistachio Cookies,
Chocolate Chip Cookie Bars, Farfel Cookies,
Mexican Chocolate Cookies*

(see "Almond flour," above). Toasting the nuts before grinding will result in a stronger flavor.

GROUND WALNUTS Good quality finely ground walnuts are readily available during Passover so there is usually no need to grind your own.

ALMOND MILK Almond milk is a recent addition to the Passover pantry. I have used plain almond milk as a substitute for soy milk or dairy milk in many recipes.

Caution: When you use almond milk in a recipe that otherwise has no nuts, remember to advise anyone with allergies that your dessert contains almond milk.

GEBROKTS

Many Jews follow a custom of not eating any matzoh or product on Passover (with the exception of the last day) derived from matzoh that is mixed with any liquid, because of the chance that the liquid might cause the matzoh to rise. The combination of matzoh and liquid is called "gebrokts" in Yiddish. As a result, these bakers do not use matzoh cake meal or farfel in their baking. I have marked desserts that are non-gebrokts so they are easy to identify.

PLAN AHEAD

As soon as you start cooking and baking for the holiday, bake a few snacks so that the moment the holiday starts, you have some nosh.

Passover Snacks

Just like days always seem longer when you don't get a snack, Passover often feels like a long holiday if you don't get a tasty treat every day. You also need recipes for snacks that are easy to carry around with you when you go places during the holiday. Below are 19 easy recipes to make sure you have a joyous holiday. Some are great for breakfast. Some are great for teatime. In fact, all of them are great for just about any time.

MODERATE

PARVE

FARFEL COOKIES
Makes 10 dozen

These are thin chocolate chip cookies that get their crunch from toasted matzoh pieces. The recipe yields many cookies so find some helpers to assist with dropping the batter onto the cookie sheets.

2 cups (120g) matzoh farfel (½-inch or smaller matzoh pieces)
½ cup (1 stick; 113g) margarine
1¾ cups (350g) sugar
2 large eggs
2 teaspoons vanilla
2 tablespoons matzoh cake meal
1 cup (120g) ground almonds
½ teaspoon salt
½ cup (90g) mini chocolate chips

PREHEAT OVEN to 350°F (180°C).
LINE A COOKIE SHEET with parchment paper. Add the farfel and spread it out in one layer. Bake for 20 minutes. Remove from the oven and slide the parchment off the sheet onto a wire rack. Let cool ten minutes.

PLACE THE MARGARINE into a large heatproof bowl and melt in the microwave for 45 seconds, or until melted. Add the sugar and use a whisk to stir. Add the eggs and vanilla and mix. Add the toasted farfel, cake meal, ground almonds and salt, and mix well. Add the chocolate chips and mix to evenly distribute. Place the dough in the fridge for at least 20 minutes (do not skip this part).

LINE COOKIE SHEETS with parchment paper. Drop teaspoons of dough onto the parchment, two inches (5cm) apart. Bake for 10 to 12 minutes, or until the cookies begin to brown on the edges. Slide the parchment onto a wire rack and let cool. Line the cookie sheets with new pieces of parchment, add more dough and bake, and then repeat for as many batches as needed. Place cooled cookies in an airtight container and store at room temperature for up to five days or freeze for up to three months. ■

EASY

PARVE

CHOCOLATE CHIP, PISTACHIO, CRANBERRY, AND HAZELNUT BISCOTTI

Makes 2 to 3 dozen

Most biscotti dough is a blank canvas onto which you can add whatever you like. You can use chopped pecans, cashews, or walnuts instead of the pistachios, as long as the amount totals ¾ cup. You can also substitute raisins or chopped apricots for the dried cranberries.

½ cup (1 stick; 113g) margarine, at room
   temperature for at least 15 minutes
1 cup (200g) plus ½ teaspoon sugar, divided
2 large eggs
1⅓ cups (175g) matzoh cake meal
⅓ cup (55g) potato starch
½ cup (60g) ground hazelnuts

¾ cup (125g) chocolate chips
¾ cup (90g) shelled pistachio nuts
½ cup (70g) dried cranberries, chopped

PREHEAT OVEN to 350°F (180°C). Line a cookie sheet with parchment paper.

IN A LARGE BOWL, with an electric mixer on medium-high speed, beat the margarine and one cup of the sugar until creamy. Add the eggs and mix well. Add the cake meal, potato starch, and ground hazelnuts, and mix again. Add the chocolate chips, pistachios, and cranberries and mix to distribute.

DIVIDE THE DOUGH in half and shape each piece into a 3 x 11-inch (8 x 28-cm) loaf. Place on the prepared cookie sheet, leaving a few inches between the loaves. Sprinkle the remaining ½ teaspoon sugar on top of the loaves.

BAKE for 35 minutes. Slide the parchment and loaves onto your counter or a cutting board and let cool five minutes. Place a new piece of parchment on the cookie sheet. Cut the loaves across into ½- (1.25-cm) to ¾-inch (2-cm) slices and place back on the cookie sheet cut-side down. Bake for 5 to 10 minutes more, 5 for soft and 10 for crunchier cookies. Remove from the oven and let cool. Store in an airtight container at room temperature for up to five days or freeze for up to three months. ■

EASY

GLUTEN-FREE • NON-GEBROKTS • PARVE

PISTACHIO COOKIES

Makes 40

Paula Jacobson, who graciously shared this recipe with me, is a professional recipe tester and editor. I always smile when I think of her, because at every event she wears a spectacular hat that rivals any royal head covering. Baking does not get much simpler than a cookie with four ingredients, and these cookies have the perfect combination of crunch and chew.

3 cups (360g) shelled, unsalted pistachio nuts
(about 1½ pounds (680g) nuts in their shells)
3 large egg whites
1 cup (200g) sugar
2 tablespoons confectioners' sugar to dust
cookies

PREHEAT OVEN to 325°F (160°C).

PLACE THE PISTACHIO NUTS into the bowl of a food processor fitted with a metal blade and process until the nuts are finely ground. In a separate bowl, use a whisk to mix together the egg whites and sugar. Add the ground nuts and mix until combined. Place in the fridge for at least 20 minutes.

COVER TWO COOKIE SHEETS with parchment paper. Scoop up a little less than 1 tablespoon of dough at a time and roll into balls. Place on the cookie sheets one inch apart.

BAKE for 16 to 18 minutes, or until lightly browned. It's OK if the cookies are still a bit soft when you remove them from the oven because they will harden while cooling. Slide the parchment onto a wire rack. When the cookies are cool, use a sieve to dust them with confectioners' sugar. Store covered at room temperature for up to four days or freeze for up to three months. ▪

EASY

GLUTEN-FREE • NON-GEBROKTS •
NUT-FREE • PARVE

BROWNIES
Makes 25 squares

This recipe requires just one saucepan for melting the chocolate and margarine and for mixing in the other ingredients. When I was growing up, my favorite Passover dessert was brownies from a mix. My only complaint was that the mix came with a pan that was too small and if I did not get to the brownies before my mother or brothers did, the brownies would mysteriously vanish.

½ cup (1 stick; 113g) margarine, plus extra for
greasing pan
8 ounces (230g) bittersweet chocolate
1½ cups (300g) sugar
4 large eggs
1 teaspoon vanilla, optional
¼ cup (20g) unsweetened cocoa
½ teaspoon salt
½ cup plus 2 tablespoons (100g) potato starch

PREHEAT OVEN to 350°F (180°C). Grease the bottom and sides of an 8-inch (20-cm) square pan with margarine. Cut a piece of aluminum foil that is larger than the pan and press it into the bottom, corners, and up the sides of the pan. Grease the foil. Set it aside.

IN A MEDIUM, HEAVY SAUCEPAN, cook the margarine and chocolate over low heat. Cook until melted, mixing often. Remove from the heat and mix in the sugar. Add the eggs, one at a time, and mix well. Add the vanilla, cocoa, and salt and mix. Finally, add the potato starch.

SPOON THE MIXTURE into the pan and bake 40 minutes, or until set. Let cool. Lift the brownie out of the pan and cut into squares. Store in an airtight container at room temperature for up to five days or freeze for up to three months. ▪

MEXICAN CHOCOLATE COOKIES

Makes 2½ to 3 dozen

These are soft, chewy chocolate cookies with confectioners' sugar on top.

⅓ cup (80ml) vegetable oil
1 cup (200g) sugar
½ cup (40g) unsweetened cocoa
2 large eggs
1 teaspoon vanilla
1 cup (160g) potato starch, sifted
¼ teaspoon salt
½ teaspoon cinnamon
⅓ cup (40g) confectioners' sugar

IN A MEDIUM BOWL, mix together the oil, sugar, cocoa, eggs, and vanilla. Add the potato starch, salt, and cinnamon, and mix well. Cover with plastic wrap and place in the fridge overnight.

PREHEAT OVEN to 350°F (180°C). Cover two cookie sheets with parchment paper. Put the confectioners' sugar into a shallow bowl. Scoop up a walnut-size piece of dough and roll it into a ball. Roll each ball in the confectioners' sugar and place it on the cookie sheet 1½ inches (4cm) apart. IF YOU HAVE ROLLED three dozen or more cookies, bake them for 12 to 14 minutes. If you have rolled two and a half to three dozen cookies, bake them for 14 to 15 minutes. The cookies are done when they are still partially soft. You can check for doneness by pressing down gently on the top of a cookie; if your finger goes down a little into the cookie, it is done and will be chewy. If you can press all the way down to the cookie sheet, the cookies need another two minutes or more to bake. Store in an airtight container at room temperature for up to five days or freeze for up to three months. ■

NOTE:
Passover potato starch often comes clumped up in the package. Use a whisk to break up the clumps or sift the potato starch before measuring.

EASY

GLUTEN-FREE • NON-GEBROKTS • PARVE

CHOCOLATE CHIP COOKIE BARS

Makes 24 2-inch (5-cm) square bars or 39 1 X 3-inch (2.5 x 8-cm) bars

This one-bowl recipe was adapted from a chocolate chip cookie recipe from my friend Limor Decter. I like to cut this into 1 x 3-inch (2.5 x 8-cm) bars to make them easier to dunk in milk.

2 cups (400g) sugar
2 large eggs
1 cup (240ml) vegetable oil, plus extra for
    greasing pan
2 tablespoons vanilla sugar
3¼ cups (390g) ground almonds
¼ cup (40g) potato starch
1 cup (180g) mini chocolate chips

PREHEAT OVEN to 375°F (190°C). Grease the bottom and sides of a 9 x 13-inch (23 x 33-cm) pan. Press in a piece of parchment paper that is big enough to cover the bottom and sides of the pan. Grease the top and sides of the parchment. Set it aside.

PLACE THE SUGAR, eggs, oil, and vanilla sugar into a large bowl and beat with an electric mixer on medium speed until combined. Add the ground almonds and potato starch and mix well. Add the chocolate chips and mix to distribute.

SPOON THE MIXTURE into the prepared pan and use a spatula to spread it evenly.
BAKE for 35 minutes, or until the edges are brown, or a toothpick inserted in the center comes out with just a few crumbs on it. Let cool. Lift out the parchment and then cut into squares or bars. Store at room temperature for up to five days or freeze for up to three months. ■

GRINDING NUTS

On Passover, dedicate a coffee grinder exclusively to grinding nuts. I find pre-ground nuts are expensive and desserts taste better if you grind the nuts fresh.

MODERATE

NUT-FREE • PARVE

FRUIT PIE BARS

Serves 15

As a mother of four, I have always had a problem with the 8-inch (20-cm) pie pan. It simply does not hold enough pie to feed my large family, and my son Sam has been known to eat an entire 8-inch (20-cm) pie in one sitting. Instead, I often make pie in a 9 x 13-inch (23 x 33-cm) pan. I make these Fruit Pie Bars with mixed berries and plums. I prefer ⅓ cup (65g) of sugar in the filling because I like my fruit desserts to be a little tart. If you like sweeter fruit fillings, use ½ cup (100g) sugar. These fruit pie bars taste better the second day.

Dough

1½ cups (240g) potato starch

1 cup (130g) matzoh cake meal

1¼ cups (150g) confectioners' sugar

1 cup (2 sticks; 226g) margarine, cut into
    tablespoons, plus one tablespoon for
    greasing pan

1 large egg yolk

1 teaspoon vanilla

2 tablespoons ice water

Filling

6 cups (24 ounces; 680g) total mixed fruit
    such as berries (blackberries, blueberries,
    raspberries) and chopped plums (cut into
    ½-inch (1.25-cm) pieces)

⅓ cup (55g) potato starch

⅓ – ½ cup (65–100g) sugar, to taste

1 teaspoon cinnamon to sprinkle on top

PREHEAT OVEN to 350°F (180°C). Grease a 9 x 13-inch (23 x 33-cm) pan and press in a piece of parchment paper large enough to cover the bottom and sides of the pan. Grease the top of the parchment and sides. Set it aside.

To make the crust

PUT THE POTATO STARCH, cake meal, and confectioner's sugar in the bowl of a food processor fitted with a metal blade and mix for 10 seconds. ADD THE MARGARINE pieces and mix for another 10 seconds, until the mixture looks like sand. Add the egg yolk, vanilla, and water, and mix just until the dough comes together.

TURN THE DOUGH CRUMBLES onto a large piece of plastic wrap and divide the dough into two pieces, two thirds and one third of the dough. Wrap the smaller piece in plastic, flatten it, and put it in the freezer. Break the larger piece of dough into pieces and scatter them over the prepared pan. Use your hands to press the dough into the bottom of the pan, covering it as evenly as possible. BAKE THE CRUST for 20 minutes, or until the edges just start to brown. Let it cool for 15 minutes.

To assemble the pie bars

PUT THE FRUIT in a large bowl. In a smaller bowl, use your fingers to combine the potato starch and sugar, and then sprinkle the mixture over the fruit. Toss the fruit until the potato starch dissolves. Spread the fruit evenly on top of the crust. Remove the piece of dough from the freezer and use the large holes of a box grater to grate the dough on top of the fruit to cover as much of the fruit as possible. Sprinkle the top with cinnamon. BAKE THE PIE for 50 minutes, or until the outside edges start to color; the top of the crumbles will remain white. Serve the pie warm or at room temperature, cut into squares or simply scoop it out with a spoon. Store in the fridge for up to three days. May be rewarmed. ■

CHOCOLATE CHIP BANANA BREAD

Serves 16

The texture of this bread is less cakelike than typical banana bread, but the taste is very similar.

3 ripe bananas

3 large eggs

1 cup (200g) sugar

½ cup (120ml) vegetable oil, plus extra for greasing pan

½ cup (120ml) orange juice

1 cup (130g) matzoh cake meal

¼ cup (40g) potato starch

¼ teaspoon cinnamon

½ teaspoon ground ginger

1 teaspoon vanilla

1 teaspoon baking powder

½ cup (90g) mini chocolate chips, or ⅔ cup (110g) regular chips

PREHEAT OVEN to 350°F (180°C). Trace the bottom of a 12-inch (30-cm) loaf pan on parchment paper and cut out the rectangle. Grease the bottom and sides of the loaf pan with a little oil. Press the parchment into the bottom of the loaf pan and grease the top. Set it aside.

MASH THE BANANAS by hand or in a food processor. Put the mixture into a medium bowl. Add the eggs, sugar, oil, and orange juice, and mix well. Add the cake meal, potato starch, cinnamon, ginger, vanilla, and baking powder, and mix well. Add the chips and mix gently to distribute. Spoon the batter into the prepared pan.

BAKE for one hour, or until a toothpick comes out clean. Let cool in the pan and then run a knife around the bread and unmold. Store covered at room temperature for up to four days or freeze for up to three months. ■

CARROT CAKE

Serves 12 to 15

This is another easy cake that is great as a snack or fancy enough to serve to guests. When I made my first version of a Passover carrot cake, I was disappointed that the grated carrot strands separated from the batter. I did some research to see how to fix the problem and learned that Shirley Corriher, author of the fabulous baking bible, *Bakewise*, recommends using finely chopped carrots instead of the grated strands. The result is a cake speckled with bright orange dots throughout.

6 large eggs, separated

1 ¼ cups (250g) sugar, divided

1 teaspoon cinnamon

2 cups (240g) almond flour

1 teaspoon baking powder

½ cup gluten-free cake meal (60g) or potato starch (80g)

2 cups chopped carrots (use a food processor with the metal blade until you have tiny pieces), about 4 large carrots

vegetable oil and 1 tablespoon gluten-free cake meal or potato starch for greasing pan

confectioner's sugar for dusting, if desired

"SOFT" PEAKS VS. "STIFF" PEAKS

SOFT PEAKS: the peaks of the egg whites are slightly bent when you lift the whisk or eggbeater out of the bowl.

STIFF PEAKS: the peak stands straight up when you lift the whisk or eggbeater out of the bowl.

PREHEAT OVEN to 350°F (180°C). Grease a Bundt pan with the vegetable oil, and then sprinkle it with the tablespoon of gluten-free cake meal or potato starch. Shake the pan to coat it evenly and tap out excess.

To make the batter

PUT THE EGG YOLKS, 1 cup (200g) of the sugar, and the cinnamon into a medium or large bowl and beat for one minute with an electric mixer on medium speed. Add the almond flour, baking powder, and gluten-free cake meal or potato starch and mix well. Add the chopped carrots and mix to distribute.

IN A SEPARATE BOWL, beat the egg whites on high speed until soft peaks form. Reduce the speed to low and add the remaining ¼ cup (50g) sugar a little at a time, and then turn the speed back to high and beat another minute. Use a silicone spatula to fold the whites into the batter in 4 to 5 parts, mixing increasingly more slowly with each addition.

POUR THE BATTER into the prepared Bundt pan and bake for 50 minutes, or until a skewer inserted comes out clean and the top is golden. Let the cake cool for one hour and then turn it out onto a wire rack to cool completely. Store covered at room temperature for up to four days or freeze for up to three months. ▢

MODERATE

GLUTEN-FREE • NON-GEBROKTS • PARVE

NUT CRUMB CAKE

16 to 20 servings

This is what you want to serve for breakfast during Passover. The taste will remind you of your favorite cinnamon buns, which is what my family always wants to eat the moment Passover is over.

Batter

4 large eggs, separated

½ cup (100g) sugar

½ cup (110g) light brown sugar, packed

2 teaspoons vanilla

3 tablespoons water

¾ cup gluten-free cake meal (90g) or potato starch (120g)

¼ teaspoon salt

oil or margarine plus 2 teaspoons potato starch for greasing pan

Streusel

2 tablespoons cinnamon

¾ cup (165g) light brown sugar, packed

1½ cups chopped walnuts and/or pecans (about 1¾ cups (210g) walnut and pecan halves)

4 tablespoons (57g) margarine, at room temperature 15 minutes

1 tablespoon gluten-free cake meal or potato starch

PREHEAT OVEN to 350°F (180°C). Grease an 8-inch (20-cm) square pan with some oil or margarine. Add the 2 teaspoons potato starch and shake to cover the pan. Tap out the excess.

To make the batter

PLACE THE YOLKS, sugar, brown sugar, vanilla, and water into a medium bowl and beat with an electric mixer for 1 minute at medium speed.

ADD THE GLUTEN-FREE CAKE MEAL and beat for two minutes on medium speed until mixed. Set it aside.

IN A SEPARATE BOWL, beat the egg whites on low speed until foamy, add the salt and then beat on high speed until stiff. Fold the whites into the batter in four parts, mixing increasingly more slowly with each addition.

SEPARATING EGG WHITES

* The best time to separate egg whites is when the eggs are cold.

* You'll need three bowls to separate the eggs: one in which to break the egg whites, one for the yolks, and a larger mixing bowl that you will use to beat the whites.

* After separating the first egg into a small bowl, dump that white into the larger mixing bowl and the yolk into the designated yolk bowl. For the second, and all subsequent eggs, separate over the small bowl and add the whites one at a time to the larger bowl and yolks to the yolk bowl. This way there is no risk that the egg will break badly and get a drop of yolk into your whites. If your yolk breaks into the small bowl, set it aside for another use.

To make the streusel

IN ANOTHER MEDIUM BOWL, mix the cinnamon, brown sugar, and chopped nuts.

To assemble the cake

SPOON A LITTLE LESS THAN HALF of the batter into the prepared pan and use a spatula to spread it around evenly. Measure out ⅔ cup of the nut mixture and sprinkle it on top of the batter. Add the remaining batter and spread it gently to cover the nuts. Add the soft margarine and gluten-free cake meal to the remaining nut mixture. Mix it with your hands until it sticks together and you have one large clump. Break the clump into smaller pieces and scatter them over the batter. Bake the cake for 45 minutes, or until a toothpick comes out clean. Serve warm. Store covered at room temperature for up to three days or freeze for up to three months. ◼

EASY

GLUTEN-FREE • NON-GEBROKTS • PARVE

CHOCOLATE HAZELNUT CUPCAKES

Makes 18 cupcakes

These are not classic sponge-type chocolate cupcakes. They are chewy and very moist, especially if you take them out of the oven when the center is still a little bit gooey, which I highly recommend. The toasted hazelnuts add crunch. Although these are in the snack section of this chapter, you can always dress them up for a Seder dessert with ganache (see page 148), a dollop of whipping cream and a raspberry, give them a dusting of confectioners' sugar, or serve them plated in a pool of berry sauce (see page 31). I prefer them straight up.

1 cup (140g) whole hazelnuts
10 ounces (280g) bittersweet chocolate
½ cup (120ml) vegetable oil
1½ cups (300g) sugar
½ cup (120ml) water
3 large eggs
½ teaspoon baking powder
½ cup (40g) unsweetened cocoa
½ cup (80g) potato starch
dash salt

PREHEAT OVEN to 325°F (160°C).

To toast the nuts

COVER A JELLY ROLL PAN with parchment paper. Spread the hazelnuts on top of the paper and bake them for 20 minutes, shaking the pan once or twice, until the nuts are golden and fragrant. Let the hazelnuts cool for 20 minutes. Raise the oven temperature to 350°F (180°C). To remove the skins from the nuts, roll the nuts between your palms. Discard the skins. Put the toasted nuts in a food processor and grind until the nuts are reduced to tiny pieces. Set them aside.

To make the cupcakes

PUT 18 PAPER CUPS into muffin tins. Break the chocolate into small pieces and melt it, either over a double boiler or in the microwave oven, for one minute and stir, heat for 45 seconds and stir, heat for another 30 seconds and stir, and, if necessary, heat for another 15 seconds, until melted. Add the oil and sugar and whisk well. Add the water, eggs, baking powder, cocoa, potato starch, and salt and whisk well. Add the toasted and ground hazelnuts and mix them in gently. Use a ⅓ measuring cup to evenly fill the 18 muffin cups with batter.

BAKE THE CUPCAKES for 35 minutes, or until an inserted toothpick comes out with just a little batter on it. It is better to underbake these cupcakes than to overbake them. Serve the cupcakes warm or let them cool first. Store in an airtight container at room temperature for up to five days or freeze for up to three months. ◼

EASY

DAIRY • GLUTEN-FREE • NON-GEBROKTS

FINANCIERS MUFFINS
(MINI ALMOND MUFFINS)

Makes 24

Every Passover, I bake muffins from a Manischewitz mix, since it reminds me of my childhood, when the only baked goods we children ate at home all year were from Passover mixes. I wanted a from-scratch muffin for Passover and remembered these French cakes—Financiers. I have always loved eating these chewy, buttery little cakes in Europe, but I rarely bake them since they're dairy; and you simply cannot achieve the traditional, deep brown butter taste from parve margarine. These little cakes are called Financiers because they are typically baked in mini rectangular pans, so they are shaped like the gold bars stored in banks. My Financiers are baked in mini muffin tins, which are useful during Passover, when sometimes all you want is a one-bite treat.

1 cup (120g) slivered almonds, plus 24 more to
    decorate the muffin tops
⅔ cup (130g) sugar
3 tablespoons potato starch
3 large egg whites
½ cup (1 stick; 113g) unsalted butter

PREHEAT OVEN to 375°F (190°C). Place mini muffin paper cups into mini muffin pans to make 24 little cakes, or bake in batches.

To make the batter

IN A COFFEE GRINDER or food processor grind 1 cup (120g) of the slivered almonds into very tiny pieces or powder. Transfer ground almonds to a medium bowl. Add the sugar, potato starch, and egg whites, and mix well with a wooden spoon or silicone spatula. In a small, heavy saucepan, melt the butter over medium-high heat. Lower the heat

to medium and cook another 2 to 3 minutes, or until the melted butter is brown and fragrant. Pour the butter into a bowl and let it cool 10 minutes. Add the butter to the batter and mix well.

To bake the cupcakes

SPOON A HEAPING TABLESPOON of batter into each muffin cup. Place one slivered almond on top of each muffin. Bake the muffins for 25 minutes, or until golden. Let them cool in the pan for 10 minutes and then turn the muffins out onto a wire rack to cool completely. Store in an airtight container for up to three days or freeze for up to three months. ■

MODERATE

GLUTEN-FREE • NON-GEBROKTS • PARVE

MARBLE CHOCOLATE CHUNK AND CINNAMON MERINGUES

Makes 8 to 10 large meringues

I first saw giant meringues on a trip to London a few years ago. While I was never a fan of meringues, I actually love these because they are crunchy on the outside and chewy on the inside. If you are not a cinnamon fan, you can omit it.

4 large egg whites, at room temperature for at
    least 2 hours
⅔ cup (130g) sugar
2 tablespoons unsweetened cocoa
1 teaspoon cinnamon
⅔ cup (80g) confectioners' sugar
4 ounces (115g) bittersweet chocolate, chopped
    into ¼-inch (6-mm) pieces

PREHEAT OVEN to 230°F (110°C). Cover a cookie sheet with parchment paper. Beat egg whites with an electric mixer at high speed until stiff. Reduce speed to low and add the sugar, a tablespoon at

CHOCOLATE CARAMEL MATZOH SANDWICH COOKIES

Makes 10

One year, just before Passover, I was in New York City doing a chocolate and pastry tour of Lower Manhattan while at the annual IACP (International Association of Culinary Professionals) conference. Among the many incredible visits was one to famous pastry chef Francois Payard's bakery. When I asked Francois, who had personally given us a tour around the bakery, about some large chocolate-covered matzohs I'd seen in a corner, he handed me his Passover specialty: two graham cracker-size matzohs with caramel between them enrobed in chocolate and decorated with white chocolate lines. He uses cracker-size matzohs. If you find them, you should use them. If not, follow the instructions below for breaking larger matzoh into the right size.

5 large pieces matzoh, or 20 3 x 3-inch (8 x 8-cm) matzoh crackers
1 cup (200g) sugar
1½ tablespoons water
⅓ cup (80ml) dairy-free whipping cream
6 tablespoons (85g) margarine
15 ounces (425g) bittersweet chocolate

To make the caramel

PUT THE SUGAR and water into a small, heavy saucepan over medium-high heat and do not stir it. Let the mixture sit until the edges start to color and then stir to dissolve the sugar. Cook over medium-high heat, stirring occasionally, until the sugar has melted and the mixture turns a deep amber color. Add the cream and margarine and stir. Transfer to a bowl. Let cool 1½ hours, stirring occasionally, until the caramel thickens.

a time, until mixed in. Raise the speed to high and beat for 10 full minutes, until thick and shiny.

SIFT THE COCOA, cinnamon, and confectioners' sugar together into a small bowl. When the egg whites are ready, spoon out about half of the whites into a separate bowl and set aside. Add the cocoa and sugar mixture to the remaining whites in the mixing bowl, along with three-quarters of the chopped chocolate, and mix on low speed to combine. Add the reserved whites back into the bowl and use a silicone spatula to mix very gently, not completely, to create a marbled effect. Using two large spoons, scoop up the meringue batter and place dollops on the prepared cookie sheet about two inches apart. Chop the remaining chocolate into smaller pieces and sprinkle on top and around the sides of the meringue clumps. Bake for two hours. Let cool. Store in an airtight container at room temperature for up to five days. ∎

To make the cookies

BREAK EACH MATZOH sheet in half as evenly as possible. Halve each piece again to make four 3-inch (8-cm) squares, roughly. Match up similar sizes and break off pieces of matzoh so the squares are the same size. Save any broken pieces for matzoh brei or Passover Whole-Wheat Fruit and Nut Granola (page 143).

COVER A COOKIE SHEET with waxed paper. Place half of the matzoh squares on top. Place a matching square next to each of the matzoh squares to serve as its cover. Divide the caramel among the 10 matzohs. The caramel will spread by itself, but use a knife, if necessary, to spread the caramel to completely cover the matzoh square. Cover the caramel with a matching matzoh square to make a sandwich. Repeat with the other squares. Place the sandwiches in the fridge for 30 minutes to firm up.

SLIDE THE WAXED PAPER and matzoh sandwiches off the cookie sheet onto the counter. Line the cookie sheet with a new piece of waxed paper.

BREAK THE CHOCOLATE into pieces and melt them, either over a double boiler or in the microwave oven as follows: heat the chocolate for 1 minute and stir, heat for another 45 seconds and stir, and then heat for 30 seconds more. Continue to heat and stir, in 15-second increments if needed, until all of the chocolate is melted.

FIRST, dip all four sides of each matzoh sandwich, where you can see the caramel, and then use a pastry brush to spread the chocolate on both matzoh sides, covering all exposed matzoh with chocolate, choosing one side to cover perfectly. The pastry brush also makes nice lines in the chocolate. Place the dipped sandwiches on the waxed paper with the prettier side facing up. Put the sandwiches in the fridge for 30 minutes to set.

REFRIGERATE for up to one week or freeze for up to three months. ■

NOTE:

You can also use whole-wheat matzoh for these cookies.

EASY

GLUTEN-FREE • NON-GEBROKTS • PARVE • VEGAN

CHOCOLATE CANDIES

Makes 40

A few years ago, I visited a kosher chocolate shop in Paris called Damyel, where I encountered the most spectacular kosher chocolates I have ever seen or tasted in my life. These candies look like the ones I've seen in many Parisian shops.

11 ounces (310g) bittersweet chocolate, chopped, divided
¼ cup (35g) dried cranberries
3 tablespoons shelled pistachios
3 tablespoons slivered almonds
¼ cup (40g) white chocolate chips

PUT 8 ounces (230g) of the chocolate into a metal bowl over simmering water (a double boiler) and melt slowly, whisking occasionally. When melted, remove the chocolate from the heat and add the remaining three ounces of the chopped chocolate and whisk it in. Place the chocolate back over the simmering water and heat until all of it is melted. Remove from heat.

COVER TWO COOKIE SHEETS with parchment or waxed paper. Pour about two teaspoons of melted chocolate on the prepared sheets. Spread the chocolate around to form a circle, about 2 inches (5cm) wide. Place one cranberry, one pistachio, a few almond slivers, and 2 to 3 white chocolate chips on top of each circle. Repeat with the remaining chocolate.

PLACE the cookie sheets in the fridge until the candies are firm, about one hour. Store in an airtight container in the fridge for up to one week or freeze for up to three months. ■

NOTE:
You can vary these candies with different nuts or dried fruits.

TEMPERING CHOCOLATE

Tempering chocolate is a method of heating chocolate to different temperatures to achieve a crisp, candy-like coating. For this recipe, I developed a simple melting method. I store these chocolates in the fridge to keep them crisp.

ROSEMARY NUT BRITTLE

Serves 10 to 12

There is no consensus among people when it comes to brittle preferences. Some like the salted version; others prefer the sweeter one. Some people like a very dark and deep caramel flavor; others swear by the lighter caramel candy that allows you to taste the rest of the ingredients. This recipe makes a medium-colored caramel, rather than a darker one, but you can cook it less or more, depending on what you like.

2 cups (about 280g) mixed shelled nuts, such as blanched almonds, cashews, and hazelnuts
1½ cups (300g) sugar
⅓ cup (80ml) water
1½ teaspoons fresh chopped rosemary, with some pieces ½ inch (1.25-cm) long
½ teaspoon kosher salt, optional

PREHEAT OVEN to 325°F (160°C). Cover a cookie sheet with parchment paper or a silicone baking mat. Scatter the mixed nuts over the parchment paper and bake them for 15 to 20 minutes, shaking the cookie sheet once or twice, or until the nuts are brown and fragrant. Let them cool. If the hazelnuts have skins, rub a bunch of the nuts together between your palms to loosen the skins, then discard them.

PUT THE SUGAR and water in a small or medium saucepan and place it over medium heat. Do not stir the mixture. Let it sit until the sugar starts to color around the edges. This takes a few minutes. Once the sugar looks amber around the edges, use a wooden spoon or silicone spatula to stir the sugar. Continue to cook the mixture on low heat, stirring occasionally, until the caramel is almost the color you want it to be and all the sugar has melted. I like the mixture to be a coffee color.

ADD THE ROSEMARY AND SALT, if using, and stir. Add the toasted nuts and stir to coat. Cook for two minutes, stirring constantly, to cover all the nuts with the caramel. Use a silicone spatula to spread the nuts on top of the covered cookie sheet. Try to spread them into one layer. Let the caramel cool and then break it into pieces; the shards can be any size you like. Store the candy in an airtight container for up to two weeks. ■

EASY

GLUTEN-FREE • LOW SUGAR • NON-GEBROKTS

DRIED FRUIT AND NUT CANDIES

Makes 28–32

These candies are so easy to make that it is almost embarrassing to call this a recipe.

⅓ cup (50g) whole, raw almonds
10 dried apricots
10 pitted dates

PLACE THE ALMONDS, apricots, and dates into the bowl of a food processor fitted with a metal blade. Process until the mixture comes together. Scoop up one teaspoon of the dried fruit and nut mixture at a time and roll it into a ball. Let the

candies sit on a plate for at least two hours to dry and then store them in an airtight container for up to five days. ■

MODERATE

GLUTEN-FREE • NON-GEBROKTS • PARVE • VEGAN

FRUIT CRISP

Serves 20

You can make this dessert with any combination of cut fruit that totals 8 cups (680g). I like to use at least three cups of berries to achieve the gooey-ness I crave in my crisps and cobblers. You can also make this into a dairy recipe by using butter instead of margarine, and then eat it with a dollop of yogurt for breakfast or with vanilla ice cream for a snack.

Fruit

3 cups (12 ounces; 340g) blueberries,
    blackberries, or raspberries
5 cups chopped stone fruit (about 6 plums
    and 2 peaches cut into ¾ inch (2-cm) cubes)
¾ cup (150g) sugar
2 tablespoons honey
1 teaspoon ground ginger
¼ cup (40g) potato starch

Topping

2 tablespoons cinnamon
¾ cup (165g) light brown sugar, packed
1½ cups (210g) chopped walnuts (about 1¾ cups
    walnut halves)
1 tablespoon gluten-free cake meal or potato
    starch
5 tablespoons (71g) margarine, at room
    temperature for about 15 minutes

PREHEAT OVEN to 375°F (190°C). Place the berries and cut fruit into a 9 x 13-inch (23 x 33-cm) pan. Add the sugar, honey, ginger, and potato starch.

With a spoon, spatula, or your hands, toss the fruit until the starch dissolves.

IN A SEPARATE BOWL, mix together the cinnamon, brown sugar, chopped nuts, and gluten-free cake meal or potato starch. Add the margarine in five pieces and use your hands to squeeze the mixture together. This takes a few minutes. It is ready when you can squeeze big clumps together.

SCATTER THE TOPPING over the fruit as evenly as possible. Bake the mixture for 40 minutes, or until the fruit bubbles through the topping. Let it cool for 10 minutes. Serve the crisp warm. Store covered in the fridge for up to three days and reheat to serve. ▨

EASY

PARVE • VEGAN

WHOLE-WHEAT FRUIT AND **NUT GRANOLA**

Makes 7 to 8 cups

I posted this recipe on my blog, www.kosherbaker. blogspot.com, for Passover 2011 and was thrilled to see that thousands of people were attracted to a Passover version of granola. Instead of oats, I use whole-wheat matzoh farfel (small pieces of whole-wheat matzoh). Whenever I am out and about during the holiday, I keep plastic sandwich bags of this granola in my handbag.

3 cups (180g) whole-wheat matzoh farfel
1 cup (50g) dried coconut flakes
1 cup (120g) pecan halves, chopped into ½-inch (1.25-cm) pieces
½ cup (60g) cashews, chopped into ½-inch (1.25-cm) pieces
½ teaspoon cinnamon
½ teaspoon ground ginger
¼ teaspoon salt
½ cup (170g) honey
2 tablespoons vegetable oil

1 tablespoon light brown sugar, packed
⅓ cup (65g) chopped apricots (about 10 halves)
⅓ cup (55g) dark raisins
⅓ cup (45g) dried cranberries

PREHEAT OVEN to 300°F (150°C). Line a jelly roll pan with parchment paper, making sure the paper goes ½ inch (1.25cm) up the sides. In a large bowl, mix together the farfel, coconut, pecans, cashews, cinnamon, ginger, and salt.

PUT THE HONEY, oil, and brown sugar into a glass measuring cup or microwave-safe bowl and heat in a microwave oven for 45 seconds, or until the honey and sugar have dissolved. Stir well. Pour over the farfel mixture and toss to coat. Spread evenly on the prepared baking pan and bake for 45 minutes, stirring every ten minutes, until the farfel and nuts are browned. Let the granola cool on the baking pan for 30 minutes. Mix in the dried fruit. Store the granola in a freezer bag or an airtight container at room temperature for up to one week. ▨

Desserts for Passover Entertaining

Growing up, I had little opportunity to eat Passover meals outside our immediate family, so my exposure to Passover desserts was extremely limited. My only options were the cakes from the mixes that we helped Mom bake, most no taller than 1½ inches (4cm) high, which served both as our snacks as well as our Seder desserts. The only truly elegant desserts I ever saw on the holiday were my grandmother's tall lemon sponge and nut Bundt cakes. For nearly 27 years my Passover dessert world was limited to fewer than eight different desserts, with not a single homemade cookie, mousse, or fresh fruit dessert among them.

The first time I had my own Passover kitchen was in 1993, when my husband and I moved to

Geneva, Switzerland. I went to the local Ikea and outfitted my kitchen with new sets of dishes and utensils to celebrate Passover in my own home for the first time. I was still working as a lawyer, and a future in desserts was still a few years off. I went through my small collection of Jewish cookbooks and found a few good recipes. After I went to pastry school in Paris and started catering in Geneva, I began developing dairy-free desserts. Every time I ran across a French recipe that had a very small amount of flour in it, or was entirely gluten-free, it sounded an alarm in my head that before me was a dessert that I could easily convert. Who knew that pastry school in Paris would teach me everything I needed to know to create delicious cookies, tarts, and mousses for Passover?

Armed with these new insights, every Passover since pastry school has been filled with delicious desserts that my friends and family happily eat all year round. The recipes in this section are your weapons to prove that Passover desserts can be both flavorful and visually stunning. ▪

MODERATE

GLUTEN-FREE • NON-GEBROKTS • PARVE

FLORENTINE BARS

Makes 20 square bars or 32 triangles

There are two completely different cookies that bear the name "Florentine." One Florentine has thin layers of sliced almonds and candied fruit, with one side covered in chocolate. Another type is the lacy kind that I grew up with in New York. They are typically made into a sandwich cookie with chocolate in between. This recipe is for a bar cookie version of the type with the sliced almonds, and I use dried cranberries rather than candied cherries, which are easier to find during Passover.

1 cup (120g) confectioners' sugar
3 large egg whites
zest of one large orange (or 2 teaspoons juice)
1⅓ cups (160g) sliced almonds (blanched or with skin)
¼ cup (35g) dried cranberries, chopped into ¼ inch pieces
1 cup (170g) dark or white chocolate chips
vegetable oil for greasing pan

PREHEAT OVEN to 325°F (160°C).

GREASE a 9 x 13-inch (23 x 33-cm) pan with vegetable oil. Press in a piece of parchment paper large enough to cover the bottom and go an inch up the sides of the pan, making sure you press it into the corners. Grease the top of the parchment. **IN A MEDIUM BOWL,** whisk together the confectioners' sugar, egg whites, and orange zest. Use a silicone spatula to gently mix in the nuts and chopped cranberries, being careful not to crush the nuts. Spoon the mixture into the pan and use the spatula or your hands to spread it evenly in the bottom of the pan. The easiest way to do this is to push the batter into the edges and corners first and then fill in the middle. You will have a thin nut layer.

BAKE the bar for 25 minutes, or until the nuts on top are golden. Cool for one hour. To lift the bar out of the pan, gently pull up the parchment paper. Put another piece of parchment on top of the bar and then turn it over onto the new parchment. Peel off the bottom parchment. Melt the chocolate chips, either over a double boiler or in a microwave oven, for 45 seconds and stir, heat for another 30 seconds and stir, and then heat for 15 seconds more, if needed, until all the chocolate chips have melted. Use a spatula to spread the chocolate on the bottom of the bar. If you like, use a serrated knife to make decorative lines, or any other pattern you like, in the chocolate. Slide the parchment onto a cookie sheet and refrigerate the bar for 30 minutes. When it has firmed up, cut the bar into squares, triangles, or rectangles. Store in an airtight container in the fridge for up to five days or freeze for up to three months. ▪

BLACK AND WHITE COOKIES

Makes 40

Black and whites cookies are actually more cake-like in texture than a cookie and are covered half in vanilla icing and half in chocolate icing. Everyone has a favorite side. You can find black and white cookies everywhere, all year long, although my Philadelphia mother-in-law, Lillian Shoyer, will always call them "New York cookies." In his tome on the history of food in Manhattan, *New York City Food,* Arthur Schwartz writes that no one knows who invented black and white cookies, but he suspects someone created them as a way to use up leftover yellow cake batter. Be careful not to overbake these cookies, as they should be light-colored. You really need a small ice cream or cookie dough scoop to create the perfect shape. Otherwise, you can use two spoons, but when done, the cookies will not sit as nicely on the platter.

Cookie

1 cup (200g) sugar

½ cup (1 stick; 113g) margarine

4 large eggs

2 teaspoons vanilla

zest of one lemon (2 to 3 teaspoons)

1¾ cups (280g) potato starch

¾ cup (100g) matzoh cake meal

1 teaspoon baking powder

dash salt

⅓ cup (80ml) almond milk

Icing

⅔ cup (130g) sugar

½ cup (120ml) water

1½ cups (180g) confectioners' sugar

½ teaspoon vanilla

½ teaspoon fresh lemon juice (from zested lemon)

2 tablespoons boiling water

3½ ounces (100g) semisweet or bittersweet chocolate, chopped into ½-inch (1.25-cm) pieces

PREHEAT OVEN to 325°F (160°C).

To make the sugar syrup for the icing

PLACE THE SUGAR and ½ cup (120ml) water into a small saucepan over high heat. Bring to a rolling boil, stir to dissolve the sugar and boil one minute. Pour into a bowl and cool for 30 minutes.

To make the cookies

PLACE THE SUGAR and margarine into a large bowl and beat with an electric mixer until creamy. Add the eggs, vanilla, and lemon zest, and beat until combined. Scrape down the bowl and mix well.

IN A SEPARATE BOWL, whisk together the potato starch, cake meal, baking powder, and salt. Add half the dry ingredients to the bowl and mix well. Add the almond milk and mix well. Add the remaining dry ingredients and mix gently until combined. You will have a thick batter.

COVER TWO COOKIE SHEETS with parchment paper or bake in batches. With a cookie dough scooper or small ice cream scoop, scoop up batter and place it on the cookie sheets, about 1½ to 2 inches (4 to 5cm) in diameter and about two inches apart. Bake for 15 to 17 minutes, or until the edges of the bottoms start to color. The top of the cookies should remain light. As soon as the cookies are out of the oven, use a spatula to move the cookies onto a wire rack to cool. These cookies are best iced as soon as they are cool.

To ice the cookies

ICE THE WHITE SIDE first. Place the confectioners' sugar into a medium bowl. Add two tablespoons boiling water, vanilla, and lemon juice and whisk well. If the mixture is too thick to spread, add the simple syrup to it by tablespoons until the consistency is thick, but still spreadable. Use a small metal spatula or knife to scoop up 1 to 2 teaspoons

of icing and spread it on half of the flat bottom of each of the cookies.

USE YOUR FINGER to rub off any extra white glaze from the edges. The icing will thicken as you ice the cookies and you will need to add some sugar syrup to make the icing smoother. If the white icing gets too loose, whisk in a tablespoon of confectioners' sugar. Let dry for a few minutes before icing the chocolate side.

MELT THE CHOCOLATE, either over a double boiler or in a microwave oven, for 45 seconds and stir, heat for another 30 seconds and stir, and then heat for 15 seconds more, or until all the chocolate is melted. Whisk in simple syrup, two tablespoons at a time, until the mixture is smooth, shiny, and spreadable. If the chocolate icing gets too thick to spread, whisk in a tablespoon or more of simple syrup to get the consistency you want. Spread the 1 to 2 teaspoons of the chocolate glaze carefully on the other half of the cookie, moving the chocolate icing back and forth across the cookie to create a straight line between the chocolate and vanilla sides. Let the icing dry for 30 minutes. Store the cookies in an airtight container for up to two days or freeze for up to three months. ■

COOKIE SCOOPS

A cookie scoop is a real time saver; you can also use it to scoop meringue for the Key Lime Pie (page 158) or to serve Strawberry Ice Cream (page 179).

EASY

GLUTEN-FREE • NON-GEBROKTS • PARVE

VANILLA CUPCAKES

Makes 12

Here is an easy gluten-free cupcake for Passover and all year long.

Cupcakes
3 large eggs, separated
½ cup (100g) plus 2 tablespoons sugar, divided
1 teaspoon vanilla
1 teaspoon almond extract
½ cup (80g) potato starch
¾ cup (90g) ground almonds

Ganache

10 ounces (280g) semisweet or bittersweet
  chocolate

1 teaspoon vanilla

1 cup (240ml) dairy-free whipping cream

2 tablespoons confectioners' sugar

2 tablespoons (28g) margarine

PREHEAT OVEN to 350°F (180°C). Place 12 paper cups into a muffin tin. Set it aside.

To make the cupcakes

PLACE THE EGG YOLKS into a medium bowl. Add the ½ cup (100g) sugar, the vanilla and almond extracts, and beat on high speed for two minutes. ADD THE POTATO STARCH and ground almonds and mix. Set aside. Place the whites into a large bowl and beat on high speed until stiff. Turn the speed to low and add the remaining two tablespoons

sugar. Turn the speed back up to high and beat another minute.

USE A SILICONE SPATULA to fold the egg whites into the yolk mixture. Spoon the batter evenly into the muffin cups. Bake for 20 minutes, or until a toothpick comes out clean. Cool the cupcakes on a wire rack.

To make the ganache

BREAK THE CHOCOLATE into small pieces and melt it in a double boiler or microwave oven for one minute and stir, heat for another 45 seconds and stir, heat for 30 seconds, and then heat and stir in 15-second increments until all the pieces have melted. Whisk in the vanilla. Heat the whipping cream until hot, not boiling. Add the whipping cream to the chocolate mixture a little at a time and whisk well. Add confectioners' sugar and margarine and beat with an electric mixer for one minute. Place the ganache in the fridge for 20 minutes to firm up.

SPOON THE GANACHE into a pastry bag fitted with a large star or other ½-inch tip. Squeeze some ganache on top of the cupcakes either to cover the surface or decorate (see photo). Store at room temperature for up to five days or freeze for up to three months. ■

MODERATE

NUT-FREE • PARVE

CHOCOLATE CHIP SPONGE BUNDT

Serves 16 to 20

This cake is based on my grandmother's most famous lemon sponge cake, and it will remind you of the tall sponge cakes that are part of the legacy of the *bubbies* of Eastern Europe. It may not be the prettiest cake, but it is definitely tasty.

9 large eggs, separated
6 tablespoons (90ml) water
1 teaspoon fresh lemon juice
2 teaspoons vanilla
2 cups (400g) sugar
½ cup (65g) matzoh cake meal, plus
    1 tablespoon for greasing
2 tablespoons potato starch
5 ounces (140g) bittersweet chocolate,
    chopped fine
½ teaspoon salt
1 tablespoon oil for greasing pan

PREHEAT OVEN to 325°F (160°C). Grease a large 12-cup tube or Bundt pan with some oil and then dust with the tablespoon matzoh cake meal. Tap out excess.

IN A LARGE BOWL, beat the egg yolks, water, lemon juice, vanilla, and sugar with an electric mixer on medium speed. Add the cake meal and potato starch and beat until mixed, about two minutes at medium speed.

IN A SEPARATE BOWL, beat the egg whites with an electric mixer on medium speed. Once they are foamy, add the salt and then turn up the speed to high and beat until stiff. Gently fold the whites into the egg yolk mixture in three parts. Add the chopped chocolate and fold in. Pour the mixture into the prepared pan.

BAKE for 70 minutes, or until a skewer comes out clean and the cake is golden brown. Remove from the oven and immediately invert pan on top of a plate and let cool. If the cake does not come out of the pan by itself when it is cool, turn the cake over and run a thin knife around the edges of the pan to loosen the cake and then turn it over onto a plate. Store at room temperature for up to five days or freeze for up to three months. ■

GLUTEN-FREE • LOW SUGAR • NON-GEBROKTS • PARVE

LOW-SUGAR CHOCOLATE ALMOND CAKE

Serves 12

My father, Reubin Marcus, is a diabetic and he loves desserts so I try to bake something for him every holiday. I invented this dessert when I happily found sugar-free chocolate chips with kosher for Passover certification in Boca Raton, Florida. As of the publication of this book, only the Gefen company makes them, but I hope more companies will join them.

6 large eggs, separated
5 tablespoons sugar, divided
2 cups (240g) ground almonds
⅓ cup (25g) unsweetened cocoa
4 tablespoons (57g) margarine, melted, plus extra for greasing pan
1 cup (170g) sugar-free chocolate chips
1 tablespoon potato starch for dusting pan

PREHEAT OVEN to 400°F (200°C). Grease a 9-inch (23-cm) round baking pan with some margarine. Dust with the tablespoon potato starch and shake out the excess. Set the pan aside.

IN A LARGE BOWL, add the egg yolks, two tablespoons of the sugar, the almonds, cocoa, and melted margarine and use an electric mixer to beat everything together. Add the chocolate chips and mix to distribute.

IN A SEPARATE BOWL, beat the egg whites until stiff. Turn the speed to low and add the remaining three tablespoons of sugar, a tablespoon at a time, and wait until each tablespoon is mixed in before adding the next one. Turn the speed to high and beat for one minute.

MIX ONE THIRD of the whites into the batter. Use a silicone spatula to fold in another third and, when mixed in, add the remaining whites and fold in gently. Scoop the mixture into the prepared pan. **BAKE** for 25 minutes, or until a skewer comes out clean. Let the cake cool in the pan for 20 minutes, and then turn it onto a wire rack. Store covered at room temperature for up to three days or freeze for up to three months. ▪

NUT-FREE • PARVE

NEVER FAIL SPONGE CAKE

Serves 16

This is another great cake from master baker Annette Lerner (see Nana's Holiday Apple Cake, page 26). I couldn't resist trying it after she told me that she possessed a Passover sponge cake recipe that didn't require separating the eggs. I was skeptical, but this really works. The result is a tall, light sponge cake that tastes as if you have incorporated beaten egg whites. Thank you, Annette, for a super easy, one-bowl cake to feed everyone at the Seder and beyond.

You need a stand mixer for this recipe because you beat the mixture for five minutes straight. I used the bowl of my 4½-quart (4.25-liter) Kitchen Aid mixer and, while the batter went all the way up to the top, it did not go over. Make sure you use a really big mixing bowl and a 12-cup (2.8-liter) or 9- to 10-inch (23 or 25-cm) Bundt or tube pan. Note that the pan does not require greasing. I followed Annette's instructions to simply wet the pan, and the cake unmolded perfectly.

9 large eggs
1½ cups (300g) sugar
zest of one lemon, about 4 teaspoons
1 tablespoon fresh lemon juice (from zested lemon)

1½ teaspoons vanilla
½ teaspoon salt
3 tablespoons potato starch
¾ cup (100g) matzoh cake meal

PREHEAT OVEN to 325°F (160°C). Place 9 eggs into a large mixing bowl of a stand mixer. Beat at high speed for five full minutes. Add the sugar and beat at high speed for another five minutes. Add the zest, lemon juice, vanilla, salt, potato starch, and cake meal and use a silicone spatula to fold them in, making sure none of the dry ingredients stick to the bottom of the bowl. Turn the mixer back on to medium speed and beat for another five minutes.

RINSE a 9- to 10-inch (23 to 25-cm) Bundt or tube pan with cold water and shake out the excess. Pour the batter into the wet pan and bang it on the kitchen counter twice to shake out any air bubbles. BAKE the cake for one hour, or until a skewer comes out clean. Turn the cake over onto a wire rack and let it cool in the pan. If you've used a silicone pan, peel the pan off the cake, or, if you used an aluminum pan, run a knife around the cake and then turn it out. Store the cake at room temperature for up to five days or freeze for up to three months. ▪

LEMON LAYER CAKE

Serves 12

The inspiration for this fresh layer cake is the lemon sponge cake my grandma Sylvia Altman was famous for, both in Brooklyn and South Florida. She would have loved to see this recipe appear in *The Kosher Baker*, be reprinted in *The Washington Post* for Passover 2011, and then be syndicated all over the United States.

Sponge Cake

4 large eggs, separated

1 cup (200g) sugar

3 tablespoons water

2 tablespoons fresh lemon juice
  (from 1 to 2 lemons)

⅓ cup (43g) matzoh cake meal

⅓ cup (55g) potato starch

1¼ teaspoons lemon zest

dash salt

margarine for greasing pan

Lemon Cream

3 large eggs plus 2 egg yolks

1 cup (200g) sugar

5 tablespoons (75g) fresh lemon juice
  (from 2 to 3 lemons)

zest of 1 large lemon

5 tablespoons (71g) margarine

1 cup (240ml) dairy-free whipping cream

fresh raspberries, strawberry halves, or
  lemon slices for decoration

To make the lemon cream

PLACE THE EGGS, yolks, and sugar in a heat-proof bowl. Set the bowl over simmering water in a medium saucepan (or use a double-boiler). Whisk in the lemon juice and zest. Cook the lemon cream, uncovered, whisking occasionally, until a thick mixture is formed. This takes approximately 30 minutes. Be patient and do not stir too much.

REMOVE THE BOWL from the heat and whisk in the margarine, one tablespoon at a time. Cool for 10 minutes and then cover with plastic wrap. Refrigerate for four hours or overnight. The lemon cream can be made three days in advance. To use it sooner, place the bowl of lemon cream over a larger bowl filled with 2 to 3 cups of ice and 2 cups (480ml) of water for 15 to 20 minutes, or until the cream is chilled. Mix occasionally.

Preparing to bake

PREHEAT OVEN to 350°F (180°C). Trace the bottom of an 8- or 9-inch-round (20- or 23-cm) baking pan onto a piece of parchment and cut out the circle. Grease the bottom and sides of the baking pan. Put the parchment circle in the pan and grease it.

To make the sponge cake

IN A LARGE BOWL, beat the egg yolks, sugar, water, and lemon juice with an electric mixer on low speed. Add the cake meal, potato starch, and lemon zest and beat until combined.

IN A SEPARATE BOWL, beat the egg whites and salt with an electric mixer on high speed until stiff. Gently fold the whites into the bowl with the egg yolk mixture and then scoop it into the prepared pan.

BAKE for 40 to 45 minutes, or until a toothpick comes out clean. Let the cake cool in the pan. Remove the cake and wrap it in plastic. Chill the cake in the freezer for one hour.

To assemble the cake

IF NECESSARY, trim the top of the cake to make it level. For a more professional look, use a knife to trim the sides of the cake to make them even. Slice the cake into thirds to create three layers. To do this, place the cake on top of a piece of waxed paper. Mark on the side of the cake where you will slice the cake to make three even layers. To cut

the first layer, slice 2 to 3 inches (5 to 8cm) into the cake while turning the cake with your other hand, palm down. Keep turning the cake until you have cut 2 to 3 inches (5 to 8cm) into it, all the way around, and then cut straight across the cake to create a slice. Place this layer on a piece of waxed paper and slice the remaining cake into two layers, using the same steps.

CUT A CIRCLE of cardboard the size of the cake or place the cake directly on a platter. In a bowl, with an electric mixer on high speed, whip the whipping cream until stiff. Place a little lemon cream on the cardboard circle or platter and attach the top slice of cake, top-side down. Tuck some pieces of waxed paper underneath the cake. Spread one third of the lemon cream on the cake. Add the second (center) piece of cake and another third of the lemon cream. Place the bottom slice, bottom side up, on top of the cream.

MIX THE REMAINDER of the lemon cream with the whipped cream. Spread the cream on the top and sides of the cake. Freeze the cake for 15 minutes. Spread some more cream on the cake to even out the sides and top and freeze for another five minutes. Dip a flat, metal blade spatula into hot water and dry it off. Slide the heated spatula all around the cake to smooth the cream. Reheat the spatula and repeat as necessary. Decorate the cake with raspberries, strawberries, or lemon slices. Keep the cake chilled in the fridge until serving. It will store for up to four days in the fridge or up to three months in the freezer. ∎

MULTIPLE STEP

PARVE

STRAWBERRY MONACO

Serves 12

When I went to pastry school in Paris, a version of this cake was one of the prettiest desserts I learned to make. The cake tastes like a strawberry shortcake, but the presentation is much more impressive. I use an ordinary Pyrex bowl to assemble the cake and give it a dome shape.

Jelly Roll

4 large eggs, separated

¼ cup (50g) sugar

2 teaspoons vanilla

¼ cup (40g) potato starch

½ cup (160g) strawberry jam, seedless if possible

Vanilla Cream

1½ cups (360ml) almond milk

2 teaspoons vanilla

2 tablespoons (28g) margarine

5 tablespoons sugar, divided

4 large egg yolks

3 tablespoons potato starch, sifted

2 teaspoons unflavored powdered gelatin

¾ cup (180ml) dairy-free whipping cream

1 pound (450g) strawberries

PREHEAT OVEN to 425°F (220°C). Trace an 8-inch (20-cm) round baking pan on parchment paper and cut out the circle. Grease the pan, press the parchment circle into the pan, and grease the top of the parchment and sides of the pan. Trim another piece of parchment paper to fit precisely inside a jelly roll pan. Set it aside.

To make the cake batter

PLACE THE EGG WHITES into a large bowl. Use an electric mixer to beat the egg whites on high speed until you have soft peaks. Turn the speed to low and add the sugar, a little at a time, mixing well after each addition. Turn the speed to high and beat another minute. In another bowl, mix the egg yolks with two teaspoons of vanilla. When the whites are beaten, sift the potato starch into the whites and add the yolk-and-vanilla mixture. Beat at low speed until almost mixed in. Finish mixing by hand.

SPOON ONE CUP of the batter into the round pan. Use a silicone spatula to spread it around evenly. Spoon the remaining batter into the jelly roll pan and use your spatula, moving back and forth, to spread the batter all the way to the sides, as evenly as you can.

BAKE the cake in the jelly roll pan for 8 minutes, or until top is golden. Bake the 8-inch (20-cm) cake for another two minutes, or until it too is golden.

LET THE CAKES cool five minutes. Run a knife around the edges of the jelly roll pan and slide the cake with the parchment onto a wire rack. Run a knife around the cake in the round pan and turn it onto a cooling rack.

TURN THE CAKE from the jelly roll pan over onto a new piece of parchment paper and carefully peel the parchment paper from the bottom. Cover with a new piece and then turn the cake over so that the browned side is facing up.

USE A SPATULA to spread the jam all over the cake, all the way to the edges. Use the parchment to lift up the top of the long side of the cake toward you about ⅓ inch (8-mm), press down, and then roll up the jelly roll. Wrap the parchment around the roll and freeze two hours or overnight. The jelly roll may be made a week in advance.

COVER the round cake with plastic, leaving the parchment stuck on the bottom, and store at room temperature. The cake may be made two days in advance.

To make the pastry cream

IN A HEAVY SAUCEPAN, bring the almond milk, margarine, and two tablespoons of sugar to a rolling boil. Meanwhile, use a whisk to beat the egg yolks and the three remaining tablespoons of sugar in a medium bowl. Add the potato starch and gelatin and mix well. Add half the hot almond milk mixture to the egg bowl and whisk. Add the other half of the mixture into the eggs and mix well. Return the mixture to the saucepan and cook on low heat for two minutes, whisking almost constantly to thicken. You will need a silicone spatula to mix the cream that collects at the edges of the saucepan where the bottom and sides meet. Remove from heat and scoop into a clean bowl. Let sit five minutes. Cover and cool for four hours or overnight. To use once the roll is chilled, place the bowl of cream over a bowl filled with 2 to 3 cups of ice cubes and two cups (480ml) of cold water for 30 minutes. Let cool, whisking occasionally. Store in the fridge until ready to assemble the cake.

To assemble the cake

LINE THE BOTTOM and sides of a 9-inch (23-cm) round glass bowl—one you might use for salad

or as a mixing bowl—with a piece of plastic wrap twice the size of the bowl, leaving the overhang. Place a second piece of plastic wrap over the first piece and press in to form an "X" so that the entire bowl is tightly lined with plastic.

BEAT THE WHIPPING CREAM until stiff. Fold half of it into the pastry cream. Add this mixture to the bowl with the remaining whipped cream and mix on high speed for 30 seconds, or until the mixture is smooth. Chill in the fridge until ready to assemble. May be made one day in advance.

WASH AND TRIM the strawberries. Cut them into ¼ to ½-inch (6mm to 1.25-cm) slices. Set the berries aside. Remove the jelly roll from the freezer. Slice the roll into ⅓-inch (8-mm) slices, no larger. You will have about 30 slices. Place one jelly roll slice in the center of the bottom of the bowl. Add slices around it with the edges touching. Continue until you have used up all the slices and they come up

the sides of the bowl evenly. Scoop up a heaping ⅓ cup of cream and place it in the bottom of the bowl, on top of the jelly roll slices. Use a silicone spatula to spread the cream until it's even, pressing down so the cream fills the holes between the cake slices in the bottom of the bowl. Cover the cream with a layer of strawberries. Add another ⅓ cup of cream and another layer of strawberries. Add the remaining cream and smooth the top as evenly as possible.

PRESS your 8-inch (20-cm) cake circle, top side down and parchment-covered side facing up, into the cream. Leave the parchment circle in place. Cover the bowl with plastic. Chill in the fridge four hours or overnight.

TO SERVE, remove the plastic and parchment circle. Turn the cake over onto a round serving plate and cut the cake into wedges. Store covered in the fridge for up to one day. ∎

MULTIPLE STEP

GLUTEN-FREE • NON-GEBROKTS • PARVE

FLOURLESS CHOCOLATE AMARETTI CAKE

Serves 12 to 16

Whenever I eat creamy flourless chocolate cakes I find that I am always missing a crunch. In creating this dessert, I solved that problem with a crust of crushed homemade almond cookies. The cookies are super easy to make and can be made several days (or much earlier) before you make the cake. And yes, you are allowed to make just the cookies and eat them, too!

Amaretto Cookies
One 8-ounce (230g) bag slivered almonds
 (about 1¾ cups)
1 cup (200g) sugar
1 tablespoon potato starch
2 large egg whites
1 tablespoon almond extract, optional

Chocolate Cake
12 ounces (340g) semisweet or bittersweet
 chocolate, roughly chopped
½ cup (1 stick; 113g) margarine, plus extra for
 greasing pan
6 large eggs, separated
½ cup (100g) sugar

PREHEAT OVEN to 325°F (160°C). Line a jelly roll pan or cookie sheet with parchment paper or a silicone baking mat.

SPREAD THE ALMONDS on the cookie sheet and toast for 20 minutes, shaking the pan after 10 minutes. When the almonds are golden and fragrant, remove them from the oven and slide the parchment off the pan onto a wire rack. Cool for five minutes.

PLACE THE TOASTED ALMONDS into the bowl of a food processor fitted with a metal blade. Process until the nuts are ground to a powder. Place into a medium bowl. Add the sugar, potato starch, egg whites, and almond extract, if using, and mix until combined. I like to use my hands, but a wooden spoon is a neater option. Line two cookie sheets with parchment.

WET YOUR HANDS and take walnut-size clumps of dough and roll them into balls about one inch (2.5-cm) in diameter. Place the balls on the prepared baking sheets, about two inches (5cm) apart. Bake for 30 minutes, or until set. Slide the parchment off the cookie sheet onto a wire rack and let cool. Store in an airtight container at room temperature for up to five days or freeze for up to three months.

PREHEAT OVEN to 350°F (180°C). Put a piece of parchment paper on the counter and trace a circle around the bottom of a 10-inch (25-cm) springform pan. Cut out the circle and set it aside. Place a large piece of foil on top of the bottom circle of the pan and fold the excess foil under the bottom of the pan. Attach the bottom piece to the sides of the pan, lock the sides in place, and then unwrap the foil and bring it up the sides on the outside of the pan. Take another piece of foil and wrap it around the bottom of the pan and up the sides again; this will prevent water from leaking into the cake as it bakes in a water bath.

USE SOME MARGARINE to grease the top of the foil in the bottom of the pan. Press the parchment circle on top of the foil. This step makes it easy to slide the finished cake onto your serving plate. Grease the parchment circle and the pan sides.

TO CRUSH THE COOKIES, place half into the bowl of a food processor fitted with a metal blade. Process until the cookies are mostly crumbs, with a few ¼ to ½-inch (6mm to 1.25-cm) pieces remaining. Pour these pieces into the bottom of the pan and spread to cover. Set aside. Place the remaining cookies into the food processor and crush, as you did the first half. Set aside to use for the top of the cake.

SAVE YOUR SPRINGFORM PAN

Ever lose your springform pan bottom because you left it with a cake at someone's house? A solution is to line the pan with a parchment circle. When you're ready to take a cake to a friend, simply separate the cake from the pan bottom and leave the bottom at home.

MELT THE CHOCOLATE and margarine together, either in a double boiler or microwave oven, for 1 minute and stir, heat for another 45 seconds and stir, and then heat for 30 seconds more and stir. Continue to heat in 15-second increments, or until all the chocolate is melted. Add the egg yolks and whisk well.

IN A SEPARATE BOWL, beat the egg whites with an electric mixer on high speed until stiff. Turn the speed down to low, add the sugar one tablespoon at a time and, once all the sugar is added, turn the speed up to high for one minute.

FOLD THE EGG WHITES into the chocolate mixture. Pour the batter into the prepared pan over the cookie crumbs. Lift the pan about two inches off the counter and then drop it down on the counter to release any air bubbles. Sprinkle the other half of the cookie crumbs on top of the batter. Cover with aluminum foil.

PLACE THE CAKE PAN into a larger roasting pan and then add boiling water to reach halfway up the sides of the cake pan. The easiest way to do this is to place the roasting pan with the cake pan in the oven and then bring the boiling water over to the oven and pour into the roasting pan around the cake.

BAKE for 40 minutes, or until the mixture is mostly set (you can tell by lifting the top of the foil and gently jiggling the pan). Remove the cake from the water bath (leave the water-filled roasting pan in the oven, after you've turned it off, until the pan is cool enough to be removed safely) and let the cake cool completely. Place the cake in the freezer a minimum of four hours or overnight.

OPEN THE SPRINGFORM and remove the sides of the pan. Use a metal flat-blade spatula to separate the parchment circle from the foil bottom, and slide the parchment and cake onto a serving plate. Heat a long knife and use it to cut perfect slices. As the cake sits out and warms up, it will soften and become creamier. Store the cake in the freezer for up to three months. ■

MULTIPLE STEP

GLUTEN-FREE • NON-GEBROKTS • PARVE

KEY LIME PIE

Serves 8

One year I demonstrated this recipe to so many audiences before Passover, I was unable to make it again when Passover finally arrived, and I *love* key lime pie. At one event in Brooklyn, New York, I made the mistake of stabbing some limes with a knife to extract more juice. All I achieved was a deep cut in my finger. I wrapped it tightly with paper towels and cellophane tape, put on a new plastic glove, and taught the class. Afterward I texted a photo of the cut to my Maryland doctor to see if I needed stitches, and thankfully, I did not. I went on to my next demonstration at New York University's kosher dining hall. (Texting my doctor for a consultation was a great use of modern technology and allowed me to continue on schedule.) The best (and safest) way to extract more juice from limes and lemons is to heat them in a microwave oven for 30 seconds, then slice the fruit in half and squeeze. Now that I know how to make this safely, I make it every Passover *and* all year round as my go-to gluten-free pie.

Crust

4 tablespoons (57g) margarine

2 cups ground walnuts (from 3½–4 cups (420–480g) walnut halves)

3 tablespoons light brown sugar, packed

Lime Filling

5 large eggs plus 3 yolks

1½ cups (300g) sugar

2 tablespoons lime zest (from 3 limes)

½ cup (120ml) fresh lime juice (from 4–6 limes or 12 key limes)

½ cup (1 stick; 113g) margarine

1 drop green food coloring, optional

Meringue Topping

⅔ cup (130g) sugar

¼ cup (60ml) water

2 large egg whites

PREHEAT OVEN to 350°F (180°C). You will need an 8- or 9-inch (20- or 23-cm) pie pan for this dessert. A disposable pan works fine, too.

To make the lime cream

PLACE THE EGGS, yolks, and sugar in a heatproof bowl set over simmering water in a medium saucepan (or a double-boiler). Stir to combine. Add the lime zest and juice and stir to combine. Cook uncovered over simmering water for 30 minutes, stirring occasionally, or until thick. Be patient and do not stir too much. Remove the bowl from the heat and whisk in the margarine, one tablespoon at a time, until the cream is smooth. Add the green food coloring, if using, and stir. Set the mixture aside.

To make the crust

HEAT THE MARGARINE in a medium microwave-safe bowl for 45 seconds, or until melted. Add the walnuts and brown sugar and mix until combined. Place this mixture into the pie pan and press to cover the bottom and up the sides. Place the pan in the oven for 15 minutes. Remove it from the oven, leaving the oven on.

WHEN THE CREAM IS READY, pour it into the prepared crust and smooth the top to make it even. Place the pie pan on a cookie sheet and bake for 20 minutes, or until the outside edges of the cream are set (the inside can remain a little wobbly). Let the pie cool and then chill in the fridge for at least two hours.

To make the meringue topping

IN A SMALL, HEAVY SAUCEPAN, bring the sugar and water to a boil, stirring to dissolve the sugar. Continue to cook the sugar until it reaches 230°F (110°C) on a candy thermometer. While the sugar is cooking, beat the egg whites in a medium bowl with an electric mixer on high speed until stiff. When the sugar is ready, turn the mixer speed to low and then slowly pour the cooked sugar into the whites, down the side of the bowl, not directly onto the wire whisk. When all of the sugar has been poured in, turn the mixer up to medium-high and beat for one minute.

USE A SILICONE SPATULA to spread the meringue over the surface of the pie or use an ice cream scoop to drop clumps of meringue on the top of the pie. You can use a blowtorch to lightly brown the top of the meringue or place the pie in a

450°F (130°C) oven for a few minutes, watching it the entire time, until the top browns (you don't want it to burn). Store the pie in the fridge for up to three days. ■

MULTIPLE STEP

GLUTEN-FREE • NON-GEBROKTS • PARVE

LEMON TART
WITH **BASIL NUT CRUST**

Serves 8

Many years ago, when I did dessert catering in Geneva, Switzerland, my lemon tart in a sugar cookie crust was one of the most popular orders. I created this gluten-free dessert so we could enjoy a lemon tart on Passover. Because I have always loved savory dishes that combine lemon and basil, I added basil to the nut crust. I make the tart in a square tart pan, but you can also use a round tart pan or a standard pie plate.

Basil Nut Crust

4 tablespoons (57g) margarine

1 cup ground walnuts (from 1¾–2 cups (210–240g) walnut halves)

1 cup (120g) ground almonds

3 tablespoons sugar

2 teaspoons chopped fresh basil leaves

Lemon Filling

3 large eggs plus 2 yolks

1 cup (200g) sugar

5 tablespoons (75ml) fresh lemon juice (from 3 lemons)

Zest of 1 lemon

5 tablespoons (71g) margarine

Meringue Topping

⅓ cup (65g) sugar

2 tablespoons water

1 large egg white

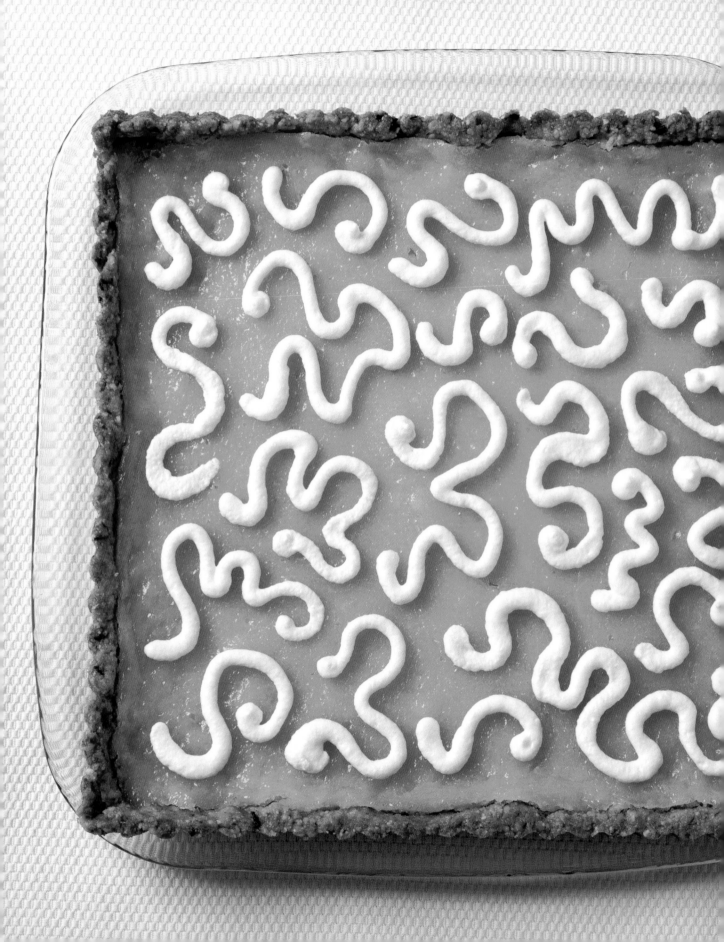

PREHEAT OVEN to 350°F (180°C). You will need an 8 or 9-inch (20 to 23-cm) pie pan with a removable bottom or pie plate.

To make the lemon cream

PLACE THE EGGS, yolks, and sugar in a heatproof bowl set over simmering water in a medium saucepan (or a double-boiler). Add the lemon juice and zest and whisk. Cook the lemon cream uncovered, whisking occasionally, until thick. This takes approximately 30 minutes. Be patient and do not stir too much. If the water in the saucepan boils too fast, turn down the heat. Remove the bowl from the heat and whisk in the margarine, one tablespoon at a time. Set it aside.

To prepare the crust

WHILE THE LEMON CREAM is cooking, melt the margarine, either in a microwave oven for 45 seconds or on the stovetop. Add the walnuts, almonds, and sugar and mix until combined. Add the chopped basil and mix it in. Drop the mixture into the pie pan in scoops and press it into the bottom and up the sides of the pan. Try to even out the rim at the top. Place the pan in the oven for 15 minutes, or until the crust starts to brown.

SPOON THE LEMON FILLING into the crust. Bake for 20 minutes, or until the outside edges of the cream are set; the inside can remain a little wobbly. Let the pie cool and then place it in the fridge for at least two hours.

To make the meringue topping

IN A SMALL, HEAVY SAUCEPAN, bring the sugar and water to a boil, stirring to dissolve the sugar. Continue to cook the sugar until it reaches 230°F (110°C) on a candy thermometer. While the sugar is cooking, beat the egg whites in a medium bowl with an electric mixer on high speed until stiff. When the sugar is ready, turn the mixer speed to low and then slowly pour the cooked sugar down the side of the bowl, not directly onto the wire

whisk. When all of the sugar has been poured in, turn the mixer up to high for one minute.

USE A SILICONE SPATULA to spread the meringue over the top of the lemon cream, or use a pastry bag and tip to make any design you like. You can use a blowtorch to brown the meringue or place the pie in a 450°F (230°C) oven for a few minutes, watching it the entire time, until the top browns. Store in the fridge for up to three days. ■

MODERATE

GLUTEN-FREE • NON-GEBROKTS • PARVE

CHOCOLATE AND PISTACHIO TART

Serves 8

This tart is prettiest made in a tart pan with a removable bottom, but it tastes just as good in a disposable pie pan (though the crust ends up a bit thicker). You can decorate the top with extra pistachio halves, grated pistachio nuts, or chocolate shavings.

Crust

2 cups (240g) shelled, unsalted pistachios

⅓ cup (65g) sugar

6 tablespoons (85g) margarine, plus 1 tablespoon for greasing pan

1 large egg white

Filling

1 cup (240ml) dairy-free whipping cream

1 tablespoon sugar

10 ounces (280g) bittersweet chocolate, finely chopped

2 large egg yolks

PREHEAT OVEN to 350°F (180°C). If you are using a round 9-inch (23-cm) tart pan with a removable bottom, trace the bottom on parchment paper and cut out the circle. Grease the bottom and

sides of the pan with one tablespoon of the margarine. Press the parchment circle into the pan and grease it. This will help make removing the slices easier. If you're using a pie plate, grease it with some margarine. Set the pan aside.

To make the crust

PLACE THE PISTACHIO NUTS into the bowl of a food processor fitted with a metal blade. Process until finely chopped. Add the sugar and pulse a few times. Place the mixture into a medium bowl. Melt the margarine on the stovetop or in a microwave oven. Add to the nuts and sugar. Add the egg white and mix with a silicone spatula or your hands until the mixture comes together.

USE YOUR HANDS to scoop up clumps of the crust mixture and press it into the sides of the pan and then into the bottom of the pan. To make the top rim look pretty, use your fingers to create a small ledge. Place the pie pan on top of a cookie sheet

and bake the crust for 15 to 20 minutes, or until the crust starts to brown a little. Remove it from the oven. If the crust puffs up a little, cover it with some parchment or waxed paper and gently press down on the crust with your hand to deflate it.

To make the filling

FIVE MINUTES BEFORE the crust is done, put the cream and sugar into a small saucepan and bring the mixture to a boil over medium heat. Stir to dissolve the sugar. Remove from the heat and add the finely chopped chocolate. Use a spoon to gently press the chocolate under the cream. Let it sit for five minutes.

STIR THE MIXTURE with a whisk until all the chocolate is melted into the cream. In a separate small bowl, whisk the egg yolks. Add ½ cup of the chocolate mixture to the egg yolks and whisk it in. Place this mixture into the saucepan with the chocolate and cream and whisk well. Spoon it into

the tart shell, place the pie pan on top of a cookie sheet and bake it for 20 minutes. Let the tart cool and then chill it in the fridge for three hours or overnight. Store the tart in the fridge for up to five days or freeze it for up to three months. ■

FRUIT PIE

Serves 8

Some people want only classic Passover desserts—sponge cake, walnut brownies, and coconut macaroons. I don't believe there is any reason why we cannot enjoy our favorite desserts on Passover. The purists will say that we can eat pie all year. My response is, any day is a good day for pie, especially during a spring holiday when you start to see some interesting fruit in the market. You can combine any fruit you like in this recipe. I don't want you to have to buy a rolling pin for Passover just for a crust, so here is a method where you can use my favorite kitchen utensils: your hands.

Crust

¼ cup (50g) sugar

2 tablespoons (28g) margarine, at room temperature for about 15 minutes, plus 1 tablespoon for greasing pan

1 large egg

2 teaspoons vanilla

⅔ cup (105g) potato starch

⅓ cup (43g) matzoh cake meal

½ teaspoon baking powder

dash salt

Filling

½ cup (100g) sugar

3 tablespoons potato starch

3½ cups (385g) berries or fruit cut into ½-inch (1.25-cm) pieces

PREHEAT OVEN to 350°F (180°C). Grease the bottom and sides of an 8-inch (20-cm) pie pan with the tablespoon of margarine. Set it aside.

To make the crust

IN A MEDIUM BOWL, beat the sugar and margarine with an electric mixer. Add the egg and vanilla and mix until combined, scraping down the bowl as needed. Add the potato starch, cake meal, baking powder, and salt and mix on low speed until combined.

USING YOUR HANDS, squeeze and flatten handfuls of dough, and press them into the sides and bottom of the pan. To make the top edge of the crust pretty, use your fingers to create a small ledge. Place the pan in the freezer for ten minutes.

To make the filling

IN A MEDIUM BOWL, combine the sugar and potato starch with your fingers. Add the fruit and mix until the starch is mostly dissolved. (If you're using only blueberries in your pie, the white-colored starch on the berries will melt away during baking.) Spoon the filling into the chilled crust and use a silicone spatula to pat down the top. Put the pie on a cookie sheet and bake it for 50 minutes to one hour, or until the fruit bubbles. Cool and store covered in the fridge for up to three days or freeze for up to three months. ■

PIE REPAIR

What to do if your pie doesn't come out as pretty as you'd like? Scoop clumps of the pie onto plates and tell your friends it's a Passover cobbler.

MULTIPLE STEP

GLUTEN-FREE • NON-GEBROKTS • PARVE

LEMON AND PASSION FRUIT PAVLOVA

Serves 8

A Pavlova is a large scooped-out meringue shell filled with whipped cream or mousse and topped with fruit. It was named after Russian dancer Anna Pavlova, and was first served in her honor when she visited New Zealand. I do not completely cover the curd with the whipped cream but rather use the cream as a border around the curd. Do not worry if you cannot find passion fruit; the dessert is delicious with any fruit you like.

Meringue
4 large egg whites, reserve 2 yolks for curd
   recipe, below
¼ teaspoon salt
1 cup (200g) sugar
1 teaspoon fresh lemon juice
2 teaspoons potato starch, sifted

Lemon and Passion Fruit Curd
2 large eggs plus 2 yolks
¾ cup (150g) sugar
2 tablespoons fresh lemon juice
1 teaspoon lemon zest (from one lemon)
3 tablespoons (42g) margarine
1-2 fresh passion fruits

Garnish
1 cup (240ml) dairy-free whipping cream
sliced strawberries, plums, mango, kiwi, or
   fresh berries

PREHEAT OVEN to 250°F (120°C).

COVER A COOKIE SHEET with parchment paper or a silicone baking mat. If you like, trace a circle around a dinner plate—about 10 inches (25cm) in diameter—on the parchment paper and use it as a

guide to make your meringue shell. Flip the parchment paper over so that the circle you've drawn is on the underside of the paper (you don't want to put your meringue on top of pencil or pen marks).

To make the meringue
PUT THE EGG WHITES in the bowl of an electric mixer. With the speed on low, beat the egg whites until they start to look foamy. Add the salt and then raise the speed to high and beat until soft peaks form. Reduce the speed to low and add the sugar, two tablespoons at a time, completely mixing it in before adding the next amount. When all of the sugar has been added, raise the speed to high and beat the meringue for one minute. Add the lemon juice and potato starch and mix to incorporate. Use a little of the meringue to glue the corners of the parchment to the cookie sheet. SPOON THE MERINGUE onto the middle of the parchment paper or silicone mat. Use a silicone

spatula to spread the meringue back and forth until you have a circle the size of a 10 to 12-inch (25 to 30-cm) wide plate. Press your spatula or the back of a spoon into the center of the meringue and press it back and forth to create a depression in the center of the meringue, leaving a border of about two inches.

IF YOU LIKE, you can use a kitchen knife or the handle of a spatula or wooden spoon to make decorative lines around the 2-inch (5-cm) border of the meringue.

BAKE THE MERINGUE for 1½ hours. Turn off the oven. Prop the oven door open with a wooden spoon and let the meringue cool inside the oven for one hour. The meringue may be made two days in advance. Store it uncovered at room temperature.

To make the curd

PLACE THE EGGS, yolks, and sugar in a heatproof bowl set over simmering water in a medium

saucepan or a double-boiler. Add the lemon juice and zest to the bowl and cook, whisking occasionally until thick. This takes approximately 30 minutes. Be patient and do not stir too much. If the water in the saucepan boils too fast, turn down the heat. The mixture should be very thick. REMOVE THE BOWL from the heat and whisk in the margarine one tablespoon at a time. Cool the curd for 10 minutes, cover with plastic, and refrigerate for eight hours or overnight. To use it right away, put the bowl of curd in a larger bowl filled with 2 to 3 cups of ice cubes and 2 cups (480ml) of water and let the curd sit until cool, about 30 minutes. Scoop the pulp and seeds out of one of the passion fruits and mix it into the curd. For a more pronounced flavor, whisk in more pulp.

Assembling the Pavlova

WHIP THE CREAM until stiff. Scoop the lemon curd into the meringue shell and spoon the whipped cream on top and around the lemon cream in order to create a whipped cream border. If you prefer, cover all of the curd with the whipped cream. Decorate the cream with sliced fruit. Store in the fridge for up to one day. ■

MULTIPLE STEP

GLUTEN-FREE • NON-GEBROKTS • PARVE

LIME MACARONS

Makes 30 to 40

You need to be patient to bake these cookies, but if you have ever eaten one, you know they are worth the effort. First, for success, your egg whites must sit out at room temperature for two hours before you make the batter. Second, after you squeeze out the cookie circles, they must sit for an hour at room temperature before baking. I tried shortcutting these steps and the macarons just did not come out as well.

Cookie

4 large egg whites, at room temperature for
  two hours
1 cup (120g) almond flour (1½ cups/180g
  slivered almonds ground extra-fine, in a
  coffee grinder)
2 cups (240g) confectioners' sugar
¼ cup (50g) sugar
green food coloring, if desired

Lime Cream

3 large eggs plus 2 egg yolks
1 cup (200g) sugar
5 tablespoons (75ml) fresh lime juice
  (from 3 limes)
zest of 1½ limes
5 tablespoons (71g) margarine
one drop green food coloring, if desired

To make the cookies

FIRST, separate the eggs when cold: store the yolks in the fridge and let the whites sit out two hours. Place the almond flour and confectioners' sugar into a food processor fitted with a metal blade. Process for three full minutes. Sift the mixture into another bowl, discarding any large pieces. It may sit out while the whites come to room temperature. LINE TWO COOKIE SHEETS with parchment paper cut to fit the sheets exactly. In a large bowl, beat the egg whites with an electric mixer on high speed until stiff. Turn the speed to low, add the granulated sugar a little at a time, and then turn up the speed to high for another three minutes. If desired, add a few drops of green food coloring and mix it in.

ADD THE ALMOND AND SUGAR MIXTURE and mix on low speed to mostly combine, scraping down the bowl to get all the dry ingredients mixed in. Finish mixing with a spatula. Place the batter into a pastry bag fitted with a ¼-inch (6-mm) round tip. Squeeze a little batter under the corners of the parchment to glue the parchment to the cookie sheet. Hold the pastry bag straight up, about ¼-inch (6mm) over the paper, and squeeze out the batter slowly until you have about a 1-inch (2.5-cm) circle. Leave two inches (5cm) of space between each circle. The circles will expand slightly while sitting. Let the cookie circles sit out at room temperature for one hour.

To make the filling

PLACE THE EGGS, yolks, and sugar in a heatproof bowl set over simmering water in a medium saucepan (or a double-boiler). Add the lime juice and zest to the bowl and whisk. Cook the cream, uncovered, whisking occasionally, until thick. This takes approximately 30 minutes. Be patient and do not stir too much. If the water in the saucepan boils too fast, turn down the heat. Remove the bowl from the heat and whisk in the margarine, one tablespoon at a time, until the cream is smooth. Add the green food coloring, if using, and stir.

COOL THE LIME CREAM for 10 minutes and then cover it with plastic and refrigerate for four hours or overnight. To use it the same day, place the bowl of lime cream in a larger bowl filled with 2 to 3 cups of ice cubes and 2 cups (480ml) of water for at least 20 minutes, or until the cream is chilled, whisking occasionally.

To bake the cookies

PREHEAT OVEN to 300°F (150°C). Bake the cookies for 20 to 22 minutes, until they have puffed up, switching the cookie sheets on the racks halfway through baking and turning the sheets around. Do not let the tops brown. To test the cookies for doneness lift one cookie off the parchment. If it comes right off, it is overbaked. Remove the cookies from the oven immediately (they are still edible, but just not as chewy as they should be). If you lift a cookie and the top comes off and you see gooey batter on the parchment, the cookies need a few more minutes. The cookies are perfect if they stick to the paper just a little, and have lines on the bottom. Slide the parchment onto a wire rack and let the cookies cool. Peel the parchment paper away from the cookies when they are cool and store them in an airtight container.

To fill cookies

ARRANGE THE COOKIES in pairs that are about the same size. Using a knife or pastry bag with a ½-inch (1.25-cm) round tip, place about 1 to 1½ teaspoons of the filling in the center of the bottom of one cookie, place the other on top, and then press gently so you can see the filling from the sides. Store in the fridge for up to three days or freeze for up to three months. ■

MULTIPLE STEP

GLUTEN-FREE • NON-GEBROKTS • PARVE

MOCHA MACARONS

Makes 30 to 40

If you are not a fan of coffee, feel free to omit it and enjoy these simply as chocolate macarons.

Cookie

4 large egg whites, at room temperature for two hours

1 cup (120g) almond flour (1½ cups/180g slivered almonds ground extra-fine, in a coffee grinder)

1¾ cups (210g) confectioners' sugar

¼ cup (20g) unsweetened cocoa

¼ cup (50g) sugar

1 ounce (28g) semisweet or bittersweet chocolate, to grate on top

Mocha Ganache

1 tablespoon instant coffee granules

5 ounces (140g) bittersweet chocolate, finely chopped

½ cup (120ml) dairy-free whipping cream

1 tablespoon confectioners' sugar

To make the cookies

FIRST, separate the eggs when cold and store the yolks in the fridge. Let the egg whites sit out at room temperature for two hours. Place the almond flour, confectioners' sugar, and cocoa into a food processor fitted with a metal blade. Process for three full minutes. Sift the mixture into another bowl, discarding any large pieces. It may sit out while the whites come to room temperature.

LINE TWO COOKIE SHEETS with parchment paper cut to fit the sheets exactly. In a large bowl, beat the egg whites with an electric mixer on high speed until stiff. Turn the speed to low, add the granulated sugar slowly, and then turn up the speed to high for three minutes. Add the almond, sugar, and cocoa mixture and mix on low speed to mostly combine, scraping down the bowl to get all the dry ingredients mixed in. Finish mixing by hand with a spatula. PLACE THE BATTER into a pastry bag fitted with a ¼-inch (6-mm) round tip. Squeeze a little batter under the corners of the parchment to glue the parchment to the cookie sheet. Hold the pastry bag straight up, about ¼-inch (6mm) over the paper, and squeeze out the batter slowly until you have a 1-inch (2.5-cm) circle. Leave two inches (5cm) of space between each cookie circle. The circles will expand slightly while sitting. Take the one ounce (28g) of chocolate and use a zester or grater with small holes to grate chocolate on top of the cookies. Let the cookie circles sit out at room temperature one hour.

To make the ganache

FIRST MAKE COFFEE EXTRACT by mixing the coffee granules with one teaspoon boiling water. Stir to dissolve the coffee and let sit 15 minutes. In a small saucepan, bring the cream to a boil. Add the chopped chocolate and let the mixture sit for five minutes. Add the confectioners' sugar and whisk well. Add one teaspoon of the coffee extract and mix. Leave the ganache in the fridge for one hour to firm up. You can leave it in longer, but then you will need to reheat it to make the consistency soft enough to squeeze out of a pastry bag and fill the cookies.

To bake the cookies

PREHEAT OVEN to 300°F (150°C). Bake the cookies for 20 to 22 minutes, until they have puffed up, switching the cookie sheets on the racks halfway through baking and turning them around. To test the cookies for doneness lift one cookie off the parchment. If it comes right off, it is overbaked. Remove the cookies from the oven immediately (they are still edible, but just not as chewy as they should be). If you lift a cookie and the top comes off and you see gooey batter on the parchment, the cookies need a few more minutes. The cookies are perfect if they come off the parchment paper, stick just a little, and you can see lines on the bottom of the cookie. Slide the parchment onto a wire rack and let the cookies cool. Peel the parchment paper away from the cookies when they are cool and store them in an airtight container.

To fill the cookies

ARRANGE THE COOKIES in pairs that are about the same size. Using a knife or pastry bag with a ½-inch (1.25-cm) round tip, place about 1 to 1½ teaspoons of the mocha ganache into the center of the bottom of one cookie, place the other on top, and then press gently so you can see the filling from the sides. If the ganache gets too hard, melt it in the microwave for a few seconds and then stir it. If it gets too soft, put the ganache back in the fridge until it firms up. Store in the fridge for up to three days or freeze for up to three months. ■

MULTIPLE STEP

GLUTEN-FREE · NON-GEBROKTS · PARVE

CHOCOLATE MOUSSE MACARONS

Serves 12 to 14

In December 2011, I took a trip to Paris to research the approximately eighty kosher pastry shops there. I only had time to visit about 12 of them, and kept seeing this dessert over and over—a French macaron cookie filled with classic chocolate mousse, the perfect combination of crunchy and creamy. These exceptional cookies make a lovely plated dessert for Passover.

Cookie

4 large egg whites, at room temperature for two hours

1 cup (120g) almond flour (1½ cups/180g slivered almonds, ground extra-fine, in a coffee grinder)

1¾ cups (210g) confectioners' sugar

¼ cup (20g) unsweetened cocoa

¼ cup (50g) sugar

Mousse

5 ounces (140g) bittersweet chocolate

1 large egg, separated

2 tablespoons sugar

½ cup (120ml) dairy-free whipping cream

To make the cookies

FIRST, separate eggs when cold and store the yolks in the fridge. Let the egg whites sit out at room temperature for two hours. Place the almond flour, confectioners' sugar, and cocoa into a food processor fitted with a metal blade. Process for four full minutes. Sift the mixture into another bowl, discarding any large pieces.

LINE TWO COOKIE SHEETS with parchment paper cut to fit the sheets exactly. Use a drinking glass or round cookie cutter to draw 28 2-inch (5-cm) circles on the parchment, two inches apart, so your cookies are exactly the same size, and then turn over the paper so the ink or pencil lead is on the bottom side.

IN A LARGE BOWL, beat the egg whites with an electric mixer on high speed until stiff. Turn the speed to low, add the granulated sugar in four parts, mixing it in completely before adding the next amount, and then turn up the speed to high for three minutes.

ADD THE ALMOND, cocoa, and sugar mixture and mix on low speed to mostly combine, scraping down the bowl to get all the dry ingredients mixed in. Finish mixing with a spatula.

PLACE THE BATTER into a pastry bag fitted with a ¼-inch (6-mm) round tip. Squeeze a little batter under the corners of the parchment to glue the parchment to the cookie sheet. Hold the pastry bag straight up, about ¼-inch (6mm) over the center of the drawn circle and squeeze out the batter slowly into the center so that it fills just the inside of the circle, about two inches (5cm) wide. The batter will expand slightly while sitting. Let the cookie circles sit at room temperature one hour.

To make the mousse

MELT THE CHOCOLATE, either over a double boiler or in a microwave oven for one minute, stir, heat for 45 seconds and stir, heat for another 30 seconds and stir, and then heat in 15-second increments, or until all the chocolate is melted. Add the egg yolk and whisk vigorously; the mixture may be pasty. In a separate bowl, beat the egg white with an electric mixer on high speed until stiff. Turn speed to low, add the two tablespoons sugar in two parts, and then turn speed to high and beat another minute. Fold the egg whites into the chocolate mixture in two parts. Whip the whipping cream until stiff. Fold it into the chocolate mixture and mix well. Place the mousse in the fridge until you're ready to use it. May be made one day in advance.

To bake the macaron cookies

PREHEAT OVEN to 300°F (150°C). Bake for 23 to 26 minutes, until the cookies have puffed up, switching the cookie sheets on the racks halfway through baking and turning them around. Do not let the tops brown. To test the cookies for doneness lift one cookie off the parchment. If it comes right off, it is overbaked. Remove the cookies from the oven immediately (they are still edible, but just not as chewy as they should be). If you lift a cookie, and the top comes off, and you see gooey batter on the parchment, the cookies need a few more minutes. The cookies are perfect if they come off the parchment paper and stick just a little, and when there are lines on the bottom of the cookie. Slide the parchment onto a wire rack and let the cookies cool. Peel the parchment

paper away from the cookies when they are cool and store them in an airtight container.

To fill the cookies

ARRANGE THE COOKIES in pairs that are about the same size. Spoon the mousse into a pastry bag with a ½ inch (1.25-cm) round tip. Squeeze nickel-size circles of mousse, about ½ inch (1.25-cm) high, around the edges of the bottom of one cookie and then fill in the center. Place the matching cookie bottom gently on top. Chill the cookies in the fridge for 20 minutes before serving. Store in the fridge for up to three days or freeze for up to three months. ■

MULTIPLE STEP

PARVE

CHOCOLATE CHOCOLATE ÉCLAIRS

Makes 60 2½- to 3-inch (6- to 8-cm) éclairs

The recent Passover certification of almond milk has transformed my baking. A huge fan of soy milk as a milk substitute, I always miss it during Passover because until recently I only had coffee creamer and whipping cream with which to create French pastries and creams on Passover; the results were, consequently, quite mixed. These éclairs are fully chocolate: chocolate pastry, chocolate pastry cream filling, and chocolate glaze.

Pastry
½ cup (120ml) almond milk
½ cup (120ml) water
½ cup (1 stick; 113g) margarine
2 tablespoons sugar
½ teaspoon salt
6 large eggs, divided
½ cup (80g) potato starch
¼ cup (20g) unsweetened cocoa
¼ cup (33g) matzoh cake meal

Pastry Cream

1¼ cups (300g) almond milk

1 teaspoon vanilla

2 tablespoons (28g) margarine

5 tablespoons sugar, divided

4 large egg yolks

3 tablespoons potato starch

1 teaspoon unflavored gelatin powder

4 ounces (115g) bittersweet chocolate, chopped into ½ inch (1.25-cm) pieces

Sugar Syrup and Chocolate Glaze

1⅓ cups (265g) sugar

1 cup (240ml) water

6 ounces (170g) bittersweet chocolate

white or chocolate chips to decorate, if desired

To make the pastry shells

PREHEAT OVEN to 475°F (240°C). Line two cookie sheets with parchment paper. Set aside.

PLACE THE ALMOND MILK, water, margarine, sugar, and salt into a medium saucepan and bring the mixture to a rolling boil over medium heat. Meanwhile, in a small bowl, whisk together the potato starch, cocoa, and matzoh cake meal.

WHEN THE MIXTURE BOILS, remove it from the heat and, with a wooden spoon, mix in the combined potato starch, cocoa, and cake meal. Put the saucepan back on the stove over low heat and cook for one minute more, stirring constantly to dry out the dough. Remove from the heat.

PLACE THE DOUGH in a medium bowl and add five of the eggs, one at a time, mixing thoroughly with a wooden spoon after the addition of each egg. Be patient, this takes time.

PUT THE DOUGH in a pastry bag fitted with a ¼- to ½-inch (6-mm to 1.25-cm) round tip. Squeeze a little dough under the corners of the parchment paper to glue it to the cookie sheet. Hold the bag at an angle, ¼-inch (6mm) above the baking sheet and pipe (squeeze out) a ¾-inch (2-cm) wide, 3-inch (8-cm) long line of dough. To do this,

squeeze a circle ¾-inch (2-cm) wide and continue to squeeze while moving the bag down to make the éclair shell 3-inches (8-cm) long. Slowly lift the tip up and over the line you squeezed out; the end will stay rounded. You will get the hang of it after a few tries. Make sure the piped dough lines are 2 inches (5cm) apart on the prepared cookie sheets.

BEAT THE SIXTH EGG in a small bowl and gently brush each pastry to smooth out the top and flatten the tip, if there is one.

PLACE THE BAKING SHEETS in the pre-heated oven and then turn off the oven. After 15 minutes, turn the oven on to 350°F (180°C). Bake the pastries another 30 minutes. They are done when the cracks on the top are the same color as the rest of the pastry; you want them to be dry. Move the baking sheets to a wire rack and let them cool. If you are filling the pastries the same day, leave them uncovered on the cookie sheet. If not, store them in an airtight container at room temperature.

To make the pastry cream

IN A HEAVY SAUCEPAN, bring the almond milk, vanilla, margarine, and two tablespoons of sugar to a boil. Meanwhile, use a whisk to beat the egg yolks and the three remaining tablespoons of sugar in a medium bowl. Add the potato starch and gelatin and whisk. Add half the almond milk mixture to the egg bowl and whisk. Add the other half of the almond milk into the eggs and whisk well. Return the mixture to the saucepan and cook on low heat for 1 to 2 minutes, whisking almost constantly, until the mixture is very thick. You will need a silicone spatula to mix the cream in the corners of the saucepan so it does not burn. Remove the saucepan from the heat and scoop the mixture into a clean bowl. Let it sit for five minutes.

MELT THE FOUR OUNCES of chocolate, either over a double boiler or in the microwave oven, for 45 seconds and stir, heat for 30 seconds and stir, and then heat for 15 more seconds, if necessary, until all the chocolate is melted. Whisk the chocolate into the pastry cream. Let it sit for five minutes. Cover the cream and leave it in the fridge overnight. To use immediately, place the bowl of cream over a bowl filled with a 2 to 3 cups of ice cubes and two cups of cold water for 30 minutes. Let the cream cool, stirring it occasionally, until it has chilled and firmed up.

To fill the éclairs

PLACE THE PASTRY CREAM into a pastry bag with a ⅛-inch (3-mm) round tip. Each éclair will have a flat side and a rounded side. Hold the pastry so the rounded side faces you. Using the pastry bag tip, or a skewer, make two holes in the rounded side of the pastry, about one inch apart. Squeeze the cream into the pastry through the holes, one at a time, tilting the nozzle to fill the entire pastry, until you feel the pastry get heavier or the cream starts coming out of one of the holes. When the éclairs are filled, make the chocolate glaze.

To make the sugar syrup for the chocolate glaze

BRING THE WATER and sugar to a rolling boil in a small saucepan. Boil one minute and then turn off the heat and let the mixture cool. May be made five days in advance and stored covered at room temperature.

To make the chocolate glaze

MELT THE CHOCOLATE, either over the double boiler or in the microwave oven, for 45 seconds and stir, heat for 30 seconds and stir, and then heat for another 15 seconds, if needed, until all the chocolate has melted. Add the sugar syrup, a few tablespoons at a time, and whisk until you get a consistency you can drizzle. If the chocolate sauce starts to harden, just add a little more sugar syrup and whisk until you get a thick, pourable consistency. Store the chocolate glaze, covered, at room temperature. Reheat the glaze in a microwave and whisk to use.

DIP THE FLAT SIDE (without the pastry cream holes) of each filled éclair into the chocolate, allowing the excess to drip off, and using your finger to wipe off any excess. Repeat with the remaining éclairs. Decorate, if desired. Store covered in the fridge for up to three days or freeze for up to three months. ■

MODERATE
GLUTEN-FREE • NUT-FREE •
NON-GEBROKTS • PARVE

CRÊPES
Makes 12

My grandma Sylvia was a master blintz maker. When she was 88 years old, she came to visit me in Washington, D.C. and promised to teach me how to make her famous cheese blintzes. I recall that she held the crêpes up to the light to show me how paper thin they were, yet still stayed intact. I did not try making them until many years later and could not achieve the thinness she could. Let this be a lesson to the wise and hungry: when learning a new recipe from a *bubbie*, the best choice is to make it again as soon as possible. This is not exactly her recipe; rather, it is the closest I could get. You can fill the crêpes with anything you like. My favorite filling is melted chocolate and sliced strawberries. Other options are any fresh or cooked fruit, pastry cream, or mousse.

½ cup (80g) potato starch

1 tablespoon gluten-free cake meal, or matzoh
cake meal

1 cup (240ml) water

4 large eggs

2 teaspoons vanilla, optional

2 tablespoons sugar

1 tablespoon oil or melted margarine for
cooking crêpes

IN A MEDIUM BOWL, whisk together the potato starch, gluten-free cake meal, water, eggs, vanilla, and sugar. Mix well. Pour the mixture through a sieve into another bowl, discarding any solids. You can make the crêpes immediately or store the batter covered in the fridge for up to three days.

TEAR OFF 12 pieces of waxed paper to place between the crêpes. Heat a 6- to 8-inch (15- to 20-cm) crêpe pan or nonstick frying pan over medium-high heat. Brush the pan with a little melted margarine or oil. When the pan is hot, take it off the stove and pour a little less than ¼ cup of the batter in the center of the pan, turning the pan clockwise three times so the batter covers the bottom of the pan. You may need to add a little more batter to cover the bottom or fill in holes. By the third crêpe, you will know just how much batter covers the pan. Return the pan to the heat.

COOK THE CRÊPE for one minute, or until the edges look brown. Lift the crêpe by sliding a spatula halfway under the crêpe and turning it over. Cook on the other side for 15 seconds and then flip it onto a plate. If the crêpes are browning too quickly, turn down the heat. Put a piece of waxed paper between each crêpe. After the stack of crêpes has cooled, wrap it in plastic wrap and store in the fridge for up to four days. Reheat and fill as desired. ◼

MULTIPLE STEP

GLUTEN-FREE • NON-GEBROKTS • PARVE

NOUGAT GLACÉ

Serves 16

In 2012, after I had eaten this frozen dessert in a fancy kosher restaurant in Paris, I wrote a blog posting called "How Does Nougat Glacé Symbolize the Survival of the Jewish People?" I was struck by the appearance of this classic French dessert in a kosher restaurant and believe it shows how French Jews fully embrace French culture, yet still retain their Jewishness. This recipe feeds a crowd, but the best part is that you can store it in the freezer for the whole Passover holiday and serve it as needed. I prefer to serve nougat glacé with a berry sauce, yet I imagine that a chocolate sauce would make it taste like a candy bar, so let me know if you try that.

Praline (caramelized almonds)
¾ cup (150g) sugar
3 tablespoons water
1 cup (120g) slivered almonds

Italian Meringue
½ cup (100g) sugar
¼ cup (85g) honey
½ cup (120ml) water
3 large egg whites
1¾ cups (420ml) dairy-free whipping cream

To make the praline

HEAT THE SUGAR and water in a heavy saucepan over medium-high heat without stirring. Let the mixture sit until it starts to turn amber around the edges. Add the nuts and stir with a wooden spoon. Reduce the heat to medium-low. The mixture will get dry, but then the sugar will melt and the mixture will turn golden. Stir often and be patient. The praline is done when the nuts are toasted, surrounded by a dark caramel, and all the sugar pieces have melted.

USE A WOODEN SPOON or silicone spatula to spread the nuts and caramel in one layer on a parchment or silicone-covered baking sheet, and let it cool for at least 15 minutes. Store the praline in a bag or container for up to one week and try not to eat it. When you're ready to use the praline, put it in the bowl of a food processor fitted with a metal blade and chop the nuts into small pieces. Some of it can be powdered, but make sure that

some pieces are about ¼- to ⅓-inch (6- to 8-mm) big so the dessert has some crunch to it. Set aside.

To make and assemble the Italian meringue
LINE A 12-INCH (30-cm) loaf pan with plastic wrap, making sure the wrap goes into the corners and goes all the way up the sides of the pan to the top. Use two pieces of plastic if necessary. You can also divide the mixture between two smaller loaf pans. Beat the whipping cream until stiff. Set it aside.

HEAT THE SUGAR, honey, and water in a heavy saucepan over medium-high heat. Place the egg whites into the bowl of a stand mixer fitted with a whisk. When the honey and sugar mixture reads 225°F (105°C) on a candy thermometer, start beating the whites on low speed; increase the speed slowly to achieve soft peaks, then stop beating. When the cooked mixture reaches 260°F (125°C), reduce the speed to low and slowly add the sugar and honey mixture down the side of the bowl. When all of the hot syrup has been poured in, turn the speed to high, cover the bowl with a clean dishtowel, and beat for five full minutes. The meringue will be thick and shiny.

USE A SILICONE SPATULA to fold the chopped nuts into the meringue. Fold in the whipped cream in four parts and scoop it into the prepared pan. Smooth the top of the mixture. Lift the pan about an inch above the counter and let it drop down onto the counter to knock out any trapped air bubbles. Cover the mixture with plastic wrap. If

you have any left over, put it in a small bowl or container. Put the pan in the freezer for 8 hours or overnight.

TO SERVE THE NOUGAT, remove the plastic and turn the loaf onto a long, rectangular plate. Serve ½- to 1-inch (1.25- to 2.5-cm) slices. Store the nougat covered in the freezer for up to three months and slice as needed. If desired, serve with a colorful fruit sauce (see page 31) or fresh fruit. ▪

(see page 31)

EASY

GLUTEN-FREE • NUT-FREE •
NON-GEBROKTS • PARVE

STRAWBERRY ICE CREAM

Serves 12 to 15

This super-easy yet elegant recipe came from Tsippy Nussbaum by way of Limor Decter. I was skeptical about the simplicity of the preparation, but it really works and results in a light, refreshing, frozen dessert. Please note that this recipe uses raw egg.

1 pound (450g) fresh strawberries, washed
    and trimmed
1 cup (200g) sugar
1 large egg white

PUT THE STRAWBERRIES in the bowl of a food processor fitted with a metal blade. Process until the strawberries are completely puréed, scraping down the processor bowl a few times to get all the pieces puréed. Pour the purée into the bowl of a stand mixer. Add the sugar and egg white and use the whisk to mix on low speed for two minutes. Cover the bowl and mixer with plastic wrap and then turn the speed up to high. Mix for 8 full minutes; the mixture will become very light and fill the entire bowl. Cover and leave the bowl in the freezer for 8 hours or overnight. Store in the freezer for up to one week. ▪

EASY

GLUTEN-FREE • NUT-FREE •
NON-GEBROKTS • PARVE • VEGAN

MOSCATO GRANITA

Serves 10

Granitas are ices that you scrape from a block of flavored ice and are really easy to make. My children love tasting these ices because it makes them feel as if they are drinking wine. I have served it for dessert and also as an aperitif, before dinner.

1 cup (200g) sugar
1 cup (240ml) water
1 bottle (750ml) Moscato wine (I like the
    Bartenura brand)
6 ounces (170g) raspberries, or 1½ cups cut fruit

BRING THE SUGAR AND WATER to a rolling boil in a small saucepan. Let boil one minute and then let cool one hour. Pour mixture into a 9- x 13-inch (23 x 33-cm) pan. Pour in the wine and whisk. Place pan in the freezer. For the first hour, stir mixture every 30 minutes and then let harden several hours or overnight until frozen solid.

TO SERVE, use the tines of a fork to scrape the ice block and then mash the remaining pieces that cannot be scraped. Spoon the granita into pretty glasses, add fruit, and enjoy. Store in the freezer for up to three months. ▪

Shavuot

Shavuot celebrates the receiving of the Torah at Mt. Sinai. The word "Shavuot" means weeks, and marks the end of counting seven weeks from the second day of Passover, when we went from slavery to becoming a nation. The seven-week period is called the Omer. According to the ancient mystical wisdom of Kabbalah, the Omer is an opportunity to strengthen and improve certain personal qualities. One week we concentrate on Chesed—loving-kindness—and consider ways in which we can improve how we treat people. During another week, we emphasize Hod—humility—and work on how we can better manage our accomplishments without belittling others. It is a period of self-refinement, reminding us that the days before Yom Kippur are not the only time when we should try to improve our behavior and relationships.

Shavuot is the only holiday when most Jewish bakers entertain with dairy desserts. When the Israelites were waiting for Moses to bring them the Torah at Mount Sinai, they did not eat any meat because they were waiting to learn the kosher laws. For many Jews, the custom is to eat only dairy meals. For a parve baker, I feel like a kid in a candy store, eating forbidden treats.

In 1995, I went to Paris to study French pastry. I was not looking for a new career and was perfectly happy as an attorney when my husband's employer, the United States government, sent us to Geneva, Switzerland, as diplomats. After working in a law-related job for two years, I enrolled in a pastry course at the Ritz Escoffier purely for fun; I had no professional aspirations. I just thought that my family would eat better. When I returned to Geneva between studies, I was very excited to bake what I had learned for my husband. Problem: our more formal meals, whether for Shabbat, holidays, or dinner parties, were always meat-based. Solution: convert classic French dairy desserts into parve ones. I bought great parve margarine and cream just across the border in France and I was ready to go. Sure, there were many "bake and dumps" until I got a recipe right, but soon enough, our Shabbat dinners were followed by parve French desserts that most guests could not believe were parve.

I went on to convert all my favorite dairy desserts into parve versions, and a new career was born. In this chapter, I bring to you some of the desserts that started me on my journey: dairy crêpes, pastry creams, napoleons, and mousses. These are my best dairy desserts. Feel free to bake them all year round.

Best Dairy Desserts

Best Dairy Desserts

This section contains desserts that don't have adequate dairy-free alternatives. For a baker accustomed to baking only parve desserts, Shavuot is your opportunity to expand your repertoire with these classic French and American dairy desserts. As the holiday of Shavuot is only two days long, I combined the snack and fancy desserts into one group.

NOTE: Use fat-free (skim) milk in the recipes in this chapter, unless it specifically calls for whole milk. Use unsalted sweet butter unless otherwise stated.

EASY

DAIRY • NUT-FREE

GG'S NOODLE KUGEL

Serves 15

My grandmother Sylvia Altman was an amazing cook and baker and made many delicious dishes, but this recipe for noodle kugel is her crowning glory. Usually, I am not a fan of kugels, as they are too heavy and generally not worth the calories. Once when I was speaking in Toledo, Ohio, about healthier holiday menus, I said that kugels should only be eaten once a year, so that our children know these traditional recipes, but not more often, as they are too high in calories. Well, this statement caused an uproar: the ladies of Toledo stormed the podium when I finished speaking. They make kugels every Shabbat and even pointed out the ladies who were their kugel mavens. Now I know to never criticize kugel in the Midwest. I am dedicating this recipe to the ladies of Toledo. Here is the best sweet kugel you will ever eat (as well as the *only* one I ever eat). I have served this as a side dish and for dessert and always bring it to the Yom Kippur break-fast I attend every year.

12 ounces (340g) medium noodles

3 tablespoons (42g) unsalted butter

3 tablespoons (42g) cream cheese (not whipped)

¾ cup (150g) sugar

1 teaspoon salt

5 large eggs

⅓ cup (75g) full fat sour cream

1½ pounds (680g) small curd, whole milk cottage cheese

2 tablespoons canola or vegetable oil

PREHEAT OVEN to 350°F (180°C). Cook noodles in a large saucepan according to package directions. Drain and then place noodles back into the saucepan. Add butter and cream cheese and mix until both have melted into the noodles. Add sugar and salt and mix well. Beat in the eggs one at a time. Add the sour cream and cottage cheese and mix to distribute.

PLACE THE OIL into a 9 x 13-inch (23 x 33-cm) baking pan and heat in the oven for five minutes. Carefully remove the pan and pour the noodle mixture into the hot pan. Bake the noodle mixture for 45 to 50 minutes, or until it has set. Serve warm. If you want the top to brown more, turn the oven temperature up to 400°F (200°C) for about five minutes, watching the kugel carefully so that the top does not burn. Store in the fridge for up to four days or freeze for up to three months. Reheat to serve ▪

FULL-FAT OR NOTHING

My mother tried switching to fat-free sour cream and cottage cheese in this recipe, and my brother Adam and I told her either to go back to the full-fat ingredients or not make the kugel anymore; it just gets too dry without the fat. Trust me, this recipe is splurge-worthy.

MULTIPLE STEP

DAIRY • NUT-FREE

HOMEMADE CANDY BARS

Makes 24 3 x 1-inch (8 x 2.5-cm) bars

I have never been a candy person, leaving the gummy treats to others, but give me a chocolate candy bar and I am a happy camper. These are my version of Twix bars, one of my favorites. This recipe took many attempts until the cookie had the right crunch, the caramel filling was deep-flavored and thick enough, and the chocolate easy to cover. My four children will happily tell you that each and every rejected version was delicious, even if the caramel was too loose or the cookies too hard.

Cookie
1 cup (125g) all-purpose flour
½ cup (60g) confectioners' sugar
½ cup (1 stick; 113g) unsalted cold butter, cut into 8 pieces, plus extra for greasing pan
1 teaspoon pure vanilla extract

Caramel
¾ cup (150g) sugar
1 tablespoon water
½ cup (120ml) sweetened condensed milk (or heavy whipping cream)
¼ cup (60ml) heavy whipping cream
1 tablespoon (14g) unsalted butter
1 teaspoon pure vanilla extract

Glaze
1⅓ cups (265g) sugar
1 cup (250ml) water
7 ounces (200g) bittersweet chocolate

To make the cookie
GREASE an 8 x 8-inch (20 x 20-cm) square pan with butter and cover the bottom with a piece of parchment paper, about 10 x 10 inches (25 x 25cm), and press it into the bottom, sides, and corners of the pan. Grease the top and sides of the parchment with more butter. Set the pan aside.

PREHEAT OVEN to 400°F (200°C). Put the flour and confectioners' sugar into the bowl of a food processor fitted with a metal blade. Mix a few seconds. Add the butter and vanilla and mix just until the dough comes together. Remove the clumps of dough and press them into the bottom of the pan as evenly as possible. Use a fork to prick the dough with holes. Place the dough in the freezer for 15 minutes. Bake the cookie dough for 12 to 15 minutes, until the edges start to color. Remove the pan from the oven and let cool 30 minutes. Refrigerate and store for up to three days.

To make the caramel
PUT THE SUGAR and water in a small or medium heavy saucepan over medium-high heat. Cook without stirring until the sugar at the edges starts to turn an amber color. This takes a few minutes. Once the sugar colors, stir the mixture with a wooden spoon or silicone spatula and cook until all of the sugar has melted and the mixture turns dark amber, stirring occasionally. Turn heat to low, remove saucepan from heat, and add the condensed milk, cream, butter, and vanilla and whisk. Be careful, as the mixture will bubble up.

TIKKUN LEIL SHAVUOT

Shavuot is celebrated with all-night Torah study (called *Tikkun Leil Shavuot*), a tradition that goes back to the 1500s. In modern Jerusalem, after learning all night, Jews walk to the Western Wall for sunrise prayers. In 2013, my older children, Emily and Sam, both on separate Israel programs, bumped into each other walking to the Wall at 4:00 a.m.

PUT THE MIXTURE BACK on the stove over medium-low heat and continue cooking, stirring constantly, until the mixture thickens and registers 230°F (110°C) on a candy thermometer. Use a spatula to scoop the caramel into a medium bowl and let sit at room temperature, uncovered, for 30 minutes, whisking occasionally, until the mixture becomes thick and hard to stir.

REMOVE THE COOKIE CRUST from the fridge and use a silicone spatula to spread the caramel on top. Spread from the center back and forth as evenly as possible to cover the cookie. Leave in the freezer for one hour or up to three days.

To prepare the sugar syrup for the glaze

PUT THE WATER and sugar in a small, heavy saucepan over medium heat. Stir to dissolve the sugar and bring to a rolling boil and cook one minute. Remove the pan from the heat. Let it sit at room temperature until you are ready to use the syrup. May be made five days in advance and stored covered at room temperature.

Glazing the candy bars

BREAK OR CHOP the chocolate into ½ inch (1.25-cm) pieces and melt it over a double boiler or in a microwave oven for 45 seconds and stir, heat for 30 seconds and stir, heat for another 15 seconds and stir, until all the chocolate is melted. Add the sugar syrup, about ¼ cup at a time, and whisk the mixture until it is shiny and pourable. You will need about one cup total syrup mixed in to start glazing the candy bars.

PLACE A WIRE RACK over a foil-covered cookie sheet to catch the chocolate drippings. Remove the caramel-topped cookie from the freezer and lift the parchment paper to get it out of the pan. Heat a large knife with boiling water until the blade is hot, dry it, and then cut the cookie into one-inch long strips. Then cut each long strip into three bars. Repeat with two more strips. Dip the caramel side of a cookie bar into the chocolate

glaze, deep enough to completely cover the sides and a little of the bottom of the bar. Allow any excess chocolate to drip off. Turn the bar over and place it on the rack, cookie side down. Repeat to dip the rest of the bars.

WHISK another ¼ cup of sugar syrup into the glaze and reheat the knife, and repeat after glazing three strips of bars. If the chocolate becomes too thick, add a little more syrup and whisk it into the glaze. You will need to cover the caramel quickly before it starts to get soft. If you have any leftover glaze, when you've finished dipping the cookies, use a whisk to drizzle lines of glaze over the candy bars.

PUT THE BARS on the rack in the fridge for 30 minutes. To serve, use a metal spatula to remove bars from the rack to a serving plate. Store the bars in the fridge for up to one week or freeze for up to three months. ■

DAIRY • NUT-FREE

CANNELÉS

Makes 30 to 32 mini pastries

Cannelés, pronounced "canelays," are small, fluted cakes that originated in the Bordeaux region of France. They have a dark, caramelized exterior and a spongy, rich, custardy interior. Use a silicone pan that makes 15 mini cakes and bake them in two or more batches. You can easily find "cannelés molds" online.

2 cups (480ml) whole milk
4 tablespoons (57g) unsalted butter, cut into pieces, plus one tablespoon to grease molds
½ vanilla bean, split and seeds scraped
dash of salt
2 large eggs plus two yolks
¾ cup (95g) all-purpose flour
1 cup (200g) sugar
2 teaspoons rum

PLACE THE MILK, butter, scraped seeds and vanilla bean pod, and salt into a small saucepan and heat over medium heat until hot, not boiling, and the butter has melted. In a medium bowl, use a silicone spatula to mix together the eggs, yolks, flour, and sugar into a paste. Strain ½ cup of the milk mixture into the eggs and whisk in. Strain in half of the remaining milk and whisk in. Strain in the remaining milk, discard the vanilla bean pod, and whisk until combined. Add the rum and stir. Strain the mixture into another bowl, discarding any solids. Let it cool for 10 minutes. Cover the bowl and refrigerate overnight.

PREHEAT OVEN to 475°F (240°C). You will need to bake the cannelés in batches, washing the pan between each batch. Place the mold on top of a jelly roll pan. Melt the remaining tablespoon of butter and use a small pastry brush to grease the

insides of the molds. Pour the batter into the molds and fill up to about ⅛ of an inch (3mm) from the top. Wipe off any excess batter on top of the pan.
BAKE for 15 minutes. Reduce heat to 375°F (190°C) and bake another 50 to 60 minutes, or until pastries are very brown on top. The pastries may puff up out of the molds at some point, but they will usually come down before they are done. If the cannelés are still puffing out of the molds after they have baked for 40 minutes, use the back of a small spoon to gently push the sides into the center and they will drop back into the molds. Do not bang the tops; this is not whack-a-mole. Remove the molds from the oven and immediately unmold the cannelés onto a wire rack to cool. Wash and dry the molds and bake another batch. Store covered at room temperature for up to three days or freeze for up to three months. ■

KOUIGH AMANN

Makes 12

This dessert is pronounced "queen amann," and I first encountered it in the Brittany region of France. It is a yeasted puff pastry filled with salted butter and sugar, and prepared as you would homemade puff pastry or a croissant, with butter between every layer of dough. My children fought over them and were angry that I had given a few to my summer intern, Annie Epstein, who had earned them, since she helped me achieve this recipe after several not-so-perfect attempts. According to recipe testers Marla and Andrew Satinsky, these pastries demand time and a lot of patience, but you will be rewarded with a croissant-type pastry that you made all by yourself. Marla said she would definitely make them again. You will want a ruler handy to measure several parts of this recipe.

Dough

1 cup (240ml) warm water

¼ ounce (1 envelope; 7g) dry yeast

1 teaspoon sugar

2 tablespoons (28g) unsalted butter, plus
    2 tablespoons for greasing

2½ cups (315g) all-purpose flour, plus extra for
    dusting

½ teaspoon salt

Filling

2 sticks (226g) salted butter, at room
    temperature for at least 45 minutes

1 cup (200g) plus 2 tablespoons sugar, divided

To make the dough

PLACE 1 CUP (240ml) warm water into a 2-cup measuring cup or a small bowl and add the yeast and one teaspoon sugar and stir. Let sit 10 minutes, or until thick. Meanwhile place the 2 tablespoons sweet butter in a small microwave-safe bowl and melt in the microwave for 15 to 30 seconds. Set it aside.

PUT THE FLOUR, salt, and melted butter in a large mixing bowl or the bowl of a stand mixer with a dough hook. Add the yeast mixture and mix on low speed until the mixture comes off the sides of the bowl and into a ball, scraping down the dough hook a few times. Turn the speed to medium and knead for three minutes, stopping a few times to scrape the dough off the hook, and turn the dough ball over until it is soft. Grease a medium bowl with 1 tablespoon (14g) butter. Shape the dough into a ball and place it in the greased bowl. Cover the bowl with plastic wrap and let the dough rise for one hour at room temperature.

WHEN THE BUTTER is soft enough to press easily, place the two sticks next to each other horizontally on top of plastic wrap and press them together. Cover butter with waxed paper and bang it with a rolling pin to press the sticks together and flatten them slightly. Press your hands against all sides of the butter to keep them straight. Roll out a 4 x 6 inch (10 x 15-cm) butter rectangle, with the longer side in front of you. Every once in a while, press your hands against the sides of the butter to keep them straight. Wrap the butter in plastic and refrigerate.

AFTER THE DOUGH has risen for one hour, remove the plastic wrap, press down on the dough and fold it over a few times. Shape the dough into a ball, cover it, and refrigerate for one hour.

REMOVE THE DOUGH and rectangle of butter from the fridge. Place the dough on a lightly floured surface. Roll out the dough into an 8-inch (20-cm) square, leaving the center of the square a little thicker than the rest. Unwrap the butter and place it in the center of the dough, horizontally, with the longer side facing you. Fold the dough over the butter and seal it, as if you were folding an envelope. Seal tightly by banging the seams with

the rolling pin. Lift up the "package" and sprinkle a little flour underneath it. Put the dough down with the long side facing you. Roll out the dough from the center, until it is three times its length, keeping the sides straight. Every once in a while, lift the dough and sprinkle more flour underneath it. Roll out the dough until it is a 10 x 16-inch (25 x 41-cm) rectangle.

SPRINKLE THE TOP of the dough with ¼ cup (50g) sugar and press it into the dough with your fingers as much as you can. Fold the bottom of the dough one third of the way up and then fold the top down to cover it. Turn the dough so that the seam is on your right and use the rolling pin to bang on the seam to seal it. You have now completed one turn.

ROLL THE DOUGH out once again until it is a 10 x 16-inch (25 x 41-cm) rectangle, keeping the sides straight. If any butter starts to come through the dough, sprinkle the area with a little flour and cover it with a piece of parchment paper. Roll over

the parchment paper with a rolling pin to smooth out the dough. Brush off any excess flour with a pastry brush. Sprinkle the dough with another ¼ cup (50g) sugar and press it in. Fold the bottom of the dough ⅓ way up and then fold down the top to cover it. Again, turn the dough so that the seam is on your right and use the rolling pin to bang the seam to seal it. You have now completed your second turn. Repeat. Roll the dough into a

10 x 16-inch (25 x 41-cm) rectangle, add the sugar, and fold the dough in thirds for two more turns, adding a little flour under the dough each time, brushing off any excess flour from the top and then sprinkling and pressing ¼ cup (50g) sugar into the dough each time.

To shape the dough

GREASE a 12-cup muffin tin with another table-spoon (14g) butter. Place a large piece of parchment on your counter. Place the dough in the middle of the parchment paper and another large piece of parchment on top of the dough. Roll on top of the parchment to roll the dough out into a 10 x 12-inch (25 x 30-cm) rectangle. Do not worry if there are a few bald spots with butter seeping through. If you can, fold some dough over to cover the spots or sprinkle them with some flour. Slice the dough into twelve 1 x 10-inch (2.5 x 25-cm) strips with a sharp knife. Roll the strips into spirals and place them in the ungreased muffin cups, spirals facing up. If any of the spirals do not sit comfortably in the bottom of the muffin cup, remove the spiral, unroll it, and trim off some of the dough to create another roll in another muffin tin. (If the rolls are too big, they will rise too far out of the cups and not bake well.) Let the uncovered dough spirals rise in the muffin tins for one hour. PREHEAT OVEN to 375°F (190°C). Sprinkle another 2 tablespoons of sugar on top of the pastries. Bake for 35 to 40 minutes, or until the tops are golden and the edges are crispy. Run a knife around the edges of the pan and then twist the pastries to remove them from the cups. Serve warm. Store the pastries in foil at room temperature for up to four days or freeze for up to three months. Reheat to serve. ■

CLASSIC CHEESECAKE

Serves 16

Cheesecake is the classic Shavuot dessert and is one of my weaknesses. I can resist overeating a lot of desserts, but cheesecake is not one of them. I had a really fun time making the fruit garland to decorate the cheesecake pictured here. First I washed, dried, and sliced the fruit I wanted to use. Then I designed a garland for the cake on a round dinner plate and moved the fruit to the top of the cheesecake in the same pattern. Decorate the cake right before serving. The fruit will start to go bad after two days, so either finish the cheesecake by then or remove the fruit from the top before it spoils.

Crust

13 graham crackers

1 tablespoon sugar

6 tablespoons (85g) unsalted butter, plus one tablespoon for greasing pan

Filling

2 pounds (900g) cream cheese (not whipped), at room temperature for at least 45 minutes

5 large eggs

1¼ cups (250g) sugar

2 teaspoons pure vanilla extract

1 teaspoon lemon zest (from one lemon)

Topping

1 cup (240g) sour cream

1 tablespoon confectioners' sugar

sliced or whole fruit and berries, optional, to decorate

PREHEAT OVEN to 325°F (160°C). You will need a 9- to 10-inch (23- to 25-cm) springform pan. Trace the bottom of the pan on parchment paper and cut out the circle. Cover the top of the pan bottom with a 20-inch (50-cm) piece of heavy-duty aluminum foil and then wrap the foil under the bottom. Attach the pan sides to the bottom, lock it in place and then unwrap the foil and wrap it up and around the sides of the pan. (This will keep water from seeping into the cheesecake while it's baking in a water bath.) Rub 1 tablespoon (14g) of butter around the bottom and sides of the pan. Press the parchment circle into the bottom of the pan and grease the top of the circle.

PUT ASIDE a large roasting pan—the sides should be more than 2 inches (5cm) high.

To make the crust

PROCESS the graham crackers in the bowl of a food processor fitted with a metal blade until finely ground. Add the sugar and mix. Heat the remaining 6 tablespoons (85g) of butter in a microwave-safe bowl for 15 to 25 seconds, until the butter softens. Add the butter to the food processor bowl and mix it into the crumbs. Spoon clumps of the mixture into the prepared pan and press it into and cover the bottom of the pan. Set the pan aside.

To make the filling

PUT THE CREAM CHEESE into the bowl of a stand mixer or blender and beat on medium-high speed until smooth. Scrape down the bowl. Add the eggs, one at a time, and scrape down the bowl each time to make sure all the cream cheese and eggs are thoroughly mixed. Add 1¼ cups (250g) sugar, vanilla, and lemon zest, and mix on medium speed until combined. The mixture should be entirely smooth.

POUR THE CHEESECAKE filling on top of the crust. Place the pan into the larger roasting pan and place it on the middle rack of the oven. Pour boiling water into the roasting pan, around the cheesecake pan, until the water reaches one-third to halfway up the sides of the cheesecake pan.

BAKE the cheesecake for 1 hour and 10 minutes. Turn off the oven and prop the door open with a wooden spoon. Leave the cheesecake in the oven for 1 more hour. Remove the cheesecake pan from the roasting pan and let it cool on a wire rack until the cheesecake is completely cool. Refrigerate it for five hours or overnight.

To make the topping

COMBINE the sour cream and confectioners' sugar and mix well. Spread the mixture over the top of the cake and decorate as desired. Store in the fridge for up to five days or freeze (without the fruit on top) for up to three months. ◼

EASY

DAIRY • LOW SUGAR • NUT-FREE

LOW-SUGAR CHEESECAKE MUFFINS WITH BLACKBERRY SAUCE

Makes 12

I was hoping to make these muffins entirely sugar free. I tried several versions with various sugar substitutes and found that every sugar replacer masked all the other flavors in the dessert. Ultimately I had to go with a low-sugar version.

Crust

16 sugar-free chocolate (or other) flavored biscuits, crushed into small crumbs
3 tablespoons (42g) unsalted butter, melted

Filling

2 8-ounce (230g) packages cream cheese (not whipped), at room temperature 30 minutes
3 large eggs
¼ cup (50g) sugar
1 tablespoon all-purpose flour

2 teaspoons lemon zest (from one lemon)
1 teaspoon pure vanilla extract, or sugar-free vanilla syrup, optional

Blackberry Sauce

10 ounces (280g) blackberries

PREHEAT OVEN to 350°F (180°C). Put 12 paper cups into a muffin tin.

To make the crust

PUT THE CRUSHED COOKIES into a small bowl. Add the melted butter and mix well with your fingers. Spoon about 2 teaspoons of the crumb mixture into each muffin cup, enough to cover the bottom.

To make the filling

PUT THE CREAM CHEESE in a large bowl and beat with an electric mixer until smooth. Add the eggs, one at a time, and mix well after each addition. Add the sugar, flour, lemon zest, and vanilla, if using, and mix well. Spoon the filling over the cookie crumbs in each of the 12 muffin cups. Bake 25 minutes, or until set. Let the muffins cool. May be made three days in advance and stored, covered, in the fridge.

To make the blackberry sauce

MEANWHILE, set aside 12 blackberries to decorate the tops of the cheesecake muffins. Put the remaining blackberries into the bowl of a food processor fitted with a metal blade. Process until puréed, scraping down the sides of the bowl a few times. Use a sieve to strain the sauce into another bowl and discard the seeds. May be made three days in advance and stored covered in the fridge.
TO SERVE, pull the paper cups off the muffins and put them on serving plates, drizzle 2 to 3 tablespoons of the sauce over each cake, and top with a reserved blackberry.
STORE in the fridge for up to three days. ◼

MODERATE

DAIRY · GLUTEN-FREE · NUT-FREE

CREAM CHEESE FLAN

Serves 12

This extremely rich and creamy dessert comes directly from Puerto Rico via Yvette Lasa, my friend Maria Sloan's mom. I make this dessert in a ceramic soufflé dish, but you can use an 8-inch (20-cm) round pan with 3-inch (8-cm) high sides or a tube pan.

1 cup (200g) sugar

1 teaspoon water

8 large eggs

one 8-ounce (230g) package of cream cheese (not whipped)

1 can (14 ounces; 400g) sweetened condensed milk (or heavy whipping cream)

½ cup (120ml) whole milk

1 teaspoon pure vanilla extract

PREHEAT OVEN to 350°F (180°C). You will need an 8-inch (20-cm) round pan with high sides and a larger baking pan that can hold the 8-inch (20-cm) pan as well as a few inches of water.

USING CREAM CHEESE IN DESSERTS

* Desserts with cream cheese will come out smoother if the cream cheese is at room temperature before you use it.

* Use regular and not whipped cream cheese for desserts.

IN A SMALL SAUCEPAN, place the sugar and water and cook over medium-high heat. When the edges start to turn amber, stir with a wooden spoon and then cook, stirring occasionally, until the sugar has melted and completely turns amber. Carefully pour the mixture into the 8-inch (20-cm) pan and swirl it around three times so the caramel colors about 1 to 2 inches (2.5 to 5cm) up the sides of the pan. Set aside.

PUT THE EGGS, cream cheese, condensed milk, whole milk, and vanilla into a blender or mixer and mix at medium-high speed until smooth. Pour the mixture on top of the caramel in the pan. Cover the 8-inch round pan with aluminum foil and put it in the larger pan. Put the larger pan on your oven rack and pour boiling water into it, until it fills the larger pan up to 1½ to 2 inches (4 to 5-cm) up the sides of the flan pan. Bake the flan for one hour.

TO TELL WHEN the flan is done, remove the foil and give the pan a gentle shake. If the custard in the center jiggles, continue baking for another 20 to 30 minutes until the mixture is fully set. Carefully remove the soufflé dish from the hot water and let it cool to room temperature, leaving the baking pan and water in the oven until they cool and can be removed safely.

WHEN THE FLAN has cooled, run a thin knife along the sides of the dish to loosen it. Place a pie pan or a platter with a rim over the top of the flan dish and turn the flan over and onto it, letting the caramel drip over the sides. If any caramel remains at the bottom of the pan, place the flan pan into a larger pan with one inch of boiling water and let sit for 2 to 3 minutes and then pour the loosened caramel over the custard. Cover with plastic and refrigerate for at least six hours or overnight. Store in the fridge for up to six days. ■

DAIRY • NUT-FREE

CARAMELIZED MOCHA AND **VANILLA BEAN** NAPOLEONS

Serves 8

Napoleons, also called "mille feuilles" for the many layers of puff pastry, are one of the most popular pastries in France. The classic recipe has vanilla cream but I added a second layer of mocha-flavored pastry cream. Don't worry—you only have to make one cream filling, which you then divide and flavor separately. When you caramelize the pastry layers, watch the pastry carefully so it does not burn.

Pastry

1 sheet frozen puff pastry (from a 17.3-ounce (490g) box)
flour for dusting pastry
1½ tablespoons confectioners' sugar

Pastry Creams

1½ cups (360ml) milk
1 vanilla bean, split and seeds scraped
3 tablespoons (42g) unsalted butter
½ cup (100g) sugar
6 large egg yolks
¼ cup (30g) flour, sifted after measuring
2 teaspoons unflavored gelatin powder
⅓ cup (80ml) whipping cream
2 ounces (57g) bittersweet chocolate
½ teaspoon coffee granules
1 teaspoon coffee extract

2 teaspoons confectioners' sugar to decorate, if desired

THAW THE PUFF PASTRY at room temperature for 45 minutes. Cut a piece of parchment the exact size of your cookie sheet and sprinkle it with flour.

Roll out a pastry sheet the size of the cookie sheet. Lift the pastry several times and sprinkle a little flour underneath. This will make it faster to roll out the dough, as the dough stretches more easily when it is not stuck to the parchment. Trim the edges to even them out. Prick the dough all over with a fork. Place it in the freezer for 30 minutes.

To bake the pastry

PREHEAT OVEN to 400°F (200°C). Put another cookie sheet on top of the pastry and bake it for 15 minutes. Take the pastry out of the oven and turn the temperature up to 450°F (230°C). Remove the top cookie sheet and sift the confectioners' sugar all over the pastry dough. When the oven temperature has reached 450°F (230°C), put the pastry back in the oven (uncovered) and bake it for another 5 to 8 minutes, or until the sugar has melted and the top is caramel-colored. Do not let the pastry burn. Immediately slide the parchment and pastry off the cookie sheet onto the counter. Trim the sides so they are straight and slice the long side into three long, even strips, and then slice each into 1½ inch (4-cm) strips so you have 24 rectangles. Let the pastry strips cool. Can be made one day in advance and stored uncovered at room temperature.

To make the pastry creams

IN A HEAVY SAUCEPAN, bring the milk, scraped seeds and vanilla bean pod, butter, and half of the sugar to a rolling boil. Whisk the mixture to separate the vanilla bean seeds. Meanwhile, use a whisk to beat the egg yolks and the remaining sugar in a medium bowl. Add the flour and gelatin and whisk well. Strain half the milk mixture into the egg bowl and whisk. Strain the other half of the milk into the egg and mix well. Use a silicone spatula to get all the cream from the sides of the bowl into the mixture.

RETURN THE MIXTURE to the saucepan and cook on medium-low heat for 4 minutes, whisking almost

constantly. Use your silicone spatula to scrape any cream on the sides of the pan into the mixture. Every 15 seconds, let the mixture sit without whisking until you see some bubbles; it should look like the mixture is breathing. When the mixture looks like thick vanilla pudding, take it off the heat and pour it into a clean bowl. Let the mixture sit for 10 minutes, then cover with plastic and refrigerate for four hours or overnight. The cream can be made three days in advance and stored in the fridge. To use the pastry cream sooner, place the bowl of pastry cream over a larger bowl filled with 2 to 3 cups of ice cubes and 2 cups of water for 30 minutes, or until chilled, whisking occasionally.

WHIP THE WHIPPING CREAM until thick. Use a silicone spatula to mix the chilled pastry cream, which will have thickened. Fold in the whipped cream in three parts. Spoon half of the cream into another bowl. Melt the chocolate and coffee granules together over a double boiler or in the microwave for 45 seconds, stir, heat for 30 seconds and stir, heat for another 15 seconds and stir, until the chocolate mixture is melted. Add the coffee extract. Then add the chocolate and coffee mixture to one of the bowls of cream and whisk well. Cover both bowls of cream and refrigerate for at least 20 minutes, or for up to one day.

To assemble the napoleons

MAKE STACKS of three pastry rectangles that are the same size. Put aside the best rectangles to be used for the tops. Put one rectangle from each of the stacks, caramelized side up, on a serving platter. Spoon each of the pastry creams into separate pastry bags fitted with round ½-inch (1.25-cm) tips. Starting on the shorter side of the pastry rectangle and going down the long side, slowly squeeze out three rows of one of the creams, about ¾-inch (2 cm) high, on each pastry. Gently place a pastry rectangle on top of the cream, caramelized side up, and cover it with three rows of the other flavor of cream. Top with the remaining pastry rectangle. Repeat with the other pastries. To decorate, sift confectioners' sugar on top. You can also place strips of waxed paper on top to make stripes or other designs. Chill the pastry for 20 minutes and serve. Store covered in the fridge for up to two days. ■

MODERATE

DAIRY • NUT-FREE

CHEESE BABKA

Serves 14

I started hearing about cheese babka recipes right before Shavuot 2012. As the chocolate babka maven, I knew I was expected to create a cheese version. People had written to me over the years that they had baked my chocolate babka using butter and they raved about it. Now I know why. When you open the oven during baking to check on the progress, you will be treated to a deep, buttery aroma.

Dough

⅓ cup (80ml) milk
¼ ounce (1 envelope; 7g) dry yeast
¼ cup (50g) plus 1 teaspoon sugar, divided

2½ cups (315g) all-purpose flour, plus one tablespoon, if needed, plus extra for dusting
½ cup (1 stick; 113g) unsalted butter, at room temperature 30 minutes
1 large egg plus 1 white (reserve yolk for glazing)

Filling

8 ounces (230g) cream cheese (not whipped)
½ cup (100g) sugar
1 large egg, divided
2 teaspoons pure vanilla extract

Crumbs

½ cup (65g) all-purpose flour
⅓ cup (75g) light brown sugar, packed
½ teaspoon cinnamon
4 tablespoons (57g) unsalted butter

To make the dough

HEAT THE MILK over the stovetop or in a microwave oven until warm, not boiling. Pour the milk into a large mixing bowl or the bowl of a stand mixer. Add the yeast and 1 teaspoon sugar and let the mixture sit 10 minutes, until thick. Add the remaining ¼ cup (50g) sugar, 2½ cups (315g) flour, butter, and egg plus one white. Combine the ingredients with a wooden spoon or with a dough hook in a stand mixer on low speed until they are all mixed together. If the dough sticks to the bowl, add the additional tablespoon of flour and mix it in; the dough should come together into a ball. Cover the bowl with plastic and let the dough rise for one hour.

To make the filling

MEANWHILE, remove the cream cheese from the fridge and put it in a medium bowl. Let the cream cheese soften for 45 minutes. Add the sugar, egg, and vanilla and combine using an electric mixer. Cover and place in the fridge until the dough is ready.

To make the crumbs and bake the babka

MIX THE FLOUR, brown sugar, and cinnamon together in a medium bowl. Add the butter and rub the mixture between your fingers until you have small clumps. Set the bowl aside.

PREHEAT OVEN to 375°F (190°C). Sprinkle a 12 x 14-inch (30 x 36-cm) piece of parchment paper with flour. Roll the dough on top of the parchment paper until you have a 12 x 14-inch (30 x 36-cm) rectangle. Sprinkle more flour on the parchment paper if the dough sticks to the rolling pin. Remove the filling from the fridge and use a silicone spatula to spread it evenly over the dough. Roll the dough up the long way. Bring the ends together into a large ring, and press them together. Use a sharp knife to make cuts in the dough, every inch or so, on the outside of the ring, but cut only about three-quarters of the way into the ring, not all the way through. After you have made all the cuts, pull the slices apart slightly and turn each one so the swirl part is facing the next slice, partly facing up. Repeat all the way around.

BRUSH THE DOUGH all over with the remaining egg yolk mixed with a teaspoon of water. Sprinkle with the crumbs. Bake for 35 minutes, or until golden. Let it cool for about 20 minutes. Store covered at room temperature for up to three days or freeze for up to three months. Reheat to serve. ■

MULTIPLE STEP

DAIRY • NUT-FREE

CHOCOLATE MILLE-CRÊPES CAKE

Serves 12 to 16

On Shavuot we generally think of using crêpes for one purpose: blintzes. This cake is really a stack of crêpes filled and held together with pastry cream. The recipe yields about 18 crêpes, not the *mille*, which means a thousand, in the recipe title. It takes some time to make the cake, but it is definitely worth your time; there are few kitchen tasks more gratifying than flipping a perfect crêpe out of a pan.

Crêpes

1 cup (125g) all-purpose flour

½ cup (40g) unsweetened cocoa

⅓ cup (65g) sugar

4 large eggs

2 tablespoons canola oil

1 teaspoon pure vanilla extract

2 cups (480ml) whole milk

4 tablespoons (57g) unsalted butter, melted

Pastry Cream

2 cups (480ml) milk

1 vanilla bean, split and seeds scraped, or
    1 teaspoon pure vanilla extract

2 tablespoons (28g) unsalted butter, plus
    1 tablespoon butter for greasing pan

⅔ cup (130g) sugar

8 large egg yolks

6 tablespoons (45g) all-purpose flour

1 teaspoon unflavored gelatin powder

To make the crêpe batter

IN A MEDIUM BOWL, whisk together the flour, cocoa, sugar, eggs, oil, vanilla, and milk. Add the melted butter and whisk it in. Strain this mixture into another bowl, press the batter through, discarding any solids. You can make the crêpes right away or store the batter covered in the fridge overnight.

To make the pastry cream

IN A HEAVY SAUCEPAN, bring the milk, scraped seeds and vanilla bean pod, butter, and half of the sugar to a rolling boil over medium-high heat. Meanwhile, use a whisk to beat the egg yolks and the remaining sugar in a medium bowl. Add the flour and gelatin and mix well. Strain half the boiled milk mixture into the eggs and whisk. Strain the other half of the milk into the eggs and whisk well.

RETURN THE MIXTURE to the saucepan and cook on medium-low heat for four minutes, whisking almost constantly. With a silicone spatula, thoroughly mix the cream into the mixture in the saucepan. Every 15 seconds, let the mixture rest without whisking until you see some bubbles; it should look like the mixture is breathing. When the mixture looks like thick vanilla pudding, remove it from the heat and pour it into a clean bowl. Let it sit for 10 minutes and then cover it with plastic and refrigerate until chilled, for at least four hours or overnight. The cream can be made three days in advance and stored in the fridge.

To make the crêpes

HEAT an 8-inch (20-cm) non-stick pan and brush it with a little melted butter. Cut off sixteen 8-inch (20-cm) pieces of waxed paper to keep the cooked crêpes from sticking to each other. When

CRÊPE PANS

I own a French crêpe pan but I prefer to use my inexpensive Teflon-coated frying pan instead.

the pan feels hot (you can tell by holding your hand two inches above the pan), lift the pan off the stove and pour a little less than ¼ cup of the batter just above the center of the pan. Turn the pan clockwise three times to spread the batter so it evenly covers the bottom of the pan. You may need to add a little more batter to cover the bottom or fill in holes. By the third crêpe, you should know just how much batter covers the pan. Return the pan to the heat.

COOK EACH CRÊPE for about one minute, or until the edges of the crepe look brown. Run a spatula around the edges of the crêpe and then lift it up, pressing the spatula into the pan under the crêpe until the spatula is about two-thirds of the way under the crêpe. Flip the crêpe over. Cook the other side for 15 seconds and then flip it onto a plate. If the crêpes begin to brown too quickly and burn, turn down the heat. Put a piece of waxed paper between each crêpe. Wrap the entire stack of crêpes in plastic wrap and chill for at least two hours. Crêpes can be stored in the fridge for up to four days.

To assemble the cake

PLACE ONE CRÊPE on a platter. Spoon two tablespoons of pastry cream into the middle of the crêpe. Use a silicone spatula to spread the cream all the way to the edges. Put another crêpe over the pastry cream, lining it up as best as you can with the first crêpe. Spread another crêpe with two tablespoons of pastry cream and top with another crêpe. Repeat with all remaining crêpes and cream, ending with a crêpe on top. Place the cake in the fridge for at least four hours or overnight; if you eat the cake right away, the crêpes will slide off the cream. Store the cake in the fridge for up to four days or freeze it for up to three months. ▪

DAIRY • GLUTEN-FREE • NUT-FREE

WHITE CHOCOLATE MOUSSE CAKE

Serves 12

When my friend Shira Jacobson Broms graduated from high school in 2005, I invented this cake and brought it to her graduation party. I did not make it again for the next seven years, so it became legendary, with people asking me if the cake was real or an urban myth. When I offered to host Shira's wedding shower in 2012, everyone asked if I was making the famous white chocolate mousse cake. I had no choice but to comply. Store this cake in the freezer until you're ready to serve it, and do not let it sit out too long; it is still tasty as it gets soft, but this cake deserves to look elegant. You can substitute strawberries for the raspberries in the sauce, or omit the sauce altogether.

Meringue
4 large egg whites, at room temperature one
    hour
⅔ cup (130g) sugar
⅔ cup (80g) confectioners' sugar

Mousse
8 ounces (230g) white chocolate, broken into
    1-inch pieces
5 large egg yolks
1½ cups (360ml) whipping cream

Raspberry Sauce
6 ounces (170g) fresh raspberries
2-3 tablespoons confectioners' sugar, to taste
2 tablespoons hot water

2-4 ounces (60–110g) white chocolate to
    decorate, if desired

PREHEAT OVEN to 230°F (110°C). Cover two cookie sheets with parchment paper trimmed to fit the bottom of the pan perfectly. Using an 8 x 2½-inch (20 x 6-cm) high dessert or flan ring (with no bottom), trace three circles on the parchments. Turn the papers over and put them on your cookie sheets. Set them aside.

To make the meringue

IN THE BOWL of an electric mixer, beat the egg whites on medium-high speed until you have soft peaks. Turn the mixer to low and add the granulated sugar, a tablespoon at a time, waiting until each addition is mixed in before adding more. Turn the speed up to high and beat another minute. Sift the confectioners' sugar into the egg whites. Turn the machine to low and mix briefly to combine.

FIT A PASTRY BAG with a ¼-inch (6-mm) round tip. Fill it with the meringue batter. Starting from the center of the drawn circles, squeeze out spirals until your circle is about half an inch (1.25cm) smaller than the drawn circle. If you do not have a pastry bag, use a silicone spatula to shape three circles of meringue batter.

SQUEEZE OUT any leftover batter into sticks or small circles about an inch wide and then lift the pastry bag to leave tips on top in the shape of Hershey's kisses, to decorate the cake later, if desired. Place the meringues in the oven, turn down the temperature to 220°F (105°C) and bake for two hours. Turn off the oven and let the meringues remain in the oven for another two hours to dry out. The meringues may be made two days in advance and stored uncovered at room temperature.

To make the sauce

PUT THE RASPBERRIES into the bowl of a food processor fitted with a metal blade and purée them, scraping down the sides of the bowl until all the fruit pieces are puréed. Add the water and sugar and mix. Taste the sauce and add more sugar if the mixture is too tart. Use a sieve to strain out the seeds and discard them. The sauce may be made two days in advance and stored covered in the fridge.

To make the mousse

MELT THE WHITE CHOCOLATE, either over a double boiler or in a microwave oven, for 45 seconds and stir, heat for 30 seconds and stir, and heat for another 15 seconds and stir, until all the chocolate is melted and smooth. Add the egg yolks one at a time and whisk well. In a large bowl with an electric mixer on high speed, beat the whipping cream until stiff. Fold the whipped cream into the white chocolate mixture and mix until well blended.

To assemble the cake

YOU WILL NEED an 8-inch (20-cm) cardboard circle. If the circle is larger than your ring, trace your ring and then cut out the circle. Line a cookie sheet with parchment paper, place the ring on top, and place the cardboard circle inside the ring. Place a tablespoon of the mousse on the cardboard to glue the meringue circle in place. Place one of the meringue circles in the ring. Pour a third of the mousse into the ring to cover the meringue. Make sure you get some mousse on the sides between the meringue and the ring. Add the second meringue circle and another third of the mousse, making sure the meringue is submerged in the mousse. Repeat with the last meringue circle and more mousse and then use a metal flat-blade spatula to smooth the top, reserving any extra mousse in a small bowl in the refrigerator to decorate the top, if desired. Freeze the cake for at least four hours or overnight.

TO REMOVE THE RING, place the cake (with the cardboard bottom) on top of a large can. Pour boiling water into a small bowl. Dip a towel or paper towel into the hot water, and then rub it around the outside of the ring; this will help release the ring from the mousse. Go around the entire ring with the hot towel. Gently slide the ring down and off the cake. Put the cake on the parchment-lined cookie sheet.

To decorate the cake

USE A VEGETABLE PEELER to scrape white chocolate curls on top of the cake or use a pastry bag with a decorative tip to decorate the top with any leftover mousse. Freeze the cake and take it out five minutes before serving to cut perfect slices. Spoon some raspberry sauce on each serving plate and lay the cake slice on top. Store the cake in the freezer for up to three months. ▪

MULTIPLE STEP

DAIRY • NUT-FREE

CHEESE BLINTZES

Makes 16

Save the blintz. No one I know makes homemade blintzes anymore. I make them to honor the memory of my grandma Sylvia, who made the most delicious cheese blintzes. Blintzes are a classic Ashkenazi dish that should be kept alive. According to my friend, and Jewish food historian, Gil Marks, the Turks introduced these thin pancakes to the Balkans in the fourteenth century. Gil also recounts that in Sholem Aleichem's Tevye stories, Tevye praises his wife's blintzes. If you know how to make crêpes, you know how to make blintzes. Please prepare blintzes this Shavuot so that your family and friends, as well as the next generation, do not lose this delicious treat.

Crêpes

1 cup (125g) all-purpose flour

3 tablespoons sugar

⅓ teaspoon salt

2 tablespoons canola oil

1¾ cups (420ml) milk

3 large eggs

3 tablespoons (42g) unsalted butter, melted

Filling

2 tablespoons (28g) cream cheese (not whipped)

1 pound (450g) farmer's cheese

⅓ cup (65g) sugar

1 large egg

1 tablespoon canola oil plus 1 to 2 tablespoons butter for frying

To make the crêpes

PUT THE FLOUR, sugar, salt, oil, milk, eggs, and 3 tablespoons of melted butter into a medium bowl and whisk vigorously. Press the mixture through a strainer into another bowl, pushing through as much batter as possible and then discard the solids. The batter may be made three days in advance and stored covered in the fridge.

To prepare the filling

PUT THE CREAM CHEESE into a medium bowl and soften it with a fork. Add the farmer's cheese and use the fork to mash it into the cream cheese. Add the sugar and egg and use a spoon to mix well. The filling may be made one day in advance and stored covered in the fridge.

To cook the crêpes

CUT OFF sixteen 8-inch (20-cm) pieces of waxed paper. Heat an 8-inch (20-cm) nonstick frying pan or crêpe pan over medium-high heat. Brush the pan with a little butter. Remove the pan from the heat, and pour a little less than ¼ cup batter into the pan, just above the middle, and then turn the pan clockwise 2 to 3 times to swirl the batter and evenly cover the bottom of the pan with batter. Add more batter to cover any holes. By the third crêpe, you will know exactly how much batter you need.

COOK EACH CRÊPE for 45 seconds to one minute and when the edges are brown, slide a silicone spatula under the crêpe to lift it up and turn it over. Cook the crêpe for another 15 seconds, then turn it onto a plate. If the crêpe starts to brown too fast, turn down the heat. Repeat with the remaining batter and put a piece of waxed paper between each crêpe. Let them cool for 15 minutes. The crêpes may be made two days in advance. Cover the stack of crêpes with plastic wrap and refrigerate.

To fill the crêpes

WITH THE BROWNER SIDE of the crêpe facing up, spoon about 2 tablespoons of cheese filling onto the crêpe, in the middle, and spread it around in a 2-inch (5-cm) wide area. Fold the right and left sides 1 to 2 inches (2.5 to 5-cm) toward the center of the crêpe and press them into the filling. Fold the top of the crêpe down over the filling and roll up the crepe over the cheese filling to close up the blintz. Set it aside. At this point you can freeze the blintzes and cook them later.

TO COOK THEM right away, heat the oil and 1 tablespoon of butter in a large frying pan over medium heat. Add the blintzes and cook them in batches for two minutes on each side, or until they've browned, adding more butter to the pan if needed. Serve hot. Stored them covered in the fridge for up to four days or freeze for up to three months. ■

LOW-SUGAR VERSION

Reduce the sugar amounts in the batter and filling to one tablespoon each.

BRIOCHE CHALLAH

Makes 2 medium loaves

Brioche is a buttery French bread that tastes like a pastry. It is typically eaten for breakfast in France, and makes the perfect dairy challah for Shavuot. When I learned how to make brioche in pastry school in Paris, we were taught how to prepare it by hand. The process of mixing and kneading the dough, and then kneading in the butter, took 30 minutes. In two separate pastry courses I had made brioche by hand, so when I had to make it a third time, I asked my teacher if I could make it with a machine. I explained that we could compare both methods and see which was superior. He only agreed because at the time I was visibly pregnant with my son Sam. The chef was sure that the hand-kneaded one would be better, but, alas, he had to admit that the taste and texture of my machine-made brioche were perfect. So in the interest of saving time, I suggest that you go the machine route.

¼ cup (60ml) warm water

4 tablespoons (50g) plus 1 teaspoon sugar, divided

½ ounce (2 envelopes; 14g) dry yeast

2½ cups (315g) bread flour, plus extra for dusting

1 teaspoon salt

4 large eggs, beaten slightly, plus 1 egg for glazing

¾ cup (1½ sticks; 170g) unsalted butter, cut into pieces, at room temperature, plus 1 tablespoon for greasing bowl

2 teaspoons water for glaze

To make the dough

POUR ¼ cup (60ml) warm water into a measuring cup, add the teaspoon sugar and yeast and stir.

Let the mixture sit five minutes, or until thick. In the bowl of a stand mixer, place the flour, salt, and four tablespoons (50g) sugar and mix. Add the four eggs and proofed yeast mixture and mix with the dough hook on low speed for two minutes, scraping down the bowl and hook two to three times. Turn the speed up to medium and knead for eight minutes, stopping to scrape down the hook and sides of the bowl three to four times. Turn the speed to low and add the 1½ sticks (170g) soft butter, two tablespoons at a time, making sure each addition is fully mixed in before adding more butter. When all the butter has been added, turn the speed to medium and mix for three minutes, stopping to scrape down the bowl once or twice.

PLACE THE DOUGH in a medium bowl greased with the tablespoon of butter. Cover the bowl with plastic wrap and let the dough rise for one hour. Remove the dough from the bowl, punch it down by folding it over a few times, then gather the dough back into a ball and return it to the bowl. Cover the dough with the plastic and let it rise for 30 minutes. Once again, remove the dough from the bowl, punch it down, return it to the bowl, and cover it. Refrigerate for 30 minutes.

LIGHTLY FLOUR your hands and kitchen counter. Divide the dough in half and braid each half into a challah, adding a little more flour to your hands if the dough feels a little sticky. Place the challahs on a parchment-covered baking sheet. Beat the remaining egg with two teaspoons of water. Brush the challahs all over with the mixture. Let them rise for one hour.

PREHEAT OVEN to 375°F (190°C). Brush the challahs again with the egg wash. Bake them for 30 minutes or until golden. When cool, wrap the challahs in foil and store them at room temperature for up to five days or freeze for up to three months. ◼

Resources

www.kosher.com
General kosher baking ingredients

www.thekoshercook.com
Kosher baking equipment
Cookie cutters

www.amazon.com
Specialty baking equipment

www.thepeppermill.com
Kosher baking ingredients and
equipment

www.surlatable.com
General and specialty baking
equipment

www.wilton.com
Cake decorating equipment

www.pastrycentral.com
Baking equipment
Cake decorating tools

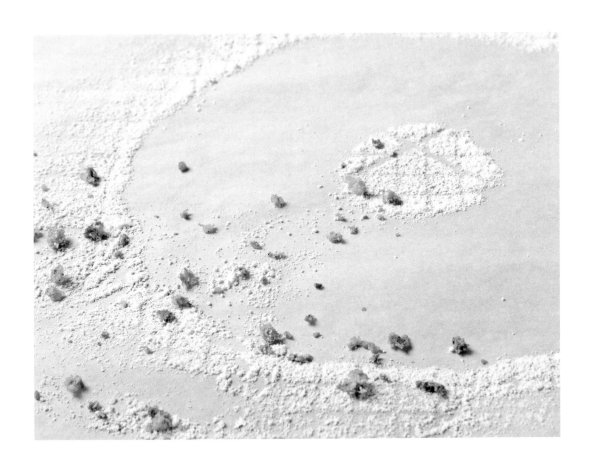

About the Author

A former practicing attorney, Paula Shoyer graduated from the Ritz Escoffier pastry program in Paris and now teaches French and Jewish baking classes in the Washington, DC, area. Paula conducts large-scale baking demonstrations across the United States and Canada. She is the author of *The Kosher Baker: Over 160 Dairy-Free Recipes from Traditional to Trendy* (Brandeis 2010) and is a contributing editor to several websites, including kosherscoop.com, as well as magazines such as *Joy of Kosher with Jamie Geller*, *Whisk*, and *Hadassah*. Paula has appeared on Food Network's *Sweet Genius*, is a frequent TV news guest, and edited the popular cookbooks *Kosher by Design Entertains* and *Kosher by Design Kids in the Kitchen* (both from Mesorah Publications, Ltd.). Paula lives in Chevy Chase, Maryland, with her husband and four children.

Acknowledgments

Thank you to my parents, Toby and Reubin Marcus, and in-laws, Arthur and Lillian Shoyer, for your love and support, which generally comes in the form of consuming my desserts and always telling me that they are all great. Thanks to my brothers, Ezra and Adam Marcus, and brother-in law, Steve, for always promoting me to everyone. Gratitude to my sisters-in-law, Tamar and Debbie, and nieces and nephews Claire, Benjamin, Yonatan, and Naomi for loving all my desserts.

I am indebted to my fabulous team of recipe testers who made sure all the desserts in this book would work in your home as well as mine. Thanks to Limor Decter, Rhonda Alexander-Abt, Elena Lefkowitz, Steve and Benjamin Shoyer, Andrew and Marla Satinsky, Mark and Melissa Arking, Esther Dayon, Amanda Goldstein, Shoshana Shemtov, Trudy Jacobson, and Andrea Neusner.

In addition to the constant support from those listed above, thank you to my other cheerleaders who always tell me to keep doing what I love, never tell me that I am crazy for working so hard, and make me feel that I can accomplish great things: Suzin Glickman, Judith Gold, Karina Schumer, Laurie Strongin, and Pamela Auerbach.

Special thanks to Limor Decter for talking through every step of this project with me from concept to final product and providing a reality check for what home bakers will realistically bake.

Special thanks to Rabbi Tzvi Marks of the Netherlands, who helped me find meaningful messages to share in the holiday introductions. Rabbi Marks gave me a private Torah study class on erev Yom Kippur. Thank you also to Nechama Shemtov for reviewing the holiday rules and rituals for accuracy and for helping me include teachings from the insightful holiday classes she has taught to our local group of Aura Jewish women over the past ten years.

I have been blessed and spoiled with fabulous interns. Shawn Eliav has worked with me on and off for two years and is a talented and creative baker who can be credited with personally developing some of these recipes. Thank you to Annie Epstein who went from basic baker to pastry hero within hours. A shout out to Samara Wald who worked with me for a mere few weeks one summer, but continues to provide great help whenever I need testing done.

The stunning photos are the work of the talented Michael Bennett Kress. I cannot imagine that anyone else could have made my desserts look more spectacular. I enjoy working with him, and we have grown together into a great food/photography team. Major thanks to Lisa Cherkasky, food stylist extraordinaire, who took my pretty desserts and made them look even more beautiful. I could not have baked the 78 desserts that we shot, or made it through the long days of shooting without the amazing help of assistant Diana Ash.

More thanks to my brother, Adam Marcus, a great writer, who served as my personal editor and helped make the writing as tight and clear as possible. I apologize that I could not send the desserts themselves as attachments.

To my literary agents, Lisa and Sally Ekus, who brought me up to the big league. You believe in me, support what I do, and inspire me to achieve great things. Every day I worked on this book, I felt your hands on my shoulder encouraging me to keep moving forward.

When I first met Sterling Senior Editor Jennifer Williams, I knew we were destined to work together; it was as if we had been friends for years. Thank you for your belief in me and this project. You are a real woman of valor. Thank you to the talented and hardworking team at Sterling: Trudi Bartow, manager, specialty & trade sales reps; Hannah Reich, project editor; Chris Thompson, art director; Elizabeth Mihaltse, jacket art director; Christine Heun, designer; Barbara Balch, designer; Molly Morrison, proofreader; Jay Kreider, indexer; Terence Campo, production manager, Rodman Neumann, managing editor, and Mary Jane Montalto, prepress manager.

Index of Recipes by Category

Dairy
Gluten-free
Low sugar
Non-gebrokts

Nut-free
Parve
Vegan

Note: Page numbers in *italics* indicate photographs.

General Index

Note: Page numbers in **bold** indicate recipe category lists. Page numbers in *italics* indicate photographs.